World Archaeology

Volume 30 No. 2 October 1998

Executive Editor Stephen Shennan *Institute of Archaeology, London**

Editorial Board Elisabeth A. Bacus *Institute of Archaeology, London*
Richard Bradley *University of Reading*
Thomas Dowson *University of Southampton*
David Gibbins *University of Liverpool*
Roberta Gilchrist *University of Reading*
Chris Gosden *University of Oxford*
Yvonne Marshall *University of Southampton*
Peter Mitchell *University of Oxford*
Peter Rowley-Conwy *University of Durham*
Kenneth Thomas *Institute of Archaeology, London*

Editor of this number Stephen Shennan

Advisory Board Professor D. P. Agrawal *Physical Research Laboratory,
   Ahmedabad*
Dr Takeru Akazawa *University of Tokyo*
Professor Sandra Bowdler *University of Western Australia*
Professor Warwick Bray *University of London*
Professor K. C. Chang *Harvard University*
Professor Barry Cunliffe *University of Oxford*
Professor N. David *University of Calgary*
Professor Pierre de Maret *University of Brussels*
Professor Kent V. Flannery *University of Michigan*
Dr Ian Glover *University of London*
Professor James Graham-Campbell *Institute of Archaeology,
   London*
Professor F. R. Hodson *University of London*
Dr Ray Inskeep *University of Oxford*
Dr Ian Longworth *British Museum, London*
Dr Rauf Munchaev *Institute of Archaeology, Moscow*
Professor Bjørn Myhre *Museum of Archaeology, Stavanger*
Dr Joan Oates *University of Cambridge*
Professor Colin Platt *University of Southampton*
Professor Derek Roe *University of Oxford*
Professor B. G. Trigger *McGill University, Montreal*

* Address: Institute of Archaeology, University College London, 31–34 Gordon Square, London
WC1H 0PY, UK.

Addresses for inquiries and submissions

Elisabeth A. Bacus
Institute of Archaeology
University College London
31–34 Gordon Square
London WC1H 0PY
UK
e.bacus@ucl.ac.uk

Richard Bradley
Department of Archaeology
University of Reading
Whiteknights
PO Box 218
Reading RG6 2AA
UK
r.j.bradley@reading.ac.uk

Thomas Dowson
Department of Archaeology
University of Southampton
Southampton SO17 1BJ
UK
tad@soton.ac.uk

David Gibbins
Department of Archaeology
University of Liverpool
14 Abercromby Square
Liverpool L69 3BX
UK
dgibbins@liv.ac.uk

Roberta Gilchrist
Department of Archaeology
University of Reading
Whiteknights
PO Box 218
Reading RG6 2AA
UK
r.l.gilchrist@reading.ac.uk

Chris Gosden
Pitt Rivers Museum University of Oxford
60 Banbury Road
Oxford OX2 6PN
UK
chris.gosden@anthropology.oxford.ac.uk

Yvonne Marshall
Department of Archaeology
University of Southampton
Southampton SO17 1BJ
UK
ymm@soton.ac.uk

Peter Mitchell
St Hugh's College
Oxford OX2 6LE
UK
peter.mitchell@prm.ox.ac.uk

Peter Rowley-Conwy
Department of Archaeology
University of Durham
Science Site, South Road
Durham DH1 3LE
UK
P.A.Rowley-Conwy@durham.ac.uk

Stephen Shennan
Institute of Archaeology
University College London
31–34 Gordon Square
London WC1H 0PY
UK
s.shennan@ucl.ac.uk

Kenneth Thomas
Institute of Archaeology
University College London
31–34 Gordon Square
London WC1H 0PY
UK
k.thomas@ucl.ac.uk

World Archaeology

World Archaeology is a peer-reviewed journal published three times per annum by the Proprietors, Routledge Journals, 2 Park Square, Milton Park, Abingdon, Oxon, OX14 4RN. Tel: (0)171 583 9855 Fax: (0)171 842 2298

© 1998 Routledge   ISSN 0043-8243

Submissions: all enquiries and correspondence concerning submission of papers to be considered for publication should be addressed to the Editors, see pp. ii and iv.

Advertising: (UK) Routledge Journals, 2 Park Square, Milton Park, Abingdon, Oxon, OX14 4RN email: jadvertising@routledge.co.uk
(USA) Susan Dearborn Publishers Communication Group, 875 Massachusetts Avenue Suite 81 Cambridge MA 01239 USA
Fax (617) 354 4804 email: sdearborn@pcgplus.com

Subscriptions: (UK) Routledge Journals Subscriptions, PO Box 362, Abingdon, Oxfordshire OX14 3WB. Tel: (0) 1235 401060 Fax: (0) 1235 401075
email: routledge@carfax.co.uk.
(USA) Routledge Journals, 29 W35th Street, New York NY 10001-2299 Tel: (21) 216 7800 Fax: (212) 564 7854
email: journals@routledge-ny.com.

A full listing of Routledge books and journals is available by accessing:
http://www.routledge.com/routledge.html

Subscription rates (1998–9):

UK/EC institutions	£96.00	UK/EC individuals	£35.00
USA institutions	$115.00	USA individuals	$55.00

Subscription rates include mailing at accelerated surface post.
Copies, including back numbers, may be obtained from the Routledge Subscriptions Department.

Members of the World Archaeology Congress (WAC) are eligible for a discounted personal subscription rate to the journal. Please apply to Routledge Subscriptions at the Abingdon address above.

Typeset by Type Study, Scarborough, North Yorkshire.

Transferred to Digital Printing 2004

Population and Demography
Edited by Stephen Shennan

Contents

Future Issues/Call for Papers

Vol. 30 No. 3   *Arctic Archaeology* ed. P. R-C. Publication in February 1999. Arctic is here defined as the Arctic and Subarctic climatic zones, wherever (and whenever) they may be found. Papers are requested on any archaeological aspect of human social, technological or economic responses to these extreme and strongly seasonal environments, with special reference to why and how particular survival strategies worked – or did not work.

Vol. 31 No. 1   *Food Technology in its Social Context: Production, Processing and Storage*, ed. K. T. Publication in June 1999. Food production, processing and storage in past societies have usually been treated from technological or environmental-cum-ecological perspectives, although the social dimensions of these phenomena, in terms of political and economic control, have sometimes been explored for more complex societies, such as those of ancient Mesopotamia. Papers are invited on any aspect of the above theme, for any type of past social or subsistence system in any part of the world. It is anticipated that published papers will include theoretical treatments as well as specific archaeological case studies or methodological/analytical approaches.

Vol. 31 No. 2   *The Cultural Biography of Objects*,* eds C. G. and Y. M. Submission by 15 December 1998 for publication in October 1999. Papers are invited which focus on the cultural biography of objects. If the meaning of objects is constructed through their contexts, then a change in context represents a change in significance. We are looking for papers which follow artefacts through such changes.

Vol. 31 No. 3   *Human Lifecycles*,* ed. R. G. Publication in February 2000. This volume will consider cultural or biological evidence for experiencing the lifecycle, including aging, symbolic identities, critical thresholds and rites of passage, in addition to the social construction of attitudes to the lifecycle, such as gender and aging.

Vol. 32 No. 1   *Archaeology in Southeast Asia*,* ed. E. A. B. Submission by 1 September 1999 for publication in June 2000. This issue will highlight Southeast Asian archaeology and its significance to issues of broad interest to world archaeology. Southeast Asia is defined here to include the countries of Brunei, Burma, Cambodia, Indonesia, Laos, Malaysia, Philippines, Singapore, Thailand and Vietnam. Submissions are invited on any area and topic of Southeast Asian prehistory, protohistory or history that draw primarily on archaeological evidence. Papers which place their work within a broader theoretical, methodological or comparative perspective are strongly encouraged, as are papers from archaeologists of this region.

*Issues at planning stage, with contributions invited. Please note that issues are made up six months before publication and the editor will plan issues about eighteen months before publication date. See Notes to Contributors at the end of this issue for more details.

Theme titles of past issues of *World Archaeology*. These are all available from Routledge Journals.

Demographic growth, environmental changes and technical adaptations: responses of an agricultural community from the 32nd to the 30th centuries BC

Pierre Pétrequin, Rose-Marie Arbogast, Christine Bourquin-Mignot, Catherine Lavier and Amandine Viellet

Abstract

In comparison with dryland settlements, peri-alpine lake-dwellings of the Neolithic represent an ideal case for the study of population growth and its consequences, owing to the better preservation of organic remains, architectural woods and artefacts. Research has been based on dendrochronological sequences divided into series of ten to twenty years and on the statistical study of hundreds of thousands of archaeological remains, preserved below the level of the water-table.

For the two lake basins of Chalain and Clairvaux at the end of the fourth millennium BC, direct correlations are proposed between a period of population growth and successive technical and economical adaptations rapidly adopted by agricultural communities trying to temporarily resolve the problems resulting from demographic growth, due in large part to the coming of immigrant populations.

Keywords

Neolithic; dendrochronology; palaeoenvironment; agriculture; demography; Europe.

Introduction

The scientific community of prehistorians is well aware of the major role that modifications in the density of the population have played and continue to play with regard to the framework of technical and cultural changes. Still, the use of contemporary models drawn from human geography has rarely been possible without encountering great theoretical and practical difficulties. As a matter of fact, much criticism has been made of the

World Archaeology Vol. 30(2): 181–192 *Population and Demography*
© Routledge 1998 0043-8243

attempts by archaeologists to deal with the growth of density in population on the basis that the imprecise and incomplete character of the archaeological record, floating in a vague chronological frame, rarely allows an unequivocal interpretation. Such a view is quite understandable considering the interactions of the processes of degradation, erosion and sedimentation on the archaeological palimpsests, of which many have already totally disappeared. We are aware both of this interest in placing demography at the centre of our research and of the limits of archaeological interpretation. Therefore, we have for more than twenty-five years devoted our research to the study of the best (or the least badly) preserved settlement sites of European prehistory. In the lake-dwelling sites, the surviving archaeological evidence has been quickly covered by either lacustral chalks or peat bogs, sealed in an anaerobic environment, waterlogged or below the water-table.

There, in this amphibious environment, sedimentation has sometimes been surprisingly rapid on the edge of the lake basins, with the consequence that the stratigraphic sequences are often expanded, and organic materials, in particular wood remains, have sometimes survived to the present day. For western Europe the remains of the Neolithic and Bronze Age lake-dwellings offer a unique case in the field of chronology by providing abundant well-preserved timber (oak and ash) that can be dated to the year (provided that the last annual growth is still preserved). The establishment of an accurate tree-ring chronology constitutes the major breakthrough in the archaeology of the last twenty years.

In this paper a case-study taking advantage of this situation is presented: a valley investigated for nearly a century, with small lakes that have been the epicentres of regional population influx during the end of the fourth and the third millennium BC.

Chalain and Clairvaux: an absolute chronology of 20-year sequences

The lakes of Chalain (Fontenu, Jura – abbreviation used on the figure captions: CH) and Clairvaux (Clairvaux-les-Lacs, Jura – abbreviation used: CL) are located in the Combe d'Ain, an enclosed alluvial valley, at an altitude of 500 metres, within the plateaux of the French Jura (Fig. 1). These two lakes have both given a long chronological sequence of lake-dwellings from *c.* 3900 BC to *c.* 850 BC (all the dendrochronological dates are expressed in calendar years).

Each year since 1970, field research has involved surveys and systematic soundings in order to evaluate the potential of the Neolithic settlements, those from the lake margins as well as those from the peat bogs or from the glacio-lacustrine terraces. These researches have also involved partial excavations of the lake-dwellings dated to the period of 3200–2900 BC, which are among the more numerous and best preserved. Villages of this time period are represented by six stratified settlement sites at the northern end of the lake of Clairvaux and seven sites at the extreme west of the lake of Chalain (Fig. 1).

To assume that we know all of the permanent establishments of this time period would be presumptuous, but new discoveries have diminished over time in spite of the intensification of the drill-soundings and subaquatic surveys. Therefore, for this time period of 300 years it can be estimated with confidence that our documentation, if not complete, is at least strongly representative of a past situation (Pétrequin 1997). It might be considered surprising that the majority of the villages were built on the edge of the lakes when the

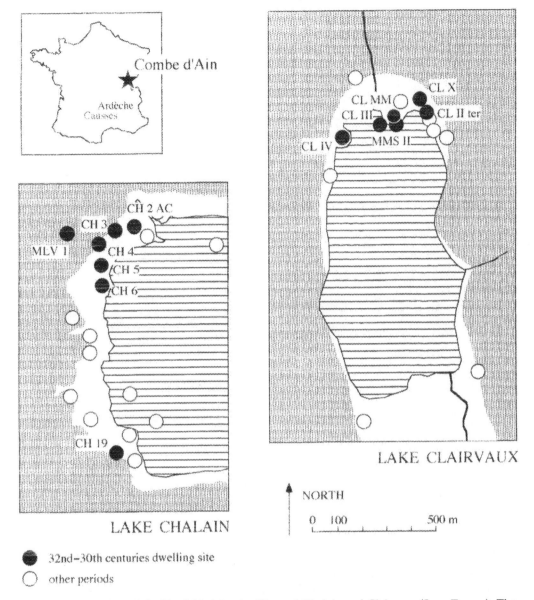

Combe d'Ain

Ardèche
Causses

CL X
CL MM
CL III
CL II ter
CL IV
MMS II

LAKE CLAIRVAUX

CÎÎ 2 AC
CH 3
MLV 1
CH 4
CH 5
CH 6

CH 19

LAKE CHALAIN

NORTH

0   100   500 m

● 32nd–30th centuries dwelling site

○ other periods

Figure 1 Location of the Neolithic lake-dwellings of Chalain and Clairvaux (Jura, France). The contemporaneous or successive villages were mostly grouped on the flattest lake shores, close to the forests on the alluvial terraces and to the best cereal lands.

rest of the valley was only slightly affected by temporary clearances but this pattern has been confirmed in the other lake basins of the region through numerous soundings and pollen diagrams (Richard 1992).

Through the combined use of the stratigraphic sequences, the modification in the tool assemblages and, above all, the dendrochronological dating of hundreds of timbers, it has been possible to count, through chronological spans of twenty years, the rise in the number of villages occupied at the same time on the lakes of Chalain and Clairvaux between the

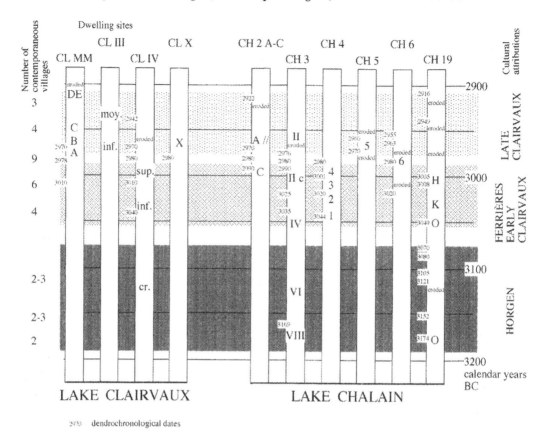

Figure 2 Stratigraphic, chronological and cultural correlations between the different Neolithic villages of Chalain and Clairvaux during the 32nd–30th centuries BC. The dendrochronological dates in calendar years BC allow one to precisely follow the variation in the number of villages on the margins of the two lakes. Those variations are the best indicators of the fluctuations in the population of the Combe d'Ain.

thirty-second and thirtieth centuries BC (Fig. 2). Dendrochronology is at the heart of this proposed method, not only because of the accuracy of the proposed dates but also because it has been the only way to tie to a chronological sequence some villages almost completely destroyed by erosion except for the wooden piles of the houses (Lavier 1996; Viellet 1997).

During this time span, the size of the small villages was nearly constant, as shown by the extensive opening up of large horizontal areas with, on average, a dozen rectangular houses, of 8 to 10 metres long and 4 metres wide and as many little cereal granaries. For the Combe d'Ain, a region of about 16km by 2 to 5km, it has thus been possible to follow the rise in the number of the villages, from a minimum of two to a maximum of nine; these figures allow us to estimate indirectly the numerical increase in the population, even if the number of inhabitants per unit remains impossible to assess.

The situation is as follows (Fig. 2, left column): around 3180 BC, only two contemporary villages would have existed, the first at Chalain, the other at Clairvaux, 12km north. By c. 3100, this number has gone up from two to three contemporaneous settlements, only a very slight increase. From 3060 to 3040, there is a sharp increase in the number of villages built at 100 or 200m from one another, at both Chalain and Clairvaux; four villages in 3040, six in 3010, nine in 2980: the number of villages (and of houses) has more than doubled in sixty years.

Newcomers and extension of the cultivated land

To discern solely from these figures (that double in less than three generations) whether the increase was due solely to the demographic growth of local communities is evidently not possible.

However, it has been shown elsewhere that the period 3060–3040 BC represents a major split in the cultural evolution of the agricultural communities of the Combe d'Ain (Giligny 1994; Giligny et al. 1995; Pétrequin 1997). Before 3060, one can speak of communities linked to the Horgen culture (a group based in the north-east and west of Switzerland), with characteristic flat-based pots (Fig. 3, bottom right) and exchange networks oriented

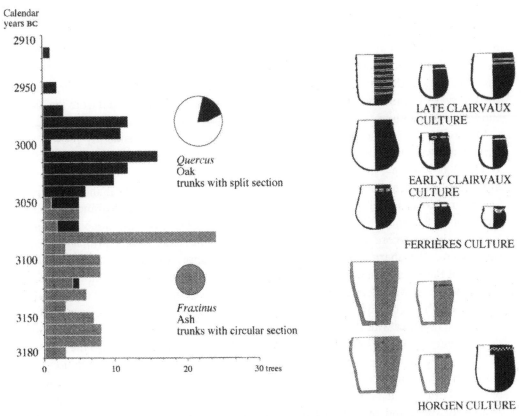

Figure 3   On the left, the precise determination together with the dendrochronological dates of the poles of the houses show, between 3080 and 3050 BC, the transition from a secondary forest of young ashes to a primary forest of old oaks. This phenomenon relates to the opening up of new deforestation fronts following on population growth, when the region was colonized by groups of agriculturalists from the south of France.

to the east and to the north-east, where the flint blades from northern Jura, together with the blades of polished stone for axes and adzes, were coming from. At this time period contacts with the south and with the Rhône Valley were only episodic, with the introduction of a few decorated pots and some types of arrowheads that imply an advanced level of technology (pressure-flaking after preheating the flint).

After 3060–3040 BC, with the increase in the number of villages (and very likely in the density of the population), the situation was immediately reversed. Although some basic techniques remained stable or changed slowly, the remainder underwent a total change. Such is the case for the pottery styles, with the exclusive adoption of decorated pots with a rounded base, well known in the Ferrières Group, in the south and south-east of the Massif Central, 250km distant from the Combe d'Ain (Fig. 3, upper right). At the same time, long-distance trading networks are reoriented, this time towards the south, with polished axes from the Lombardes Alps and very long flint blades from Forcalquier in the Alpes-de-Haute-Provence (Beugnier 1997).

Global analysis of the phenomenon (Pétrequin 1997) tends to suggest that the demographic growth of the Combe d'Ain resulted mainly from the arrival of successive human groups: the first around 3060–3040 coming from the Ardèche region, a second around 2980 BC coming from the area of the Grands Causses. These immigrants would have rapidly mingled with the local population, imposing their pottery styles with rounded bases and new technology to manufacture them (Martineau 1995). The mutual acculturation between local populations and immigrants quickly led to a hybridization of the Horgen assemblages and the Ferrières styles. In less than a generation, a specific cultural group, the Clairvaux Group, developed in the Jura and the south of Switzerland from the end of the fourth millennium.

Moreover, the very rapid demographic growth may be independently proved by a careful study of the timber used during that period of time (Fig. 3, left) (Viellet 1997). Before 3060–3040 BC, most of the timbers are young straight ash poles from the secondary forest, spring shoots from stumps. Contemporary phytosociological and ethnographical examples suggest that this type of tree grows well after forest clearance in shifting agriculture (Pétrequin 1996, 1997). In contrast, after 3060–3040, ash almost disappears from the timber record. Ash poles were replaced by old oaks from the primary forest. In our opinion, this sharp modification in the timber supply would have been the consequence of the expansion of the cultivated land into the primary forest, following the new demographic growth (Pétrequin 1996). Total clearance of the young forest due to shifting agriculture through sequences of 30 to 70 years must have been the way that this happened, together with the opening up of new clearance fronts; both were the result of deep changes in cultivation habits; the forest could not be regenerated into the thin poles of regular size that were so well adapted to the architecture of the wooden houses.

Both recession and degradation of the local forest may also be seen through analyses of the soil litter in the lake villages. The litter was largely made up of the accumulation of bundles of sticks and small branches; their role was to stabilize moist ground, liable to flooding and with no mechanical resistance. Botanical identification of wooden material of less than a centimetre in diameter suggests what could have been the feeding of livestock: the elm is more abundant together with ash, ivy and mistletoe: these species were recovered in the stables of the Middle Neolithic of north-eastern and central Switzerland,

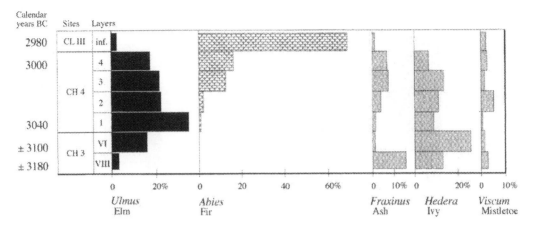

Percentage distribution of the more representatives taxa

Figure 4　Determination of elm twigs of less than 1cm in diameter, used for the feeding of live-stock. Ash, ivy and mistletoe were also used. This indicates that early on young sprouts from stumps were over exploited. From 3000 BC, the low-altitude forests were so degraded that agriculturalists had to turn to the plateau firs to feed the livestock in winter and obtain certain building timbers.

in association with thick layers of stable litter and of sheep and goat dung (Troels-Smith 1960; Rasmussen 1993). At Chalain, one should note the speedy disappearance of the best winter forage (elm, ash and ivy) at the exact time that the number of villages occupied simultaneously reached its maximum (Fig. 4). This may constitute another sign of forest degradation. The new adaptation seems to have been to fetch the lower branches of the firs (*Abies alba*); that is, to go to the plateaux at an altitude of above 700m, one hour's walking distance away.

It is thus possible to postulate that, after the clearance of the thirty-first century for extensive agriculture, the grazing of the livestock in the forest may have been the cause of the general degradation of the woodlands of the Combe d'Ain; livestock grazing on the shoots from the stumps led to a difficult and incomplete regeneration of the secondary forest.

Investigating diet: the part played by cereals and the part played by meat

A way to gain knowledge of the short-term transformations of the woodland environment in the Combe d'Ain is to stress the problem in terms of subsistence strategies during the phase of population growth which has been identified (Fig. 5). Nevertheless, even though there are long well-documented lists of cereals and vegetables, gathering products, and bone remains of both domestic and hunted animals found in the excavations by their hundreds of thousands (Lundstrom-Baudais 1986; Arbogast and Pétrequin 1993; Arbo-gast 1997; Pétrequin 1997), the record is in all cases biased: to directly assess the weights and volumes of the food that has been consumed is not possible.

Nevertheless, we propose, with caution, a method that could well indirectly reflect the pattern of consumption during the thirty-second to thirtieth centuries BC. The sole data

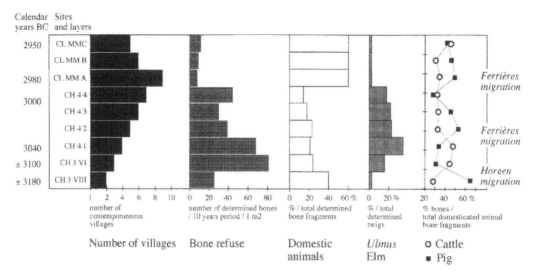

Figure 5 Demographic growth is indirectly shown by the rise in the number of villages between 3180 and 2980 BC. This growth, marked by the successive arrival of two groups of immigrants, quickly led the agricultural communities to adopt new technical choices: reduction of the animal protein part in the diet; an increase in hunting leading to the exhaustion of the local potential; the development of animal husbandry in forest areas and then on the cleared lands; finally, the sudden emphasis on pig breeding every time the Combe d'Ain was subjected to a new wave of immigration.

available are the discarded animal bones in the refuse areas in front of the houses. In lime-rich milieux, risks of the disappearance of these faunal remains are quite low. Moreover, plant litter and lake deposits have quickly covered them up, preserving them from attrition by dogs. It has been shown that nearly all of the anatomical pieces are present (Arbogast 1997) and that most of the carcasses of wild or domestic animals must have been butchered within the village enclosure (although this does not imply that all of the meat was brought in as carcasses). As it has been possible to precisely circumscribe the areas of the refuse deposits, and because of the remarkably precise sequences gained through dendrochronology, we have tried to calculate the rate of deposition of bone fragments, which could give an idea of the way the consumption of meat may have evolved. Rate of discard was defined as the total number of bones divided by ten-year periods in the occupation of the village, divided by the size of the refuse areas in square metres. Many other tests were performed on the basis of the total weight or the total number of the bone remains, the results being more or less the same (Pétrequin 1997).

In Figure 5, the left-hand columns allow us to trace the variations in this rate of bone deposition in relation to the demographic growth (number of villages). As the newcomers arrive, the 'animal protein consumption' tends to grow rapidly and stay constant for about 200 years. The central column of Figure 5 suggests that this was based more on wild animals than domesticated ones. It appears that, at first, subsistence problems connected to the population growth were solved by increasing the hunting strategies rather than animal husbandry (Arbogast and Pétrequin 1993). In fact, during this phase of population growth and colonization, domestic animals in general do not appear to have been the object of special care. They seem to be slowly decreasing. The high percentages of elm branches (Fig. 4 and Fig. 5, right) could well attest to a decision to feed the livestock with forest shoots. Direct evidence of such practices (analyses of faeces) is still missing; however, only a very slow development of specific areas devoted to grazing is to be seen. The impression thus suggested is more consistent with what is known of the environment of secondary forests with a quick regeneration rate, where young poles of light species (Fig. 3, left) are dominant. Globally speaking, the consumption of animal protein must have been quite high.

The situation is totally changed when the highest number of villages occupied simultaneously is reached, that is in 2980 BC, following the coming of a new migration front that seems to originate from the Grands Causses. Products of hunting abruptly diminish, together with evidence of livestock feeding on forest products. Husbandry is now predominant. The consumption of meat, however, is reduced, as judged by the discarded bone in the domestic refuse areas. It is as if the potential of the region in game had been temporarily exhausted and the solution adopted to sustain a more numerous population was to increase the cereal portion, a cheap source of food compared to husbandry, in terms of occupation and use of land. Animal husbandry itself seems to have then been more focused on open spaces. This can be inferred from the reduction in forage of forest origin but also by the increase in the pollen spectra of the pollen of *Plantago major/media*, the expansion of which is favoured by trampling rather than by cereal cultivation (Richard and Géry 1993).

However, cereal fields seem also to have expanded, as shown by the increase in the amount of pollen due to cereal crop processing in the lake-edge villages (Bourgeois 1989) and by the stock of weeds, the latter resulting from a greater permanence of wheat and barley cultivation (Lundstrom-Baudais 1986).

In this reconstruction, the period of demographic growth sees a simultaneous accentuation of the traditional patterns of shifting agriculture and the development of hunting and husbandry based on forest products. Later, at a time period when the limits of the previous pattern seem to have been reached, leading to the establishment of permanent fields, the development of a husbandry based on grazing land can be seen as the consumption of meat decreases. Such a reconstruction fits well with the current results of the stratigraphical and pedological studies conducted at the foot of the slopes of the basin of Chalain. In these sequences of clay colluvial deposits related to the glacio-lacustrine terraces, the contrast is unquestionable between two forms of agricultural techniques: before 3000 BC, a slash and burn agriculture in a forest environment only produced a slight erosion of deposits rich in small wood charcoals; after 3000 BC, the erosion is rapidly accentuated as the traces of fires set to burn the grass-cover before the land can be cultivated for cereals become more frequent (Pétrequin et al. 1996; Le Jeune 1997).

Such an opposition must exist in the dwelling sites themselves, where wooden tools were preserved below the water level. Digging and ploughing sticks to work the surface and weed the fields are well represented during the Horgen phase, before 3060 BC; after this date they disappear. This must surely coincide with the introduction of the ard, at the same time as erosion of the slopes starts to become accentuated. This date fits well with what is known of the first ploughing marks in the Val d'Aosta, in the north of Italy (Pétrequin and Pétrequin 1989).

Conclusion

In order to follow the technical and economic readjustments of agricultural communities subjected to successive waves of immigrants over three centuries, only the most significant features of this synchronous evolution have been outlined. More features do exist and one may cite the case of pig breeding, which is regularly marked at each arrival of a migratory movement (Fig. 5, right) and then diminishes in importance. In fact, it appears as if demographic growth had consequential effects on all aspects of life. However, it is not yet possible to distinguish internal adaptations within the Neolithic communities from those associated with new technical and economic patterns brought by immigrants from the south of France.

Outside the technical realm though we may cite an example drawn from the realm of culture. More than 600 ornament objects have been recovered on the two sites of Chalain and Clairvaux. Statistical study of these beads and pendants (Giligny et al. 1995) – which according to our western eyes do not have a straightforwardly technical function – shows nevertheless that changes in the fashion of personal adornment (Fig. 6) could be just as good an indicator of the opening up of the forest milieu and of the changes in the environment as the architectural timbers, vegetation remains, pollen or bone fragments: pierced teeth and other symbols related to hunting gradually give way to smooth pendants and limestone beads where male symbolism is explicit, as shown by the representation of male sexual attributes.

There is a striking parallelism between this cultural vision of the modified environment and the choice in the building materials for the houses. Before 3060, when villages are still involved in cycles of shifting agriculture in secondary forest, short-lived young ash poles

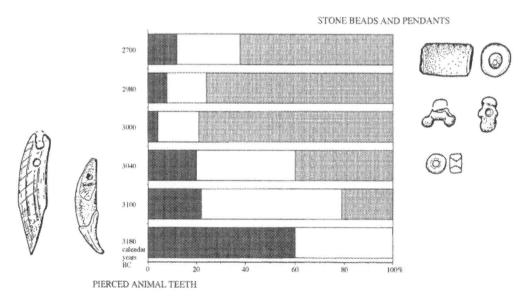

Figure 6 The rapid and drastic deforestations of the Combe d'Ain from 3180 to 2700 BC seem to have some consequential effects on the cultural system as shown by the decrease in ornaments of wild animal teeth to the benefit of beads and pendants in polished stone.

were picked. Then, after 3040, when villages had been settled for quite a while, in an open environment with permanent fields and grazing lands, large long-lasting trunks of old oaks were chosen.

The history of the agricultural communities of Chalain and Clairvaux from the thirty-second to the thirtieth centuries BC offers in brief a unique view of the typical non-linear consequences of demographic growth. The number of villages then decreased after 2970 and the local groups were strongly affected by the climatic degradation at the end of the twenty-ninth century (Magny 1993). This cyclical history then started again later on in the Combe d'Ain, after a pause when the human pressure on the environment seems to momentarily fade away. However, the reality of the effects of the climatic variations on the output of the cereal fields and as a consequence on the density of population (Arbogast et al. 1995) still remains to be determined. Unfortunately, to do this means leaving behind the waterlogged environments and therefore losing the irreplaceable accuracy of the dendrochronological calendar.

Translated by Laurence Garenne-Marot

Laboratoire de Chrono-Ecologie
UMR 6565, CNRS and Université de Franche-Comté
UFR Sciences, 16 route de Gray
France 25030 Besançon Cedex

References

Arbogast, R.-M. 1997. La grande faune de Chalain 3. In *Les sites littoraux néolithiques de Clairvaux-les-Lacs et de Chalain (Jura), III, Chalain station 3. 3200–2900 av. J.-C.* (ed. P. Pétrequin). Paris: Editions de la Maison des Sciences de l'Homme, vol. 2, pp. 641–91.

Arbogast, R.-M. and Pétrequin, P. 1993. La chasse du cerf au Néolithique dans le Jura: gestion d'une population animale sauvage. In *Exploitation des animaux sauvages à travers le temps*. 13e Rencontres Internationales d'Archéologie et d'Histoire d'Antibes, Juan-les-Pins: Editions APDCA, pp. 221–31.

Arbogast, R.-M., Magny, M. and Pétrequin, P. 1995. Expansions et déprises agricoles au Néolithique: populations, cultures céréalières et climat dans la Combe d'Ain (Jura) de 3700 à 2500 av. J.-C. In *L'homme et la dégradation de l'environnement*. XVe Rencontres Internationales d'Archéologie et d'Histoire d'Antibes, Juan-les-Pins: Editions APDCA, pp. 20–41.

Beugnier, V. 1997. L'usage du silex dans l'acquisition et le traitement des matières animales dans le Néolithique de Chalain et de Clairvaux. Thèse, Ethnologie et Préhistoire. Université de Paris X, Paris.

Bouchet, F., Pétrequin, P. and Dommelier, S. 1995. Première approche paléoparasitologique du site néolithique de Chalain (Jura, France). *Bulletin de la Société de Paléoparasitologie Expérimentale*, 88: 265–8.

Bourgeois, E. 1989. Microanalyses palynologiques d'un niveau néolithique de la station 2 AC du lac de Chalain. Mémoire de maîtrise, Histoire des Arts et Archéologie. UFR Lettres, Université de Franche-Comté, Besançon.

Giligny, F. 1994. Variabilité et transferts techniques dans le Jura à la fin du IVe et au IIIe millénaires av. J.-C. In *Terre cuite et Société*. Actes des Rencontres Internationales d'Archéologie et d'Histoire d'Antibes, Juan-les-Pins: Editions APDCA, pp. 365–80.

Giligny, F., Maréchal, D. et al. 1995. La séquence Néolithique final des lacs de Clairvaux et de Chalain. Essai sur l'évolution culturelle. In *Chronologies néolithiques. De 6000 à 2000 avant notre ère dans le bassin rhodanien* (ed. J. L. Voruz). Actes du Colloque d'Ambérieu-en-Bugey, Genève: Documents du Département d'Anthropologie et d'Ecologie de l'Université, pp. 313–46.

Lavier, C. 1996. Dendrochronologie appliquée à l'Archéologie: élaboration d'une chronologie du chêne (*Quercus* sp.) pour le Néolithique à partir des sites lacustres de Clairvaux-les-Lacs et de Chalain (Jura, France). Mémoire de DEA, Méthodes et Techniques Nouvelles en Sciences Humaines. UFR Lettres, Université de Franche-Comté, Besançon.

Le Jeune, Y. 1997. Etude de l'érosion des sols sur la rive occidentale du lac de Chalain (Jura): une manière d'appréhender l'histoire des paysages. Mémoire de DEA, Environnement et Archéologie. Museum National d'Histoire Naturelle, Paris.

Lundstrom-Baudais, K. 1986. Etude paléoethnobotanique de la station III de Clairvaux. In *Les sites littoraux néolithiques de Clairvaux-les-Lacs (Jura), I, Problématique générale. L'exemple de la station III*. Paris: Editions de la Maison des Sciences de l'Homme, pp. 311–92.

Magny, M. 1993. Un cadre climatique pour les habitats lacustres préhistoriques? *Comptes-rendus de l'Académie des Sciences Paris*, 316(II): 1619–25.

Martineau, R. 1995. Approche expérimentale de la céramique néolithique: le cas du Néolithique moyen et du Néolithique final de Chalain et de Clairvaux (Jura). Mémoire de maîtrise, Préhistoire et Ethnologie. Université de Paris X-Nanterre, Paris.

Pétrequin, A. M. and Pétrequin, P. 1989. *Le Néolithique des lacs. Préhistoire des lacs de Chalain et de Clairvaux*. Paris: Editions Errance.

Pétrequin, A.-M., Pétrequin, P. and Croutsch, C. 1996. Marigny (Jura), Parking. Rapport d'evaluation archéologique. Service Régional de l'Archéologie, Franche-Comté, Besançon.

Pétrequin, P. (ed.) 1989. *Les sites littoraux néolithiques de Clairvaux-les-Lacs (Jura), II, Le Néolithique moyen*. Paris: Editions de la Maison des Sciences de l'Homme.

Pétrequin, P. 1996. Management of architectural woods and variations in population density in the fourth and third millennia B.C. (lakes Chalain and Clairvaux, Jura, France). *Journal of Anthropological Archaeology*, 15(1): 1–19.

Pétrequin, P. (ed.) 1997. *Les sites littoraux néolithiques de Clairvaux-les-Lacs et de Chalain (Jura), III, Chalain station 3. 3200–2900 av. J.-C.* Paris: Editions de la Maison des Sciences de l'Homme, 2 vols.

Rasmussen, P. 1993. Analysis of goat/sheep faeces from Egolzwil 3, Switzerland: evidence for branch and twig foddering of livestock in the Neolithic. *Journal of Archaeological Science*, 20: 479–502.

Richard, H. 1992. Analyse de l'anthropisation du milieu à partir de quelques exemples de variations de pollens d'arbres et d'arbustes. In *L'homme et la dégradation de l'environnement*. XVe Rencontres Internationales d'Archéologie et d'Histoire d'Antibes, Juan-les-Pins: Editions APDCA, pp. 143–59.

Richard, H. and Géry, S. 1993. Variation in pollen proportions of *Plantago lanceolata* and *P. major/minor* at a neolithic lake dwelling, Lake Chalain, France. *Vegetation History and Archaeobotany*, 2: 79–88.

Troels-Smith, J. 1960. Ivy, mistletoe and elm. Climate indicators – fodderplants. *Danmarks Geologiscke Undersøgelse iv, Rockke*, 4: 1–32.

Viellet, A. 1997. Etude dendrochronologique des chênes et des frênes (*Quercus* sp. – *Fraxinus* exc.) provenant du site Néolithique final de Chalain-station 19 (Jura). Mémoire de DEA, Histoire et Cultures des Sociétés Antiques. UFR Lettres, Université de Franche-Comté, Besançon.

Rock art and socio-demography in northeastern Australian prehistory

Bruno David and Harry Lourandos

Abstract

The late Holocene witnessed widespread cultural change in northeastern Australia. These changes incorporated: 1) novel food processing technologies allowing new levels of food production; 2) the commencement of new lithic types; 3) major increases in intensities of site occupation; 4) increases in intensities of regional land use; and 5) a regionalization of rock art styles. Regional demographic models need to account for both the quantitative and qualitative aspects of these changes. In particular, we argue that demography needs to be considered as a social, as well as a 'biological' or ecological phenomenon. Demography in this sense includes population sizes and densities and their socio-organizational principles. We conclude by arguing that a regionalization of artistic behaviour in Cape York during the late Holocene points to an increased compartmentalization of people–land relations, culminating in the establishment of new territorial structures after ~2000 BP, approximating those observed ethnohistorically.

Keywords

Rock art; regionalization; Australia; prehistory; sociodemography.

Introduction

This paper addresses the dynamics of socio-demography as a question of relations between people, and between people and their environments. We attempt this through an analysis of the rock art of southeast Cape York (northeastern Australia), a behavioural product that is more or less permanently fixed in the landscape. Such an approach, we argue, can be adopted because activities that are grounded in specific locales (such as rock art, which 'signs' the landscape for extended periods of time) also are subject to political processes linking people to land and to each other. That is, they are implicitly territorially-based. This is so not so much because rock art is necessarily a means of marking territory, but because the individuals who mark the land are linked to it politically in a variety of ways. These include, for example, rights of access, land ownership sanctioned by formal legislature, appropriation, or a reclaiming of the land through perceived traditional rights or self-identification with specific locales (as evidenced by some modern graffiti). By investigating the changing configuration of specific cultural conventions – such as rock art styles – associated with a marking of the land, we aim to address the *dynamics* of relations between people and between people and land across the landscape and through time (see also Bradley 1997).

While the rock art of Cape York has been known for a long time, this is not so of the distinctive, *regional character* of the late Holocene paintings, which we argue emerged from an older, more widespread and homogeneous artistic tradition (see also Maynard 1976). Here we explore the history of rock art regionalization in Cape York, in archaeological context, together with its social and demographic implications. For regionalization of rock art suggests a sociocultural compartmentalization of the landscape, and therefore the emergence of a new socio-demographic order. We take a sociocultural approach (David and Lourandos 1997; Lourandos 1997; also David and Chant 1995) which has much in common with prior approaches to Australian material using different archaeological and palaeoanthropological data (Pardoe 1988, 1990, 1995; see also Jochim 1983).[1] One of the main assumptions employed here, however, is that it is the sociocultural context that primarily influences and shapes decisions taken, and therefore sets the historical trajectory. In this case the sociocultural context is linked to regionalization, territory and competitive intergroup politics. Decisions themselves are taken within the limits (and influences) set by the natural environment at different points in time (Ingold 1980, 1988; also Ellen 1982).

Rock art, place and people

Rock art involves a marking of the land by people who do more than wander around a politically neutral, open landscape. As Conkey (1990: 15) notes with reference to art styles, what artistic practices 'can tell us about is not culture or groups per se, but the contexts in which group or other social/cultural phenomena are mobilized as process' (see also Smith 1992). Social and political conventions act to *structure* and *regulate* behaviour on the ground, via locally and regionally recognized principles that serve to control relations between people, and between people and land.

The ability to mark the land, such as in the creation of rock art or the construction of monuments (e.g. cemeteries, earth mounds), is likewise subject to access to place. Rock art is a means of socializing the land, not only through a symbolling process that attributes metaphysical meaning to place, but in the process also by externalizing the cultural self onto the landscape (see also Taçon 1993, 1994). Rock art in this way plays a role in the definition of territory. Australian examples abound in the literature of this link between artist, land and sense of place mediated by belief system, which together articulate aspects of territoriality. For the arid zone, Taçon (1994) documents that specific rock art styles delimit land ownership and its relationship to particular ancestral Dreamings, who give identity to the land. In Yarralin country, in semi-arid Australia, people talk of rock art as a 'photo' that identifies that land with its Dreaming beings (Rose 1992; see also Lewis and Rose 1987). There is knowledge associated with this art; some of this is public, and some is restricted, even highly secret. It is, however, always linked to the shape, to the history, to the people, to the spirits and/or to the law of the land. The latter are given to local groups by ancestral beings in the Dreaming.

For Arnhem Land, Morphy (1991) has argued that named moieties and clans *own* particular songs, ceremonies and artistic motifs (see also Taylor 1996). 'Paintings', he writes, 'are part of the ancestral . . . inheritance of clans. They are as much the property of clans as the land itself' (Morphy 1991: 57). The creation and use of art are circumscribed by strict socio-political conventions, which involve a consideration of kin links, territorial concerns, ritual roles and contexts of use and presentation (which are interrelated concerns) (see also Williams 1986). Similarly, in Wardaman country of the Northern Territory, paintings and engravings portray specific historical events and/or designate the identity of the local Dreaming spirits, which give identity to place (David et al. 1994; Merlan 1989). Further to the west, in the Kimberley region of Western Australia, Layton (1985, 1992) has shown how Wandjina and associated paintings are linked to local clans, landed groups descended from those very Dreaming beings. The late David Mowaljarlai, a Ngarinyin elder from the Kimberley, noted that in his homeland rock art is united *with* the land on which it occurs, as both are expressions of the same Dreaming beings that people, and events that shape, the landscape, thereby giving it territorial order and meaning (Mowaljarlai and Malnic 1993). In southeast Cape York, Trezise (1969, 1993) recorded oral traditions from local elders showing that rock paintings identify local ancestral beings and sorcery figures, both of which are grounded in the local landscape.

In each case, the art documents local history and being, as represented by actual events between people and between people and metaphysical realities, each of which is grounded in the local landscape. In each case also, the art not only relates directly to the land on which it is created and to the spirit beings it portrays, but it is said by local, traditional landowners that the beings sit in the rock, having positioned themselves in the landscape during the Dreaming. That is, the 'art' is not art, but the spirit beings themselves, much as in Christian religion the Eucharist is said to be the 'body of Christ' itself, not a mere representation (see also Rose 1992: 42–3). The only people who can 'create' this art are members of social groups officially sanctioned to do so by law, as given to them in the Dreaming. This right is defined by appropriate affiliation with local ancestors, the land and its Dreaming spirits, which together define territorial integrity. As Rosenfeld (1997: 291) has noted, although the relationship between people, place and rock art is complex,

> it is clear that most, if not all Aboriginal rock art has in some sense a meaningful relationship to the locale in which it is executed. There are cultural constraints of varying severity on artists that influence who may paint and what it is appropriate to paint at any locality.

Regionalization

During ethnographic times, therefore, rock art in Australia was intimately linked with place, the Dreaming beings that gave the land its identity, and the people who were affiliated with, and given social identity by, both the land and the Dreaming. Rock art, therefore, was a signpost to the land's identity and history, documenting both actual and metaphysical relationships. Consequently, changes in the distribution of specific markings across the landscape, we argue, reflect broader issues concerned with people and their relationships with the land; it has implications also for a metaphysical marking of the land.

Be it through a broadening or narrowing of the distribution of specific rock art styles or motifs, the implications are that the formal expression of landed behaviour changed. Regionalization – a process that we argue is visible archaeologically in our region – is embedded therefore in broader socio-demographic processes relating people and their numbers to land. The ecological and socio-political aspects of these processes are now discussed.

Territoriality

In general, territorial size among the hunter-gatherer Aboriginal populations of Australia has a close, but not necessarily deterministic, relationship with environmental productivity. Birdsell (1953, 1957, 1968, 1971, 1977) demonstrated that a general gradient existed in territorial sizes, with the largest occurring in the central Australian arid zones and the smallest in the better watered regions, including more fertile coastal areas. Birdsell and others (Tindale 1974; Dixon 1976) also pointed out that denser, more territorially bounded populations resided in the latter zones. Birdsell (1953) modelled the Australian hunter-gatherer populations as clustering in 'dialectal tribes' of some 500 people, which generally formed socio-political, landed units (also Tindale 1974). Sutton (1991: 50) has argued that such landed groups mark 'the lands whose owners under Aboriginal customary law were given particular languages during the mythic foundation of the world, the Dreaming, and it plots those land/language associations'.

Patterns of land ownership and use, however, were more complex. In general, land was owned (inherited) by clans (descent groups) and used by less formally composed 'bands' (local groups) of related people and their allies who were often drawn from various clans (Hiatt 1962; Stanner 1965; Sutton and Rigsby 1982). Both these groups were smaller in size than the 'dialectal tribe'. The politics of land ownership, and its inheritance and control (including that of its natural resources) were mediated by and competed for by clan elders. Their ends were achieved by a manipulation of marriage arrangements, knowledge, ritual, exchange, inter-group ceremonial events and access to territory and resources (Lourandos 1997; Rose 1987; Sutton and Rigsby 1982; Williams 1986).

Fissioning

Using ethnographic data, Birdsell (1953) and others (e.g. Tindale 1974) have demonstrated that these socio-demographic units (tribes, clans, bands) subdivided and formed new units when groups became too large. While the thresholds of group sizes varied (see critique of Birdsell by Hiatt 1968), this process of group fissioning has been widely reported across ethnographic Australia. McNiven's (in press) recent review indicates that fissioning involved a host of ecological and socio-political factors, including overpopulation, resource stress, political disputes, leadership rivalries (among elders, for example), inter-group rivalries and the like. Overpopulation in this case, however, involved not only overall group size, but also the potential number of elders a group could sustain (Rose 1987: 148). Moreover, splinter groups often located themselves in more marginal terrain than that of the core group (McNiven, in press). In Cape York, comparable processes of fissioning have been reported by Sutton and Rigsby (1982: 161), who describe it as a general solution to disputes arising when band size doubled. Other instances also were reported from northeastern Queensland (Dixon 1976: 213; Tindale 1974: 123, 168) and from the North Wellesley Islands in the Gulf of Carpentaria (Memmott 1983: 39; McNiven, in press).

Climatic gradients

Overall, this information allows us to suggest that in time the sizes of both groups and territories would have varied with changing climates and rates of environmental productivity, following a gradient of larger territories in less fertile and smaller sizes in more productive regions. And as numbers of people and population densities rose, groups subdivided into more numerous socio-political units. We should avoid, however, viewing this process merely in environmentally deterministic terms, for socio-political factors, among others, also mediated these events. The latter, for example, help shape micro-demographic factors, socio-cultural structures and historical patterns, and influence the timing of events. Futhermore, some apparently 'fertile' or 'rich' areas may be effectively resource-poor if the material or ideological means to exploit them are not available.

The interrelationship between ecological and socio-political factors was clearly demonstrated by Yengoyan (1968, 1976), who argued that complex socio-political practices acted as elaborate support systems that helped to bind together larger, relatively 'open' social networks in harsh arid areas of central Australia during ethnographic times (see also Gamble 1986). Complex social networks, however, also operated ethnographically in the more productive regions of Australia (such as the southeast) where, it may be argued, they served similar purposes, while at the same time mediating relations between denser and more competitive Aboriginal populations (Lourandos 1997; David and Lourandos 1997). From this evidence, we argue that both ecological/climatic and socio-cultural factors need to be considered in the general socio-demographic process under discussion, taking place in both space and time.

The general model

In order to assess the archaeological evidence from Cape York, we present the following general socio-demographic model. We argue that increasingly 'closed' territorial behaviour among hunter-gatherer populations led to more dynamic relations between people (see below). More 'open', flexible and fluid social formations were documented for ethnographic populations of lower density and reduced patterns of aggregation, like those of more arid Australian regions. These 'open' formations were mediated by kin systems that allow extensive but ordered relationships with both people and their territories (e.g. the 'eight-class' system, which enables geographically distant individuals to be incorporated into socially close kin networks). Alternatively, more 'closed' and territorially bounded formations are generally found among populations of higher density and increased levels of aggregation, as in the more fertile or ecologically diverse regions of Australia (see also Casimir 1992). Indeed, a gradient exists between the two categories, with most Australian populations having some combination of both 'open' and 'closed' characteristics.

More 'open' systems are characterized by more homogeneous cultural traits (Gamble 1986), whereas in more 'closed' systems there is a greater emphasis on territoriality, social hierarchy, and resource intensification, as well as levels of aggregation. These are all means of marking, legitimating and controlling the land and social relationships, not only as economic capital, but also as social and political resources. They are, to use Hodder's (1990) words, means of domesticating the land. For example, the maintenance of physical or conceptual 'boundaries' is often expressed through territorial marking (e.g. rock art), ritual (e.g. population aggregation for ceremonies) and formalized exchange (Bender 1981, 1985, 1993; Jochim 1983; McBryde 1984; Gamble 1986; Wobst 1976; Lourandos 1993, 1997; Pardoe 1988). 'Closure' can be accentuated by increases to population size and density, either as a result of changes in resource productivity, ecological relationships, and/or social and political organization and decision making. 'Closure' can also be associated with the formalized 'opening' up of relations at other levels (e.g. through ceremony and exchange) – an attempt at overcoming the territorial and social constrictions of 'closure' (Lourandos 1993, 1997). Once established, formal boundaries become incorporated in legal frameworks defining conditions of *integration*. Thus, once operationalized, the 'closing' of systems forges more dynamic social relations and formations, as 'boundaries' and social relations, among other things, are negotiated and renegotiated. These processes are not solely the product of environmental change or population increase, but also of particular historical conditions, and can take place in any environment.

The region

Cape York is Australia's largest peninsula, its tip forming the northern-most point of mainland Australia, jutting north of latitude 17°30′S (Fig. 1). It was attached to the island of New Guinea to the north during the terminal Pleistocene when sea levels were lower. The peninsula is environmentally diverse, including a broad range of landforms such as low-lying plains, plateaux, rainforests, mangrove systems and dissected gorges. The climate is tropical, receiving much of its rain during the monsoonal months of November to April, the rest of the year being typically dry. Very high rainfall occurs on parts of the east coast, while inland to the west of the ranges is a rain-shadow area exhibiting dry weather from May to October (the dry season). The wet season months bring about 90 per cent of the annual rain, which totals 800–1,100mm. Microhabitats vary considerably, including limestone karst outcrops, sandstone gorges and sandy plains. To the south, the peninsula opens up to wide plains that lead to Australia's arid core, more than 500km away.

Palaeoenviroments

For the general region, long-term environmental trends are based upon pollen studies and estimates of past rainfall from Atherton as well as from lake levels from the same general area of southeastern Cape York. The general pattern indicates that climate was very dry during the last glacial maximum (22,000–17,000 BP), some parts of the study region receiving about one third of today's rainfall levels. Arid conditions prevailed until the terminal Pleistocene, 14,000–13,000 BP, when precipitation levels began to increase. Climatic amelioration may not have taken place until just prior to about 10,000 BP on the Atherton Tableland, where the intensity of rainfall changes was probably most severe (Hiscock

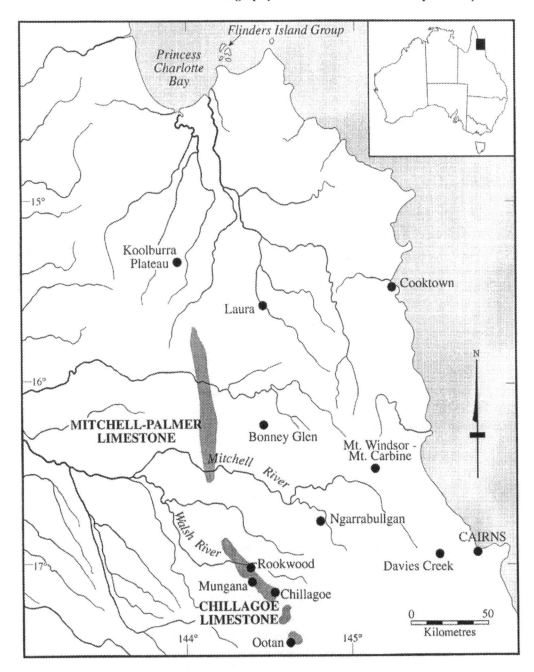

Figure 1   Southeast Cape York, showing places mentioned in text.

and Kershaw 1992: 47–9, 54). The highest levels of precipitation and temperature were recorded in the early Holocene after 10,000 BP. During this time, and within the space of only about 2,000 years, precipitation levels became as much as 285 per cent those of the terminal Pleistocene. They continued to climb during the mid Holocene, when forests (and rainforest in Atherton) were most extensive, so that by 6500 to 5900 BP they were more than 460 per cent what they had been during the preceding terminal Pleistocene (Hiscock and Kershaw 1992: 54–8; Rainfall estimates calculated from rainfall curves presented in Kershaw 1974, 1983, 1986, 1994: fig. 3; Williams et al. 1993). Rainfall levels after 3000 BP decreased slightly, and became driest between 2600 and 1400 BP, with more open (sclerophyll) vegetation (Chappel et al. 1983; Hiscock and Kershaw 1992: 58; Kershaw 1986).

Ethnography

Southeast Cape York was peopled by approximately forty language groups when Europeans first arrived in the region in the mid- to late 1800s. The sizes of territories varied greatly, from approximately $400km^2$ (e.g. Gunggandji, along the coast) to $14,800km^2$ (Ewaman, in the more arid southwestern corner of the region), although Tindale (1974) argued that the population of each group was roughly the same, around 500 individuals. Early historical accounts (e.g. Leichhardt 1847) repeatedly documented that the highest densities of people were along permanent rivers and coasts during the dry season.

Two broad, separate interaction networks have been identified for southeast Cape York (David and Cole 1990). To the north of the Walsh and Mitchell Rivers, formalized exchange relationships were established, often between individuals. Exchange relations involved short-distance travels, often between neighbouring groups. The principal times for trade both here and to the south were during times when food was plentiful, enabling the harvesting of sufficient staple plant foods to support population aggregations. Trading routes usually followed coastlines and river valleys. Many of these travels were undertaken along well-beaten paths, preserved up to the present day (McCracken 1989). While behaviour tended towards 'exclusivity' (also Pardoe 1990: 61), with closely-spaced territories being clearly differentiated and regional behaviour encoded in distinct languages, ceremonies, artistic behaviour and the like, interaction between some groups was intensive, leading Anderson and Robins (1988: 186) to conclude that they constituted a single 'cultural and linguistic bloc'.

To the south of the Walsh and Mitchell Rivers operated a largely distinct network of territorial groups. Exchange relations often involved huge areas and geographically distant kin, with travel involving distances over 300km to attend formalized, planned ceremonies being common. During such agglomerations, exchanges of both material goods and ideas took place, such as new dances, songs and the like. It was also during such times that marriages were sealed and initiations conducted. The meeting of peoples who traditionally resided in distant regions, and the sharing of cultural innovations, resulted in a broad spread of sociocultural conventions, at a geographical scale not evident to the north (David and Cole 1990; David and Chant 1995). Pardoe (1990) termed such networks 'inclusive'.

The rock art of southeast Cape York

Much of Cape York is devoid of rock art, for the simple reason that rock outcrops are not widespread. The southeastern corner of the Cape, however, is one of the world's great rock art regions, early-on coined 'Quinkan Country' by rock art enthusiasts, after the local Quinkan spirits documented from local indigenous groups (Trezise 1969). However, as we shall see below, this broad-brush characterization does not accurately tag the region's rock art, for there is no evidence of the ethnographically recorded Quinkan images before the mid- to late Holocene, part of a series of cultural innovations that changed the shape of Cape York prehistory. More critically, Quinkan rock art only appeared along the Laura sandstones, stylistically one of many more or less geographically distinct and discrete bodies of rock art to emerge in Cape York during the late Holocene (see David and Chant (1995) for multivariate statistical analyses of this trend).

The art

Systematic recordings have been made in Cape York of 10,746 rock pictures from 398 sites, representing nineteen geographically distinct areas (Fig. 1). It is from these recordings that the art's spatial and temporal patterning are here investigated. Both the geographical distribution of specific conventions, and the motif proportion of each region are considered.

Spatio-temporal trends

The earliest rock art of Cape York consists of heavily patinated peckings (petroglyphs) of abstract motifs and animal tracks (Plate 1). These have been found in a number of regions where rock surfaces are relatively stable: the Koolburra Plateau and Laura sandstones, and the Mitchell River, Palmer River, Rookwood, Mungana and Chillagoe limestones. In each case, this art shows evidence of considerable antiquity, at least dating to the early Holocene and more probably to the late Pleistocene. In the Koolburra Plateau, it is dominated by pits, single and multiple lines and mazes believed to date to at least 8500 BP by association with occupied sites (Flood 1987). At Laura, Rosenfeld (Rosenfeld et al. 1981) has uncovered similar motifs – linear designs, including simple and multiple lines, circles and their variants, and mazes – buried below sediments dated to ~13,000 BP, indicating their minimal age. Again, these are heavily patinated. In the Palmer and Mitchell Rivers nearby, similar heavily patinated motifs are again found. The only two such excavated sites – Hearth and Hay Caves – have revealed occupation dating to more than 21,000 and 13,000 BP, respectively (David and Chant 1995). To the south of the Walsh and Mitchell Rivers, the Rookwood, Mungana and Chillagoe limestone outcrops also possess a similar range of heavily patinated, pecked motifs. Motif forms again include mazes, pits and linear designs. The only two sites excavated with such art are Walkunder Arch Cave and Fern Cave, both of which have revealed Pleistocene occupation (>16,000 and 26,000 BP, respectively) (Campbell 1982; David 1991). At Walkunder Arch Cave, micro-stratigraphic dating of the layered cortex that overlies one such pecking (radiating lines) has returned a *minimum* age of 7085 ± 135 BP for the art (Campbell and Mardaga-Campbell 1993).

In some areas, such as Laura, this art appears to continue into more recent times, along with new motif forms. In others (e.g. Mitchell and Palmer Rivers), it does not. In all areas, however, the more recent rock art becomes highly regionalized, with specific stylistic attributes restricted to much smaller regions. We see this regional network throughout Cape York, including areas where earlier art has not survived. The northern-most example is Princess Charlotte Bay and the Flinders Island Group, where each of the five areas investigated is dominated by paintings of moths/butterflies and zoomorphs with crescent heads (Table 1). The paintings are certainly of late Holocene antiquity, if only because earlier paintings could not survive the exposed, maritime conditions.

Plate 1　Patinated engraving from Fern Cave, Chillagoe.

Table 1　Proportions of painted motif forms, in percentages, by region (from north to south). 1987; Maynard 1976; Grahame Walsh, pers. comm. 1994.)

Region	Marine fauna	Eel/fish	Zoomorph with crescent head	Moth/butterfly	Turtle/tortoise	Bird	Snake	Crocodile/lizard	Dog	Echidna	Bat	Macropod
Clack Is.	7	1	49	18	7	2	1	1	1			
Cliff Is.	9	6	19	30	6	4	2	4				
Flinders Is. Group	6	1	20	23	10	4	1	3	2			
Bathurst Head	5	1	22	31	9	1	1	3	1			
Jane Table Hill	2		19	49	3	2	1	1				
Koolburra Plateau		2			3		<1	7				
Jackass Station		4				1		2		2	42	2
Jowalbinna		8		2	2	1	1		3	1	8	2
Laura R.	<1	9			4	7	2	1	1	1	5	6
Palmer R.						<1			2			
Mitchell R.		1			1	1		<1	3	<1	5	
Bonney Glen									3			
Mt. Windsor/Carbine												1
Bare Hill		4				5			4			7
Ngarrabullgan							1	1				
Rookwood												
Mungana				<1		1						
Chillagoe								1		1		
Ootan												

In the Koolburra Plateau, 80km to the south, paintings become common after 1800 BP. This dating is based on the presence of sub-surface art, patterns of superimposition, weathering and patination, the presence of dogs in the pigment art (which must date to the last 4,000–3,500 years due to the timing of their arrival in Australia), fragile pigments (kaolinite), stratified pigments beneath painted panels, and by the association of painted surfaces with dated occupational events (see David and Chant, 1995: 450–1). Unlike the earlier engravings, the paintings are dominated by zoomorphs and anthropomorphs. The predominant motifs are echidna-human beings (therianthropes), a type not present anywhere else (Plate 2) (Flood 1987).

To the east are the Laura sandstones, an extensive, 400km-long arc of rugged hills, gorges and rocky outcrops. Paintings here (including the areas of Jackass and Jowalbinna Stations and the Laura River) include a very broad range of motif forms, mainly zoomorphous and anthropomorphous, at times larger than life-size. Internal decorations such as stripes, dots or rectilinear partitions are often depicted. Elaborations such as head-dresses, pendants, and distorted body parts are also commonly found, particularly on the so-called 'Quinkans' that give this body of rock art its regional name (see Cole 1992) (Plate 3). This painting tradition was initially argued by Rosenfeld et al. (1981) to be less than 5,000 years old. David and Chant (1995) revised this figure, arguing that its period of florescence dates to the last ~1,900 years (although here, like elsewhere in Australia, rock painting as a technique almost certainly has a much greater antiquity; see Cole et al. 1995 for a more detailed chronology of Laura rock art) (see also Flood 1987). The only direct radiocarbon dates yet obtained on the paintings, from two anthropomorphs, have revealed dates of 725±111 BP and 730±75 BP (Watchman and Cole 1993).

To the immediate south are the Palmer and Mitchell Rivers limestone outcrops. The

(Sources: Clegg 1978; Cole and David 1992; David and Chant 1995; David and Cole 1990; Flood

Contact fauna	Beehive/ bees	Unident. zoomorph	Echidna/ human	Human	Hand/ foot	Animal track	Item of material culture	European letters	Abstract
		2		1		3	3		6
						19			
		8		1	<1	5	10		7
				2	2	7	7		5
						9	5		10
		3	28	22		13	1		21
		3		24		7		8	5
<1	1	2		55		1	1		12
				42	1	2	2		17
				83		2	<1		13
<1		<1		70		3	5		12
				62		3			32
		3		73					24
		7		52		1			20
				8		6			85
				3		28			69
				3		12			84
				<1		10			88
				2		18			79

Plate 2 Painted human-echidna therianthropes from the Koolburra Plateau (photo by Josephine Flood).

Plate 3 Painted 'Quinkan' from the Laura region.

Plate 4   Painted dog and anthropomorphs. Mitchell-Palmer limestone zone.

paintings here consist of a narrow range of motifs, predominated by 'simple' anthropomorphs devoid of formal elaboration (Plate 4). This stands the Mitchell-Palmer paintings apart from those of surrounding regions. However, as elsewhere, the paintings date to the late Holocene, stratified pieces of ochre from excavated deposits always peaking during the last 3,900 years. The great majority date to the last 1,500 years. This is consistent with the presence of painted dogs and the use of fragile pigments (white kaolinite, local muds), and with their often relatively 'fresh' appearance.

To the east are Bonney Glen station, Mt. Windsor and Mt. Carbine, and Bare Hill (Davies Creek). The first two of these areas contain paintings similar to those of the neighbouring Palmer and Mitchell Rivers limestone (B. David, in press; M. David 1989, 1990). At Bare Hill further east, endemic anthropomorphs also predominate, all of which have down-bent legs and up-bent raised arms (Clegg 1978). In each region, the art is unlikely to be very old. This is because of various factors, including their 'good' state of preservation in active environmental settings, the presence of dogs, and the presence of unstable pigments. It is likely that the paintings are hundreds rather than thousands of years in age.

Eighty kilometres south of Bonney Glenn is the sandstone mountain of Ngarrabullgan. Here, the art's character changes dramatically. The paintings are now dominated by abstract, linear motifs such as grids, radiating lines, single and multiple lines (Plate 5). Such motifs contribute 85 per cent of all the paintings of this region. Their antiquity is less than 5400 BP – and probably considerably less – as indicated by the distribution of stratified and used pieces of ochre from Ngarrabullgan Cave (analysis still in progress). Here, a paint palette dated to 3990 ± 70 has also been excavated. At the Lookout Shelter, rock art of this character dates to between 1900 and 1600 BP.

Plate 5   Paintings from Ngarrabullgan.

To the southwest, some 50km south of the Mitchell-Palmer limestone belt, are the lime-stone outcrops of Rookwood, Mungana and Chillagoe. While microscopic traces of pigment have been found embedded between crust layers on cave walls, and dated as far back as 28,100 ± 400 BP by AMS dating of associated oxalates (Watchman and Hatte 1996), we do not yet know what this pigment art looked like, as they have so far only been revealed in cross-section. We do know, however, that by 3500 BP a rock painting tradition began to flourish. Eleven radiocarbon dates have so far been obtained directly on the art (Table 2). It is significant that none of these is older than 3500 BP, in line with the purported late Holocene antiquity of paintings from other parts of Cape York, based mainly on circumstantial dating evidence (see above). At Rookwood-Mungana-Chillagoe, however, the paintings are similar formally to those of Ngarrabullgan to the immediate northeast (Plate 6). There is no south–north gradient in predominant motif forms as one approaches the Mitchell-Palmer region to the north, where figurative motifs predominate. And further to the south, around Ootan, abstract rock paintings continue. No excavations have yet been undertaken here, but again the paintings are likely to date to the late Holocene, with about one third of paintings occurring in the fragile white pigment, kaolinite. Significantly, Ngarrabullgan, Rookwood-Mungana-Chillagoe and Ootan represent the northeastern-most extremities of the long-distance exchange network documented ethnographically (see above).

In summary, the art of Cape York consists of an early, widespread tradition of pecked pits, circles, mazes and other linear designs and animal tracks, dating to the late Pleisto-cene and possibly continuing into the early Holocene. This is followed by regionally distinctive bodies of painting, beginning around 3500 BP and blooming into full-blown, regional traditions by 1900 BP (Fig. 2) (see also Morwood and Hobbs 1995). In many areas,

Table 2 AMS radiocarbon determinations obtained on rock paintings from the Rookwood, Mungana and Chillagoe regions.

Laboratory Code	^{14}C age, in years BP	Reference
OZA576	Modern	David et al., in press
OZA577	Modern	David et al., in press
OZA578	Modern	David et al., in press
OZA579	Modern	David et al., in press
OZA573	400 ± 60	David et al., in press
OZA575	440 ± 55	David et al., in press
OZA574	840 ± 70	David et al., in press
OZB586 + OZB765 (averaged)	1220 ± 220	Armitage et al., in press
NZA2738	2056 ± 81	David 1992
OZB587 + OZB782 (averaged)	2500 ± 250	Armitage et al., in press
OZB783	3350 ± 350	Armitage et al., in press

Plate 6 Non-figurative paintings, Walkunder Arch Gallery, Chillagoe.

motif forms during this latter period have diverged noticeably from those of their historical antecedents. Before we can discuss the social and demographic implications of this regionalization of artistic behaviour, however, we consider the contemporary archaeological trends in Cape York and in wider Australia.

The archaeology of Cape York

What characterizes settlement in Cape York prehistory, we ask, for settlement systems document formalized access to place in much the same way as rock art documents an access to mark the land? Is there evidence for trends in site and regional *occupational* strategies

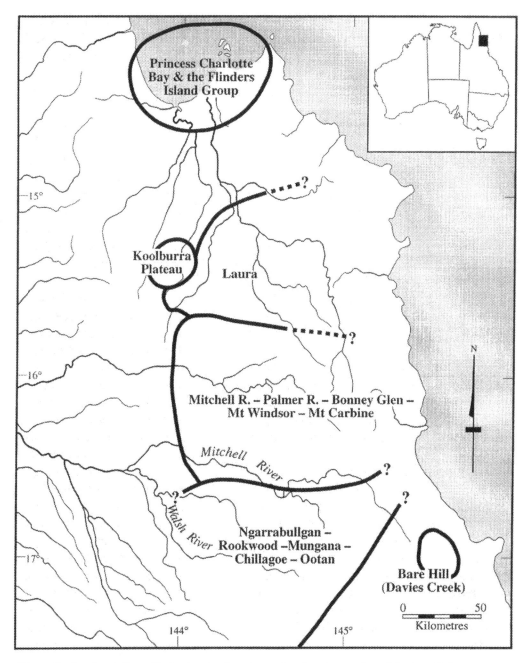

Figure 2   Southeast Cape York, showing locations of regional art styles of the late Holocene.

to accompany the rock art trends documented above? The only site types yet investigated in Cape York are rockshelters and caves, which occur wherever rock outcrops of sufficient size occur, and shell middens near the coast. During the late Holocene period, the rock-shelters show evidence of a change in intensities of both site and regional land use. Twenty-nine rockshelters and caves have been excavated and radiometrically dated from southeast Cape York – one of the largest regional samples in Australia. Of these, all but one show marked increases in intensities of site occupation, rates of hearth construction, artefact deposition and sediment build-up during the Holocene, with peak rates during the late Holocene. In addition, there are also marked increases in rates of site establishment and in the number of sites occupied within the region at this time. This information has been derived using a variety of different indices (David and Lourandos 1997, in press; David and Chant 1995; see also Morwood and Hobbs 1995). We suggest that while methodological problems remain in modelling and evaluating these trends, broadly comparable patterns and trends have been obtained from disparate data which strengthens the overall general results.

At this time also, new stone artefact types and technologies appear, such as Burren Adzes, blades and blade technologies, mostly after ~2400 BP. Significantly, it is also around this time that specialized seed-grinding stones first come into general use, both here and further afield (see below). In Australia, few artefacts can unambiguously be said to be directly related to food processing. Of these, seed-grinding stones are the only type reported from the study region. Here, they have not been found in contexts older than 1900 BP (they also occur in the very upper, undated levels of Giant Horse Gallery, a site whose base is dated to ~3800 BP) (Morwood 1995).

Coastal shell middens are mainly small in size, rarely exceeding a few tens of centi-metres in thickness. At Princess Charlotte Bay in the east and Weipa in the west, however, massive, mounded middens, often exceeding 3m in height, begin to appear around 1700 and 2500 BP respectively (Bailey et al., 1994; Beaton 1985: 8–9). In both cases, they consist almost entirely of *Anadara* cockle shells, obtained from nearby mangrove shell beds; they occur on cheniers, sandy beaches and beach ridges. At Princess Charlotte Bay, the chenier plains themselves developed before 4000 BP, and probably around 6000 BP, but the archaeological sites were formed well after the stabilization of local landforms.

As such, mound construction implies the beginnings of new resource exploitation strat-egies focused on the systematic exploitation of the mangrove species, *Anadara granosa*. Mounds also imply the establishment of focused and centralized consumption bases late in the region's occupied history. Through time, there is no evidence for a change in faunal diet breadths as such, for earlier sites reveal a similar range of fauna to the mound economies, dating at least as far back as 4760 ± 90 BP (Beaton 1985; Cribb 1986). The difference is one of scale, forcing us to consider settlement and dispersal activity as components of broader behavioural systems. The systematic exploitation of mangrove beds during the late Holocene, especially *A. granosa*, implies the beginnings of a new, specialized and focused subsistence strategy. This strategy is unlikely to have had compar-able historical precedents given that, despite concerted efforts, no earlier evidence for such a scale of locally-focused subsistence activity has yet been obtained. The mounds imply that people were not only obtaining large quantities of shellfish from geographi-cally circumscribed areas during, and only during the last 2,000 years or so, but that they were returning to those very spots time and again. Together, an alteration in land use, resource management strategies, settlement, disposal patterns and methods of living on the land (people–land relations) after 2500–1700 BP are implied.

Cape York in broader perspective

Broadly comparable patterns have been reported from other Australian regions during the late Holocene period. Many of these have already been reviewed elsewhere (David and Chant 1995; Lourandos 1997), and for lack of space only two such innovations will be discussed here. From the neighbouring north Queensland rainforests, Horsfall (1987) has argued that the first conclusive evidence for the exploitation, treatment (detoxification) and consumption of toxic plants takes place after ~2000 BP at the Mulgrave 2 site, and after ~1000 at Jiyer Cave. Before that time, plant remains are present, but none are identified as toxic species. These important results herald the addition of a large range of relatively common plants to the diet, both from the rainforest and beyond (e.g. cycads, *Pandanus* spp.). Similar results have been obtained further afield by Barker (1995) from the Whitsunday Islands for the period after ~500 BP, and by Beaton (1977) from the Central Queensland Highlands after ~4300 BP. In both cases, this was accompanied by a marked increase in intensities of site and regional land use, as well as in the incidence of rock painting (Barker 1995; Morwood 1979). In the Whitsunday Islands, these changes have been explained as accompanying the emergence of new, bounded territories, enabling specific groups to control socially, politically and economically individual off-shore islands (Barker 1995).

Significantly, these changes came roughly at a time when in more arid parts of Australia grass seeds began to be systematically exploited (Smith 1986). Seed-grinding stones of a standard form occur in the archaeological record around 3000 BP (but see Gorecki et al. 1997), and from then on become relatively common. The ramifications of such innovations are not exclusively 'economic' or demographic, but also imply changes in the way people interacted with and symbolized their immediate surroundings, transforming grasslands to harvestable 'fields'. These changes have a bearing on the scheduling of everyday life and seasonal cycles: with these plants securing their place as staples, people's movements became retuned to novel resources. There is an implication here for the use and management of the land, altering relations between people and between people and their environments (see also David and Lourandos, in press). The general issue of late Holocene cultural changes in Australia has been widely debated for some time. It has more recently also been compared to cultural changes of earlier periods, such as the terminal Pleistocene and early Holocene (Lourandos 1997; see also Beaton 1985; Bird and Frankel 1990; David and Chant 1995; David and Lourandos 1997; Hiscock 1994; Hiscock and Veth 1991; Hughes and Lampert 1982; Lourandos and Ross 1994; O'Connell and Allen 1995; Ross 1985; Smith 1986; Veth 1989).

Discussion: rock art, climate and socio-demographic dynamics

To sum up: in Cape York, the late Holocene witnessed a regionalization of rock art styles; increased use of sites and of the region as a whole; the beginnings of new, standardized stone artefact types and technologies; the first evidence of systematic exploitation of grass seeds – a major potential food staple; and the establishment of large, centralized base camps along some parts of the coast. In each case, these new developments reached their zenith after 1900 BP or shortly beforehand. We argue that this temporal coincidence of innovations in qualitative (e.g. stone artefact types, settlement-subsistence systems) and quantitative (e.g. increases in site and regional occupation) factors, coupled with a shift in organizational principles (rock art regionalization), is not fortuitous.

Rock art is part of the cultural landscape peopled by groups and communities with social, political and economic organization. Why is the early rock art of all parts of southeast Cape York dominated by abstract designs and animal tracks? The question is not so much why figurative elements are so rare or absent before the late Holocene, but why a single or very similar sets of abstract images, of limited range, are in use throughout the region where early art has been found in Cape York – an area covering more than 38,000km². Why do we not see notable regional variation during this early phase (e.g. there are no triangles, squares, diamonds or rectangles)? One likely scenario, we argue, is due to the operation of a single, more or less unified system of territoriality, land use and information exchange, linking each area symbolically, socially, culturally and politically. But by 3500 BP, and especially after 1900 BP this changed. The art became regionally distinctive, a phenomenon which, we argue, suggests the emergence of regionally-specific networks of interaction and symbolic frameworks. In all areas where both earlier and late Holocene art have been found, the same trend towards late Holocene regionalization was identified; artistic change across southeast Cape York followed much the same course. Far from signifying the operation of separate regional processes, a single, general late Holocene demographic trend towards regionalization in people–people and people–land relations is implied. The use and marking of the land became a more local concern, increasingly independent of neighbouring territories.

To understand adequately these trends we need to position innovations in their historical contexts. We argue that during the *early* to *mid*-Holocene, Aboriginal populations were rising. This was a time when natural levels of bioproductivity were high as a result of increased levels of effective rainfall. When such productivity eventually decreased with a change to drier climate during the mid- to late Holocene, Aboriginal populations were faced with two main options. These were either (a) to re-attune population sizes to the current availability of natural resources by *lowering* population sizes; or (b) to maintain or increase population levels and follow the more 'novel' strategy of regionalization, for which there is far less evidence in earlier times. That the latter option was selected suggests that the sociocultural context, out of which decisions arose, had now changed. Thus, sociocultural patterns appear different to those evident in prior dry or drier periods, such as the glacial maximum and terminal Pleistocene. This change in strategy resulted in the following.

1 The emergence of new territorial systems that served, among other things, to regulate access to resources, which themselves came in increasing demand as a result of rising populations, and possibly also of changing population structures. This was operationalized by further formalizing and enforcing territorial protocols, resulting in a regionalization of social behaviour and the emergence of relatively small territories. A geographically more patchy mosaic of formal landed groups and territorial blocs, some closely inter-related and others not so, emerged. It is possible that patchiness itself may to some extent have been the product of drier climates. We make the point, however, that in Australia levels of environmental patchiness were, and continue to be, influenced by people during ethnographic times, such as in the management of habitats and resources through the use of fire and other practices (e.g. Harris 1977; Hynes and Chase 1982). Good examples of this are the geographically well-demarcated, managed yam

grounds in southwestern Australia (Hallam 1975), and the *Pandanus* and cycad groves criss-crossed by well-defined footpaths in Queensland (e.g. Leichhardt 1847; see also Beaton 1982), both of which were observed by the earliest European explorers. We suggest here that risk-management strategies that may have emerged during the late Holocene to cope with more patchy conditions, as argued by Hiscock (1994) to explain the advent of new, specialized stone tool types, should be considered in such a context of *effective* (that is, socioculturally-mediated) rather than purely 'natural' environmental patchiness – that is, territoriality itself constructs patchiness.

2 Enlarging diet breadths, incorporating a new range of staple plant foods capable of being collected in large quantities and over extended periods of time. The advantage was two-fold, firstly broadening everyday diets and thereby minimizing risks associated with resource fluctuations – and even depletion – and secondly enabling the demands of mass consumption, such as at times of feasts or ceremonies, to be met. During the ethnographic period, such feasts are known to have taken place at regular intervals in many parts of Australia, and often involved groups of >500 individuals congregating for up to weeks at a time. Without such mass foods, events of this kind would not have been possible (see also Flood et al. 1987; Gould 1980; Lourandos 1988).

3 Restricting the ranges of resource extraction and settlement to shorter-spaced and/or more commonly reused areas. That is, residential bases became more marked as a result of higher levels of use and reuse – perhaps over longer periods than previously – and a decreasing incidence of long-distance mobility (but not necessarily exchange) with increasing political definition of bounded homelands, especially in the more resource-rich areas. One implication of such historical trends would be their archaeological visibility in places such as quarries and other centralized places of resource extraction, where control over land and resources was heightened (see also point 1 above, concerning effective patchiness). We predict that in Cape York, and possibly elsewhere, the politically formalized control of such centralized resource targets mostly dates to that period of increasing territorial circumscription – the late Holocene. So far, no quarries have yet been investigated, although they are known to exist.

Elsewhere, we also note that – on independent, skeletal evidence – Pardoe (1990) has argued for a similar pattern of Holocene (including late Holocene) regionalization of social behaviour and territorial organization along the Murray River, some 2000km to the south of Cape York (see also Lewis (1988) for Arnhem Land to the west).

Through such innovations, relations between people and between people and land were altered (see also Layton 1992; Lewis 1988). This allowed both individuals and groups to cope with lowered levels of natural resource productivity during the drier late Holocene period, together with increasing population densities, as suggested by the occupational trends (above). Such conditions also would have heightened levels of inter-group competition. Indeed, they enabled social and political trajectories set in motion during the preceding early to mid-Holocene period to continue – such as increasing intensities of site and regional land use. Rather than revert to prior demographic conditions, the regionalization process severed the socio-demographic principles of previous periods of lower environmental productivity (the terminal Pleistocene), which had taken place before the early Holocene climatic 'amelioration', when the process here described was set in motion. Once fragmented into more or less distinct and discrete social and political blocs (each with their own territorial interests and at least in part directing economic routines), historical conditions favoured an on-going momentum towards maintaining, and possibly accentuating, a compartmentalized cultural landscape and its associated alliances. Individual territorial interests by now may have been legitimized by association with the Dreaming, itself steeped in territoriality. Together, this process became expressed archaeologically by heightened levels of land use and a regionalization of social, cultural and territorial behaviour, as is expressed in northeastern Australia in a marking of the land through rock art. We therefore view this process as a complex set of events, involving an interrelationship between climate, demography (including population increase and patterns of dispersal) and sociocultural factors (relating to the sociopolitics of territoriality). We also have avoided merely attributing this course of events to 'prime movers' such as climatic change or population increase.

Conclusion

In this paper, we have attempted to integrate both external environmental conditions and social-historical foundations in modelling palaeodemographic trends in Cape York prehistory. We have argued that a regionalization of artistic behaviour in Cape York during the late Holocene indicates an increased compartmentalization of relations between people and land, resulting in the establishment of new territorial structures after about 2000 BP, reminiscent of those observed in the more recent ethnohistoric period.

Acknowledgements

We thank the Australian Institute of Nuclear Science and Engineering for radiocarbon grants to date rock art; Professor Marvin Rowe, Ruth Ann Armitage, Ewan Lawson and the Australian Nuclear Science and Technology Organisation's ANTARES AMS laboratories for chemistry and radiocarbon dating; Bryce Barker, Ian McNiven, Meredith Wilson, and Stephen Shennan for comments; Gary Swinton, Department of Geography and Environmental Science, Monash University for Figures 1 and 2; Monash University for a Logan Fellowship to BD; and two anonymous referees for their helpful, constructive comments.

Bruno David
Department of Geography and Environmental Science
Monash University
Victoria 3168, Australia
E-mail: Bruno.David@arts.monash.edu.au

Harry Lourandos
Department of Anthropology and Sociology
University of Queensland
Queensland 4072, Australia
E-mail: H.Lourandos@mailbox.uq.edu.au

Note

1 This paper has not included sociobiological approaches, as pointed out to us by one anonymous referee. While inclusion of such may be a profitable extension of the arguments developed here – e.g. by discussion of contrasting non-human examples and the effects of the processes presented here on genetics – it is beyond the scope of the theoretical and substantive aspects of our paper. We have worked within the literature (both ethnographic and archaeological) on the sociocultural side of this wider debate.

References

Anderson, C. and Robins, C. 1988. Dismissed due to lack of evidence? Kuku-Yalanji sites and the archaeological record. In *Archaeology with Ethnography: An Australian Perspective* (eds B. Meehan and R. Jones). Canberra: Australian National University, pp. 152–205.

Armitage, R. A., David, B., Hyman, M., Rowe, M. W., Tuniz, C., Lawson, E., Jacobsen, G. and Hua, Q. in press. Radiocarbon determinations on Chillagoe rock paintings: small sample Accelerator Mass Spectrometry. *Records of the Australian Museum*.

Bailey, G., Chappell, J. and Cribb, R. 1994. The origin of Anadara shell mounds at Weipa, North Queensland, Australia. *Archaeology in Oceania*, 29(2): 69–80.

Barker, B. 1995. The sea people: maritime hunter-gatherers on the tropical coast. A late Holocene maritime specialisation in the Whitsunday Islands, central Queensland. Unpublished PhD thesis. St. Lucia: University of Queensland.

Beaton, J. M. 1977. Dangerous harvest. Unpublished PhD thesis. Canberra: Australian National University.

Beaton, J. M. 1982. Fire and water: aspects of Australian Aboriginal management of cycads. *Archaeology in Oceania*, 17: 59–67.

Beaton, J. M. 1985. Evidence for a coastal occupation time-lag at Princess Charlotte Bay (North Queensland) and implications for coastal colonisation and population growth theories for Aboriginal Australia. *Archaeology in Oceania*, 20: 1–20.

Bender, B. 1981. Gatherer-hunter intensification. In *Economic Archaeology* (eds A. Sheridan and G. Bailey). Oxford: British Archaeological Reports International Series 96, pp. 149–57.

Bender, B. 1985. Prehistoric developments in the American midcontinent and in Brittany, northwest France. In *Prehistoric Hunter-gatherers: The Emergence of Cultural Complexity* (eds T. D. Price and J. A. Brown). Orlando, Florida: Academic Press, pp. 21–57.

Bender, B. 1993. *Landscape: Politics and Perspectives*. Oxford: Berg.

Bird, C. F. M. and Frankel, D. 1991. Chronology and explanation in western Victoria and southeast South Australia. *Archaeology in Oceania*, 26: 1–16.

Birdsell, J. B. 1953. Some environmental and cultural factors influencing the structuring of Australian Aboriginal populations. *American Naturalist*, 87: 171–207.

Birdsell, J. B. 1957. Some population problems involving Pleistocene Man. *Cold Spring Harbor Symposia on Quantitative Biology*, 22: 47–69.

Birdsell, J. B. 1968. Some predictions for the Pleistocene based on equilibrium systems among recent hunter-gatherers. In *Man the Hunter* (eds R. B. Lee and I. DeVore). Chicago: Aldine Publishing Company, pp. 229–40.

Birdsell, J. B. 1971. Ecology, spacing mechanisms and adaptive behavior in Aboriginal land tenure. In *Land Tenure in the Pacific* 9 (ed. R. Crocombe). Melbourne: Oxford University Press, pp. 334–61.

Birdsell, J. B. 1977. The recalibration of a paradigm for the first peopling of Australia. In *Sunda and Sahul* (eds J. Allen, J. Golson and R. Jones). London: Academic Press, pp. 113–67.

Bradley, R. 1997. *Rock Art and the Prehistory of Atlantic Europe: Signing the Land*. London: Routledge.

Campbell, J. B. 1982. New radiocarbon results for north Queensland prehistory. *Australian Archaeology*, 14: 62–6.

Campbell, J. B. and Mardaga-Campbell, M. 1993. From macro- to nano-stratigraphy: linking vertical and horizontal dating of archaeological deposits with the direct dating of rock art at 'The Walkunders', Chillagoe (north Queensland, Australia). In *Time and Space: Dating and Spatial Considerations in Rock Art Research* (eds J. Steinbring, A. Watchman, P. Faulstich and P. Taçon). Melbourne: Australian Rock Art Research Association, pp. 57–63.

Casimir, M. 1992. The determinants of rights to pasture: territorial organisation and ecological constraints. In *Mobility and Territoriality* (eds M. Casimir and A. Rao) Oxford: Berg, pp. 153–203.

Chappell, J., Chivas, A., Wallensky, E., Polach, H. and Aharon, P. 1983. Holocene palaeoenvironmental changes, central to north Great Barrier Reef inner zone. *Bureau of Mineral Resources Journal of Geology and Geophysics*, 8: 223–35.

Clegg, J. 1978. Mathesis words, mathesis pictures. Unpublished MA (hons) thesis. Sydney: University of Sydney.

Cole, N. 1992. 'Human' motifs in the rock paintings of Jowalbinna, Laura. In *State of the Art: Regional Rock Art Studies in Australia and Melanesia* (eds J. MacDonald and I. Haskovec). Melbourne: Australian Rock Art Research Association, pp. 164–73.

Cole, N. and David, B. 1992. 'Curious drawings' at Cape York: a summary of rock art investigation in the Cape York Peninsula region since the 1820s and a comparison of some regional traditions. *Rock Art Research*, 9(1): 3–26.

Cole, N., Watchman, A. and Morwood, M. 1995. Chronology of Laura rock art. In *Quinkan Prehistory: The Archaeology of Aboriginal Art in SE Cape York Peninsula, Australia* (eds M. Morwood and D. Hobbs). *Tempus* 3. Brisbane: University of Queensland, pp. 147–59.

Conkey, M. W. 1990. Experimenting with style in archaeology: some historical and theoretical issues. In *The Uses of Style in Archaeology* (eds M. W. Conkey and C. A. Hastorf). Cambridge: Cambridge University Press, pp. 5–17.

Cribb, R. 1986. Sites, people and archaeological information traps: a further transgressive episode from Cape York. *Archaeology in Oceania*, 21 (3): 171–5.

David, B. 1991. Fern Cave, rock art and social formations: rock art regionalisation and demographic changes in southeastern Cape York Peninsula. *Archaeology in Oceania*, 26: 41–57.

David, B. 1992. An AMS date for north Queensland rock art. *Rock Art Research*, 9(2): 139–41.

David, B. in press. Rock art of southeast Cape York Peninsula: Bonney Glen Station. *Memoirs of the Queensland Museum*.

David, B. and Chant, D. 1995. *Rock Art and Regionalisation in North Queensland Prehistory. Memoirs of the Queensland Museum*, 37 (2).

David, B. and Cole, N. 1990. Rock art and inter-regional interaction in northeastern Australian prehistory. *Antiquity*, 64: 788–806.

David, B. and Lourandos, H. 1997. 37,000 years and more in tropical Australia: investigating long-term archaeological trends in Cape York Peninsula. *Proceedings of the Prehistoric Society*, 63.

David, B. and Lourandos, H. in press. Landscape as mind: land use, cultural space and change in north Queensland prehistory. *Quaternary International.*

David, B., McNiven, I., Attenbrow, V., Flood, J. and Collins, J. 1994. Of Lightning Brothers and White Cockatoos: dating the antiquity of signifying systems in the Northern Territory, Australia. *Antiquity*, 68: 241–51.

David, B., Tuniz, C., Lawson, E., Hua, Q., Jacobsen, G., Head, J. and Rowe, M. in press. Dating charcoal drawings from Chillagoe, north Queensland. To be published in a book (title unknown) edited by G. Ward and C. Tuniz, Canberra: Australian Institute of Aboriginal and Torres Strait Islander Studies.

David, M. 1989. An archaeological survey of the Mt. Carbine and Mt. Windsor tablelands region, northeast Queensland. Conducted as part of the ANZSES 'Devil's Thumb' expedition, 1988–1989. Unpublished report, Archaeology Branch, Brisbane.

David, M. 1990. Beyond the Calamus: an archaeological survey of the Mount Carbine Tableland and Baker's Blue Mountain region. Conducted as part of the ANZSES 'Daintree Falls' expedition, 1989–1990. Unpublished report, Archaeology Branch, Brisbane.

Dixon, R. M. W. 1976. Tribes, languages and other boundaries in northeast Queensland. In *Tribes and Boundaries in Australia* (ed. N. Peterson). Canberra: Australian Institute of Aboriginal Studies, pp. 207–38.

Ellen, R. 1982. *Environment, Subsistence and System.* Cambridge: Cambridge University Press.

Flood, J. 1987. Rock art of the Koolburra Plateau, north Queensland. *Rock Art Research*, 4(2): 91–126.

Flood, J. David, B., Magee, J. and English, B. 1987. Birrigai: a 21000 year old site in the A.C.T. *Archaeology in Oceania*, 22(1): 9–26.

Gamble, C. 1986. *The Palaeolithic Settlement of Europe.* Cambridge: Cambridge University Press.

Gorecki, P., Grant, M., O'Connor, S. and Veth, P. 1997. The morphology, function and antiquity of Australian grinding implements. *Archaeology in Oceania*, 32(2): 141–50.

Gould, R. A. 1980. *Living Archaeology.* Cambridge: Cambridge University Press.

Hallam, S. 1975. *Fire and Hearth.* Canberra: Australian Institute of Aboriginal Studies.

Harris, D. R. 1977. Subsistence strategies across Torres Straits. In *Sunda and Sahul* (eds J. Allen, J. Golson and R. Jones). London: Academic Press, pp. 421–63.

Hiatt, L. R. 1962. Local organisation among the Australian Aborigines. *Oceania*, 32: 267–86.

Hiatt, L. R. 1968 Discussion, Part V. In *Man the Hunter* (eds R. B. Lee and I. DeVore). Chicago: Aldine, pp. 245–8.

Hiscock, P. 1994 . Technological responses to risk in Holocene Australia. *Journal of World Archaeology*, 8: 267–99.

Hiscock, P. and Kershaw, A. P. 1992. Palaeoenvironments and prehistory of Australia's tropical Top End. In *The Naive Lands: Prehistory and Environmental Change in Australia and the Southwest Pacific* (ed. J. Dodson). Melbourne: Longman Cheshire, pp.43–75.

Hiscock, P. and Veth, P. 1991. Change in the Australian desert culture: a reanalysis of tulas from Puntutjarpa rockshelter. *World Archaeology*, 22: 332–45.

Hodder, I. 1990. *The Domestication of Europe.* Oxford: Blackwell.

Horsfall, N. 1987. Living in rainforest: the prehistoric occupation of north Queensland's humid tropics. Unpublished PhD thesis. Townsville: James Cook University of North Queensland.

Hughes, P. J. and Lampert, R. J. 1982. Prehistoric population change in southern coastal New South Wales. In *Coastal Archaeology in Eastern Australia* (ed. S. Bowdler). Canberra: Australian National University, pp. 16–28.

Hynes, R. A. and Chase, A. K. 1982. Plants, sites and domiculture: Aboriginal influence on plant communities in Cape York Peninsula. *Archaeology in Oceania*, 17: 38–50.

Ingold, T. 1980. *Hunters, Pastoralists and Ranchers*. Cambridge: Cambridge University Press.

Ingold, T. 1988. Notes on the foraging mode of production. In *Hunters and Gatherers: History, Evolution and Social Change* (eds T. Ingold, D. Riches and J. Woodburn). Oxford: Berg, pp. 269–85.

Jochim, M. 1983. Palaeolithic cave art in ecological perspective. In *Hunter-gatherer Economy in Prehistory* (ed. G. N. Bailey). Cambridge: Cambridge University Press, pp. 212–19.

Kershaw, A. P. 1974. A long continuous pollen sequence from north-eastern Australia. *Nature*, 251: 222–3.

Kershaw, A. P. 1983. Considerations nouvelles sur la vegetation Australienne. *L'Espace Geographique*, 3: 185–94.

Kershaw, A. P. 1986. Climatic change and Aboriginal burning in north-east Australia during the last two glacial/interglacial cycles. *Nature*, 322: 47–9.

Kershaw, A. P. 1994. Pleistocene vegetation of the humid tropics of northeastern Queensland, Australia. *Palaeogeography, Palaeoclimatology, Palaeoecology*, 109: 399–412.

Layton, R. 1985. The cultural context of hunter-gatherer rock art. *Man* (n.s.), 20: 434–53.

Layton, R. 1992. *Australian Rock Art: A New Synthesis*. Cambridge: Cambridge University Press.

Leichhardt, L. 1847. *Journal of an Overland Expedition in Australia*. London: T. & W. Boone.

Lewis, D. 1988. *The Rock Paintings of Arnhem Land, Australia: Social, Ecological and Material Culture Change in the Post-glacial Period*. Oxford: British Archaeological Reports, International Series 415.

Lewis, D. and Rose, D. B. 1987. *The Shape of the Dreaming: the Cultural Significance of Victoria River Rock Art*. Canberra: Aboriginal Studies Press.

Lourandos, H. 1988. Palaeopolitics: resource intensification in Aboriginal Australia and Papua New Guinea. In *Hunters and Gatherers: History, Evolution and Social Change* (eds T. Ingold, D. Riches and J. Woodburn). Oxford: Berg, pp. 148–60.

Lourandos, H. 1993. Hunter-gatherer cultural dynamics: long- and short-term trends in Australian prehistory. *Journal of Archaeological Research*, 1(1): 67–88.

Lourandos, H. 1997. *Continent of Hunter-Gatherers: New Perspectives in Australian Prehistory*. Cambridge: Cambridge University Press.

Lourandos, H. and Ross, A. 1994. The great 'intensification debate': its history and place in Australian archaeology. *Australian Archaeology*, 39: 54–63.

McBryde, I. 1984. Kulin greenstone quarries: the social contexts of production and distribution for the Mt William site. *World Archaeology*, 16: 267–85.

McCracken, C. 1989. Some Aboriginal walking tracks and camp sites in the Douglas Shire, north Queensland. *Queensland Archaeological Research*, 6: 103–13.

McNiven, I. in press. Fissioning and regionalisation: the social dimensions of changes in Aboriginal use of the Great Sandy Region, South East Queensland. In *Australian Coastal Archaeology* (eds J. Hall and I. J. McNiven). Research School of Pacific and Asian Studies, Australian National University, Canberra.

Maynard, L. 1976. An archaeological approach to the study of Australian rock art. Unpublished MA thesis. Sydney: University of Sydney.

Memmott, P. 1983. Social structure and use of space amongst the Lardil. In *Aborigines, Land and Rights* (eds N. Peterson and M. Langton). Canberra: Australian Institute of Aboriginal Studies, pp. 33–65.

Merlan, F. 1989. The interpretive framework of Wardaman rock art: a preliminary report. *Australian Aboriginal Studies*, (2): 14–24.

Morphy, H. 1991. *Ancestral Connections: Art and an Aboriginal System of Knowledge*. Chicago: University of Chicago Press.

Morwood, M. 1979. Art and stone: a prehistory of central western Queensland. Unpublished PhD thesis. Canberra: Australian National University.

Morwood, M. 1995. Excavations at Giant Horse. In *Quinkan Prehistory: The Archaeology of Aboriginal Art in SE Cape York Peninsula, Australia* (eds M. Morwood and D. Hobbs). *Tempus* 3. Brisbane: University of Queensland, pp. 101–6.

Morwood, M. and Hobbs, D. 1995. *Quinkan Prehistory: the Archaeology of Aboriginal Art in SE Cape York Peninsula, Australia. Tempus* 3. Brisbane: University of Queensland, pp. 101–6.

Mowaljarlai, D. and Malnic, J. 1993. *Yorro Yorro*. Broome: Magabala Books.

O'Connell, J. F. and Allen, J. 1995. Human reactions to the Pleistocene-Holocene transition in Greater Australia: a summary. *Antiquity*, 69: 855–62.

Pardoe, C. 1988. The cemetery as symbol. The distribution of prehistoric Aboriginal burial grounds in southeastern Australia. *Archaeology in Oceania*, 23: 1–16.

Pardoe, C. 1990. The demographic basis of human evolution in southeastern Australia. In *Hunter-Gatherer Demography: Past and Present* (eds B. Meehan and N. White). Sydney: Oceania Monograph 39, University of Sydney, pp. 59–70.

Pardoe, C. 1994. Bioscapes: the evolutionary landscape of Australia. *Archaeology in Oceania*, 29: 182–90.

Pardoe, C. 1995. Riverine, biological and cultural evolution in southeastern Australia. *Antiquity*, 69: 696–713.

Rose, D. B. 1992. *Dingo Makes Us Human*. Cambridge: Cambridge University Press.

Rose, F. G. G. 1987. *The Traditional Mode of Production of the Australian Aborigines*. North Ryde: Angus and Robertson.

Rosenfeld, A. 1997. Archaeological signatures of the social context of rock art production. In *Beyond Art: Pleistocene Image and Symbol* (eds M. Conkey, O. Soffer, D. Stratmann and N.G. Jablonski). *Memoirs of the Academy of Sciences*, 23: 289–300.

Rosenfeld, A., Horton D. and Winter, J. 1981. *Early Man in North Queensland. Terra Australis* 6. Canberra: Australian National University.

Ross, A. 1985. Archaeological evidence for population change in the middle to late Holocene in southeastern Australia. *Archaeology in Oceania*, 20: 81–9.

Smith, C. 1992. Colonising with style: reviewing the nexus between rock art, territoriality and the colonisation and occupation of Sahul. *Australian Archaeology*, 34: 34–42.

Smith, M. 1986. The antiquity of seed grinding in central Australia. *Archaeology in Oceania*, 21: 29–39.

Stanner, W. E. H. 1965. Aboriginal territorial organisation: estate, range, domain and regime. *Oceania*, 36: 1–26.

Sutton, P. 1991. Language in Aboriginal Australia: social dialects in a geographic idiom. In *Language in Australia* (ed. S. Romaine). Cambridge: Cambridge University Press, pp. 49–66.

Sutton, P. and Rigsby, B. 1982. People with 'politicks': management of land and personnel on Australia's Cape York peninsula. In *Resource Managers: North American and Australian Hunter-gatherers* (eds N. Williams and E. Hunn). Boulder, CO: Westview.

Taçon, P. 1993. Regionalism in the recent rock art of western Arnhem Land, Northern Territory. *Archaeology in Oceania*, 28(3): 112–20.

Taçon, P. 1994. Socialising landscapes: the long-term implications of signs, symbols and marks on the land. *Archaeology in Oceania*, 29: 117–29.

Taylor, L. 1996. *Seeing the Inside: Bark Painting in Western Arnhem Land*. Oxford: Clarendon Press.

Tindale, N. B. 1974. *Aboriginal Tribes of Australia*. Los Angeles: University of California Press.

Trezise, P. 1969. *Quinkan Country*. Sydney: Reed.

Trezise, P. 1993. *Dream Road: A Journey of Discovery*. St Leonards: Allen & Unwin.

Veth, P. 1989. Islands of the interior: a model for the colonization of Australia's arid zone. *Archaeology in Oceania*, 24: 81–92.

Watchman, A. and Hatte, E. 1996. A nano approach to the study of rock art: 'The Walkunders', Chillagoe, north Queensland, Australia. *Rock Art Research*, 12(2): 85–92.

Watchman, A. and Cole, N. 1993. Accelerator radiocarbon dating of plant-fibre binders in rock paintings from northeastern Australia. *Antiquity*, 67: 355–8.

Williams, M. A. J., Dunkerley, D. L., De Deckker, P., Kershaw, A. P. and Stokes, T. 1993. *Quaternary Environments*. London: Edward Arnold.

Williams, N. 1986. *The Yolngu and their Land*. Canberra: Australian Institute of Aboriginal Studies.

Wobst, H. M. 1976. Locational relationships in palaeolithic society. *Journal of Human Evolution*, 5: 49–58.

Yengoyan, A. A. 1968. Demographic and ecological influences on Australian Aboriginal marriage sections. In *Man the Hunter* (eds R. B. Lee and I. DeVore). Chicago: Aldine, pp. 185–99.

Yengoyan, A. A. 1976. Structure, event and ecology in Aboriginal Australia: a comparative viewpoint. In *Tribes and Boundaries in Australia* (ed. N. Peterson). Canberra: Australian Institute of Aboriginal Studies, pp. 121–32.

'Terra deserta': population, politics, and the [de]colonization of Dacia

L. Ellis

Abstract

This article explores the demographic history of Dacia/Romania during and after Roman coloniz-ation as a study in the effects of colonialism and de-colonization in the core area vs. the periphery, the identification of local vs. transitory populations, the development of cultural identity, and the more ominous issue of political manipulation of archaeological data. Archaeological surveying and excavations in Romania and peripheral regions, as well as a re-evaluation of ancient literary evidence, suggest a more complex settlement history, rather than a 700-year 'terra deserta'. The post-Roman era has demonstrated an abundant archaeological record of burial and settlement, along with a continuation in distribution of Roman objects throughout former core and peripheral areas. A more thorough analysis of Roman colonization and de-colonization, together with the role of the Roman military, coinage, and commerce, are recommended as avenues towards resolution of the population continuity issue for Dacia.

Keywords

Demographic history; population continuity; Dacia; Romania; Roman Empire.

Introduction

Archaeological population studies in Eastern Europe and the Balkans have never been without controversy. Even after the demise of the Iron Curtain in 1989–90, a political tapestry, two millennia in the making, still casts a long shadow over research efforts in the social sciences. The demographic history of Romania, and its territorial antecedent Dacia, is no less an enigma – partly because the region within its shifting boundaries has been divided in various configurations and partly because Dacia/Romania occupied a geo-graphic location conducive to the economic or geo-political interests of the Roman and later Byzantine, Ottoman, Habsburg, Romanov, and Soviet empires. The combined effects of external and internal political interests on the one hand, and the fact that most of the literature is not published in a west European language on the other, have made understanding of the archaeology of Romania elusive.

Despite the difficulties, the ancient demography of Dacia/Romania should have a general archaeological interest for its informative value as a study in effects of colonialism and de-colonization in the core area vs. the periphery, the identification of local vs. transitory populations, the development of cultural identity, and the more ominous issue of political manipulation of archaeological data. This study will explore the aforementioned issues surrounding archaeological research on the population history of Dacia, from the period prior to, during, and after Roman colonization.

Historical background

The Dacians first entered written records through Herodotus (IV, 93), on an expedition in 514 BC. In the archaeological record, Dacian settlements flourished during the latter half of the Iron Age (La Tène period), i.e. fifth century BC to 70 BC. The period comprising the first century BC and the first century AD is often referred to as the 'classical period' of Dacian socio-political development, not only for the appearance of monumental architecture (stone sanctuaries and citadels), but also for the unification of a number of tribes, beginning with the Dacian leader Burebista (Strabo VII, 3, 11–12).

Between AD 101 and 106, the Dacian population under the leadership of Decebal was involved in two brutal wars with the Roman Empire, which were later memorialized on Trajan's Column in Rome. The two Dacian wars were the ultimate efforts of Roman imperial expansion. Although Roman commercial interests in Dacia date back to the second century BC, Dacia became the last Roman colony until the Aurelian withdrawal in AD 270–5. The Romans, however, only secured control over central and southern Dacia, what is today Transylvania and western Wallachia; eastern Wallachia was very likely under Roman control but was not officially incorporated into a Roman province. Dobrudja had become part of Moesia Inferior/Scythia Minor, so that the Romans controlled both banks of the lower Danube. The Roman Empire did not establish military control in the area to the west, north, and east and, therefore, this 'free Dacia' (Pârvan 1928) remained a buffer zone against barbarian populations during the second to third centuries AD (Figs 1 and 2).

The eventual reduction in Roman military commitment and the retreat during the reign of Aurelian by 275 created a power vacuum, contributing to the global crises of the third century AD. The late third and fourth centuries AD saw the movement of populations through the Carpatho-Danubian region, among them the Goths. Roman forces were still protecting Moesia and the Roman military lines along the Danube with access to the Black Sea. This demographic and cultural mosaic – instigated by Roman colonization, continued in Late Antiquity with the successive arrivals of the Goths, Huns, and Slavs, and made even more complicated by subsequent population movements during the early Medieval period – has provided an enormous challenge to both archaeologists and historians trying to sort out who was where and when.

Geo-politics and population issues

In addition to the migrations of transitory populations, Dacia/Romania has also been the object of competing power interests in the region and of disputes over territory. Dacia

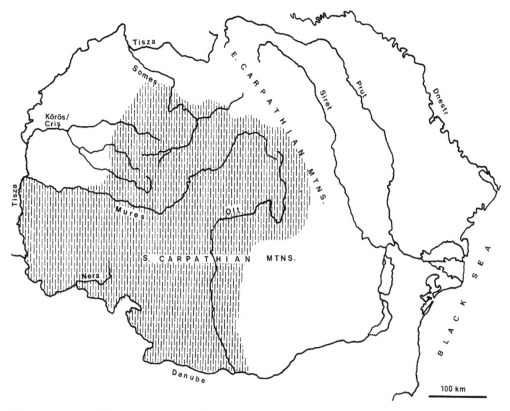

Figure 1   Area of Roman province of Dacia during the first half of the third century. The western extension of provincial Dacia to the Tisza River (currently Yugoslav territory and western Banat) is uncertain and disputed (cf. unbiased discussion of the evidence by Tudor 1968: 52–6). This region was sparsely settled probably due to past extensive moors and/or sandy soils; however, there is evidence of a number of *vici* (rural villages), occasional Roman troop movements, and several earthen wall constructions – the latter of uncertain date (Horedt 1974; Vulpe 1974).

was cut in half in the Roman period; the Black Sea region (Dobrudja) was incorporated into the Byzantine Empire; the entire territory was later divided between Habsburg and Ottoman interests; and, finally, the eastern region of Bessarabia and some adjoining areas were annexed by imperial Russian and later Soviet regimes.

However, it is the period of the Austro-Hungarian Empire and the relations among ethnic groups (Romanians, Hungarians, and Saxons) in Transylvania which is particularly pertinent to the archaeological discussion on demography. Ethnic politics in Transylvania have been a dilemma for centuries (cf. Verdery 1983). The Hungarians had settled in the region of Pannonia at the end of the ninth century and entered Transylvania in the tenth century, making the province part of the Hungarian kingdom in the eleventh century. Colonies of German-speaking Saxons were established in the urban centers of Transylvania during the twelfth century. The controversy centers around the origin of the Romanian population and its relationship with respect to the period of Roman colonization and to the indigenous Dacians. Two diametrically opposed opinions flourished during the

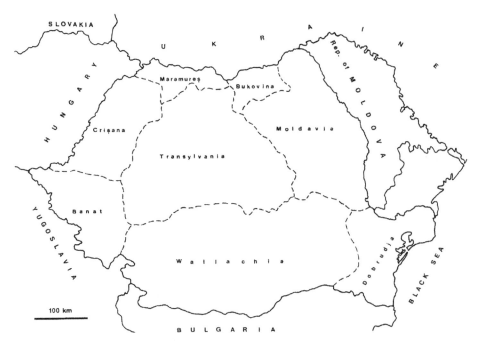

Figure 2   Current political map of Romania with provincial subdivisions (broken lines) and international boundaries (solid lines).

fervor of nineteenth-century nationalism: the Austro-Hungarian worldview saw Transylvania as uninhabited land prior to Hungarian/Saxon settlement; Romanian nationalists saw Transylvania as part of their linguistic and territorial heritage dating back to the Roman colonization of Dacia. Of the numerous publications written in the eighteenth and nineteenth centuries on the origins of the Romanians, two authors in particular stand out for their propagation of a *terra deserta* hypothesis. The historical treatises of Sulzer and Roesler have had a daunting effect on how twentieth-century archaeological research into population history has been conducted in Romania.

The Swiss Franz Joseph Sulzer (d. 1791) had a career primarily in the military and later the law. He became a captain in the Habsburg imperial regiment (1759–73), moved to Transylvania and married into a wealthy Saxon family. He had a short career in jurisprudence and later re-entered the army as an officer in 1782. Sulzer is mostly remembered as an amateur historian who wrote a 3–volume history of the Romanian provinces entitled, *Geschichte des transalpinischen Daciens, das ist Walachei, Moldau und Bessarabiens, im Zusammenhange mit der Geschichte des übrigen Daciens*, published in 1781–3 in Vienna. In the second volume of this work, he developed the theory that Dacia was totally vacated of population after the withdrawal of the Roman Empire. His contention was that, since Romanian-speaking peoples are never mentioned in documents during Late Antiquity and the early Medieval period, they must have moved somewhere south of the Danube by the end of the third century and then migrated back into present Romanian territories in two waves, beginning at the end of the twelfth century and early thirteenth century. Sulzer cited as 'evidence': 1) the influence of Slavic on the Romanian language (which could not have occurred except further south on the Balkan Peninsula), 2) the absence of political rights among the Romanians in Transylvania, 3) their Orthodox Christian faith (which could only have been embraced south of the Danube and in contact with the Byzantine church), and 4) the ancient literary sources which state that Dacia was depopulated as a result of the Aurelian withdrawal.

In 1871, Robert Roesler, a Moravian philologist trained in Vienna, Lvov and Graz, published a revised version of Sulzer's theories in *Rumänische Studien. Untersuchungen zur älteren Geschichte Rumäniens* (Leipzig). Roesler's writings, in particular, contained rather blatant ethnic vilification of Romanians and also referred derogatively to the demands of Romanians for equal rights in Transylvania. Roesler thereby crossed a subtle border from the writing of academic history to the writing of history for political purposes.

Habsburg influence in Romania did not extend to the eastern provinces (Bessarabia and Moldavia) nor to the south (Wallachia and Dobrudja), which would have intruded into Romanov and Ottoman spheres of interest. Moreover, historians were not concerned with the issue of population continuity in these southern and eastern Romanian territories, even though there is a similar paucity of epigraphic or literary references to Dacians in the Roman and post-Roman eras. Therefore, the writings of the early proponents of the *terra deserta* theory are suspect because they cannot be separated from the political aims of the Habsburg Empire, whose policies fomented ethnic unrest throughout the Balkans and led to tragic consequences for the twentieth century.

In the post-Second World War era, Soviet annexation of Bessarabia resurrected pre-First World War Romanov territorial interests in a majority control over the Black Sea coastline with access to the Danube Delta region. Reminiscent of Habsburg interests in Transylvania, Soviet publications on the archaeology of the re-named 'Moldavian SSR' hesitated in their discussion of Dacian-period sites. Some authors even referred euphemistically to Dacian wheel-made pottery as 'kiln products' (cf. Ellis 1996 for review). In the aftermath of the Second World War, Soviet archaeology was also uncomfortable with the presence of fourth-century Goths, albeit a transitory Germanic population, on both Romanian- and even Ukrainian-speaking territories. Publications covering the archaeology of the Iron Age to the post-Roman migration period in the Moldavian SSR are noteworthy for their brief discussion of the Dacian and Germanic presence, with significant emphasis on Scythian, Sarmatian, and especially Slavic populations. Furthermore, the USSR made concerted efforts to manipulate the cultural identity of Romanians in Bessarabia/Moldavian SSR through de-Romanization of both spoken and written Romanian and classification of 'Moldavian' as a separate language (Gabinschi 1997).

The Romanian Communist Party was also not without its controversial claims on archaeological populations. In the Stalinist era of the 1950s, much of the archaeology of Late Antiquity was focused on documenting and emphasizing the presence of Slavic populations in Romania. In 1953, the orthography of the name of the nation itself was changed to substitute the letter î (which exists in Russian phonetically and orthographically) for â so that 'Romînia' would not imply a connection to Roman history, although the spelling was later reversed in 1965. Linguists at Romanian universities were required to confirm that Romanian was a Slavic language and not a member of the Romance family. Archaeologists and historical linguists who did not agree with these ethnic changes were summarily incarcerated in forced labor camps on the Danube Canal construction – many did not return.

During the Ceauşescu era, archaeology was no less affected by totalitarian politics. Demographic history and ethnic identity were manipulated yet again, only this time the Ceauşescu government, in a dramatic turnaround, claimed for the Romanians direct descent back to the Dacians (cf. Deletant 1991). Simultaneously, the Roman contribution to population history was de-emphasized, as this period represented imperialism and exploitation of the masses. In one of its many attempts to strengthen the pre-Roman lineage, the Ceauşescu régime organized a celebration in 1980 of 2050 years of the establishment of a 'centralized, unified and independent Dacian state'. Even though scholars were consulted, the government selected a rather arbitrary date of 30 BC as the starting point for the genealogy of the nation. One of the foci of celebrations was the Dacian site of Bâtca Doamnei at the town of Piatra Neamţ, where archaeological excavations during the 1950s and 60s had revealed a sanctuary and dwellings dating to the first century BC, together with stone construction genuinely considered to be the remnants of defense fortifications. Subsequent excavations of a larger surface area beginning in 1980, however, revealed the stone 'fortification' to be supporting walls for terraces, although it still represented a significant construction effort (Mihăilescu-Bîrliba 1997). However, for the 2050 celebration, the Communist Party had plans to rebuild the walls, erect flags on them, and station soldiers dressed up in ancient military uniforms. More realistic archaeological interpretation was therefore ignored (Mihăilescu-Bîrliba 1997). Ceauşescu not only discouraged cogent analysis of archaeological data, but these excessive nationalist policies also tragically detracted from the work of competent archaeologists (of various ethnic backgrounds) in Romania.

Hundreds of publications have been written over the past 300 years, mostly by authors of Hungarian and Romanian ancestry, and an article of this brevity cannot do justice to this complicated topic (cf. Köpeczi 1994 and Pop 1996 for extensive discussions of Hungarian and Romanian viewpoints, respectively). It also should be noted that there is a variety of opinion as to specific details of the general hypothesis presented above. Two issues, however, have been inextricably combined in the literature on this controversy and perhaps should be considered separately (*vide infra*): the ethnicity of the inhabitants of Dacia during the period of Roman colonization and the depopulation of Dacia by the Roman Empire, both as a result of the Trajanic wars and of the Aurelian withdrawal.

Archaeological data on demography

After the Second World War, archaeological fieldwork was reorganized through the Institutes of Archaeology in major cities and through a network of regional museums located in each county in Romania. In this highly centralized system, annual funding for archaeology originated from the national government in Bucharest and was subsequently allocated throughout the country. Since Romanian archaeologists conducted field campaigns each year and presented and published the results annually, the volume of archaeological research escalated logarithmically in contrast to the corpus of fieldwork prior to the Second World War.

In addition to excavation, some archaeologists also undertook the compilation of inventories of archaeological sites and finds, for all periods, complete with bibliographic documentation, illustrations, and maps. The first published archaeological inventory, and the most ambitious to date, covered all chronological periods for the entire province of Moldavia (Zaharia et al. 1970; updated by Teodor 1997 for the fifth to eleventh centuries). Subsequent inventories have been on a more intensive county-by-county basis for Botoşani (Păunescu et al. 1976), Iaşi (Chirica and Tanasachi 1984, 1985), Neamţ (Cucoş 1992), Vaslui (Coman 1980), Cluj (Horaţiu et al. 1992), Alba (Moga and Ciugudean 1995), Mureş (Lazăr 1995), Braşov (Costea 1995), and Brăila (Harţuche 1980) (Fig. 3). This preliminary level of site documentation comprised all known published information about sites and records of museum collections, together with archaeologists' own knowledge based on both excavations and established relations with rural, agricultural populations in their respective counties. Systematic surveying programs have also been conducted on a district-by-district basis (Păunescu and Şadurschi 1983, 1989a, 1989b, 1994) or focused on larger zones (Ioniţă 1967; Dumitroaia 1992) within counties, as well as along major river systems (Ioniţă 1961; Şadurschi and Ursulescu 1989; Ursachi et al. 1992; Andronic 1997).

Because these published inventories were compiled on a voluntary basis, not as a result of a national directive, only a select number of counties have published archaeological gazetteers. However, their contribution to the knowledge base has vastly changed the image of the archaeological landscape and has provided especially valuable information

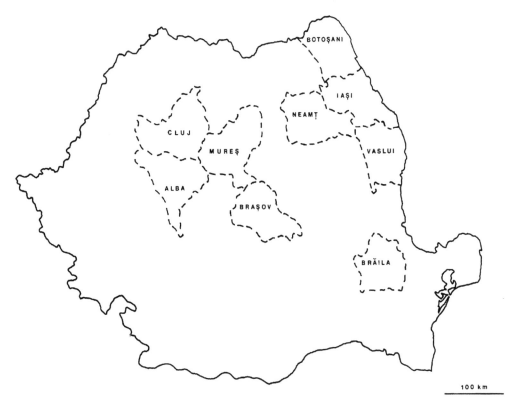

100 km

Figure 3 Current political map of Romania showing counties (broken lines) for which published inventories of archaeological sites exist.

for population studies. Combined with extensive settlement pattern studies of Transylvania and the Banat regions (Rusu 1977), as well as in the Apuseni Mountains (Dumitraşcu 1980), what has emerged from the decades of excavation, surveying, and inventorying of archaeological data is a more complex view of settlement history which clearly outlines the importance of population studies in archaeology.

Tables 1 and 2 provide summaries of six site inventories for Moldavia and Transyl-vania, respectively, for the purposes of contrasting the settlement history of non-Roman (periphery) vs. Roman provincial (core) areas. These gazetteers include precise documentation of finds from settlements, fortresses, coin hoards and isolated finds, cemeteries and burial

Table 1 Number of locations with archaeological materials from gazetteers published for three counties in Moldavia (eastern Romania) from the Iron Age to the early Medieval period (including settlements, burials, cemeteries, sites with cursory remains; numbers in parentheses indicate additional locations of possible but uncertain date; authors' original chronological groupings of sites are preserved here).

Century	Botoşani (1976)	Vaslui (1980)	Iaşi (1984–5)
5th BC–1st AD	51 (?11)*	205 (?8)	229
2nd–3rd AD	23 (?4)	89 (?3)	172
3rd–4th	204 (?8)		
4th		348	535
4th–5th	8 (?2)		27
5th	3		22
5th–6th	1		35
end 4th–beg. 6th		111 (?5)	
6th–7th	10	68 (?3)	
7th–8th			48
8th–11th	35 (?3)	344 (?8)	133

* Authors indicated insufficient field research for first century AD.

Table 2 Number of locations with archaeological materials from gazetteers published for three counties in Transylvania (central Romania) from the Iron Age to the early Medieval period (including settlements, burials, cemeteries, sites with cursory remains; authors' original chronological groupings of sites are preserved here).

Century	Cluj (1992)	Alba (1995)	Mureş (1995)
5th BC–1st AD	59	111	252
Roman	144	155	332
3rd–4th			79
5th			49
6th			48
7th			40
8th			39
9th			19
10th			16
4th–10th cumulative	40		
5th–10th cumulative			211
11th–13th	47		
4th–13th cumulative		67	

grounds, isolated burials, and other find spots. Roman and post-Roman sites are dated by standard archaeological seriation techniques via multi-component sites, tracing items of commerce (especially Romano-Byzantine imports), and using coinage (an exceptionally prevalent find in all classical and post-classical periods). Most notable are the effects of Roman de-colonization in Cluj and Alba counties – a reduction in number of sites, but not the purported *terra deserta*. Moreover, the data from Mureş county warn us against generalizing about population history across a wider territory, and in fact show more consistent settlement in the post-Roman period. Based on this preliminary evidence, the abandonment theory is certainly questionable and a closer analysis of post-Roman human settlement is warranted. At this juncture, we now have to examine the dynamics of colonization and decolonization by the Roman Empire.

Colonization and de-colonization

Both ancient literary sources and archaeological data need to be examined in order to ascertain the effects of Roman colonialism and de-colonization, not only in the core area (provinces of Dacia and Scythia Minor) but also throughout the peripheries (non-Roman, 'free' Dacia). Unfortunately, not all arguments or evidence can be examined in an article of this brevity, thus some selectivity has been employed to permit a concise presentation and to elucidate larger issues surrounding population studies. But first, two issues, *ethnic* continuity and *population* continuity, need to be separated, since they have become muddled amidst centuries of political fray.

With reference to the population continuity issue, there have been two arguments presented against Romanian historical claims for Transylvania: first, that the Dacian population was completely annihilated by the two wars with Trajan, i.e., as a result of Roman colonization; second, that the province of Dacia was completely depopulated during the Roman withdrawal, i.e., as a result of de-colonization. Turning to the ethnicity issue, the first hypothesis implies the destruction of a native, Dacian-speaking population; the second hypothesis, the removal of a colonial population speaking Latin and probably other languages. The primary faults with these eighteenth-century population models are that they rely on a singular cause (colonization or de-colonization) for population changes amidst major political, economic, and military events and also fail to address the complexity of human behavior. Nevertheless, these issues can be addressed by re-evaluating the ancient literary evidence and examining excavation data both in Romania and in surrounding countries.

Colonial period

The theory of the annihilation of Dacia's native population as a result of Roman colonization, relied significantly on ancient historical texts, principally the *Breviarium ab urbe condita* of Eutropius (316–87) which was written during the reign of Valens (364–78). The *Breviarium* consists of ten books which synthesize the major historical events of Rome and the Roman Empire. Eutropius makes four references to Dacia (*Breviarium* VIII, 2; VIII, 6; IX, 8; and IX, 15). The first critical edition of the *Breviarium* was published by

Hans Droysen in 1879, using eight codices which contained the word *viris* in the final sentence of *Breviarium* VIII, 6: 'Dacia enim diuturno bello Decibali *viris* fuerat exhausta' (Dacia, in fact, had been depleted of *men* in the lengthy war with Decebalus). However, not all existing manuscripts of the *Breviarium* are consistent and some contain copyists' errors. In 1979 Carlo Santini republished Eutropius' work using twenty-four codices. Five codices (dating to the ninth to thirteenth centuries) contain the variant *res* ('Daciae enim diuturno bello Decibali *res* fuerant exhaustae'); two codices (thirteenth and fourteenth centuries), the variant *vires* ('Daciae enim diuturno bello Decibali *vires* fuerant exhaustae'); and yet another group (also dating to the ninth to thirteenth centuries) contains the variant *viris* ('Dacia enim diuturno bello Decibali *viris* fuerat exhausta'). The variant *vires* may be an erroneous derivative from *res*, since the syntax is the same for both. The variant *viris*, however, has significant differences in syntax and grammatical agreement when compared to the other two variants (Diaconescu 1993: 350). The variant *res* would imply then that Dacia was depleted of *things* or perhaps more appropriately, *resources*. Given that the Roman Empire's primary interests lay in the economic resources of its colonies, expecially Transylvania's gold mines, the transcription of *res* as opposed to *viris*, appears more logical to this author. But, more importantly, we as archaeologists must accept some degree of uncertainty when relying on copyists' versions of classical texts as sources for precise data on the ancient world.

As to whether or not the native population continued in existence directly after Roman conquest, it would be difficult to envisage the annihilation of every person across terrain measuring 250,000 to 300,000 square kilometers. Well-documented Roman military and colonial policies included maintaining a local power élite in addition to establishing opportunities for resettlement of Roman citizens and veterans, the latter of which was recorded for provincial Dacia (Eutropius VIII, 6). Although speculative, the logistics of removing both settlements, as well as potentially recalcitrant populations from the southern Carpathians, would have been a daunting task for the Roman legions; even late twentieth-century military technology has been stymied in the mountainous regions of the Balkans.

The second supposition, that the province of Dacia was completely depopulated as a result of Roman de-colonization, does not consider the initial divisive nature of colonization in this region. The Romans only secured the southern and central parts of Dacian territory to organize the province of Dacia in 107. However, neither administrative nor military control was achieved north-west, north and east of the province. The area beyond the eastern Carpathian Mountains (Moldavia) was especially perilous and was used as a buffer zone against 'barbarian' populations during the second to third centuries AD.

Archaeological data from the colonial period (second to third centuries) is exceptionally rich and well published (cf. Ioniță 1982; Bichir 1973, 1984). Ceramic manufacturing traditions continue from the pre-Roman to the Roman period, both in provincial and unoccupied Dacia and well into the fourth and even early fifth centuries (Ellis 1996). Settlements likewise continue in non-Roman Dacia throughout the second and third centuries. Other Roman products – glass, amphorae, coin hoards of hundreds or even thousands of Roman silver coins in Dacian pottery vessels – are numerous in the sub-Carpathian region of Moldavia (Mihăilescu-Bîrliba 1980, 1994).

Cemeteries also continue into the Roman period. Burial ritual among Dacians consisted of cremation, a centuries-old practice dating to the Iron Age, and continued during the second and third centuries, both in the Roman province (Diaconu 1965; Protase 1971, 1976) and beyond the frontier in free Dacia (Ioniță and Ursachi 1988). Cremation was the preferred rite for adults; the remaining bones were placed in a ceramic urn, with or without a lid, or placed directly inside a pit. This pattern is consistent on every necropolis. Inhumation was also practiced among Dacians, but appears to have been used primarily for children or adolescents. Dacian cremation and inhumation burials were usually quite modest in inventory (usually glass beads, a fibula, a couple of pots, etc.) – a pattern similar on both sides of the Roman frontier.

Post-colonial era

After Roman withdrawal, likewise we do not see a *terra deserta*, neither in the provincial core zone nor in the peripheries. However, the late third and fourth centuries did bring significant cultural and population changes as a result of de-colonization – not only in Romania, but also in the Republic of Moldova and Ukraine. Archaeologists in the region have designated these changes the 'Sântana de Mureș Culture' in Romania (Ioniță 1966; see note on spelling *infra*) and the 'Černjakhov Culture' in the Ukraine (Rybakov 1960; Magomedov 1987) and the Republic of Moldova (Federov 1960), both terms deriving from the first type sites in these respective nations. These sites date from the late third to the early fifth centuries – a period contemporaneous with the migrations of the Goths, who traversed the Carpathian region for approximately 100 years following Roman de-colonization. So we are faced not so much with depopulation as with the ethnic continuity issue and identification of migratory peoples.

The most visible changes in the archaeological record of the post-Roman period are the method of burial (from cremation to inhumation) and the augmentation of burial inventories. Inhumation, with corpses oriented north–south, became a principal and widespread burial method from the late third century and continuing to the early fifth century. In contrast to the relatively poor contents of Dacian cremation burials, inventories of post-Roman period inhumations averaged 10–12 pottery vessels (Rybakov 1960; Ioniță 1966, 1977; Vulpe 1957: 276–96). This pottery comprised mostly fine gray ware (50 percent or more) identical in technology to colonial and pre-colonial period sites, together with a melange of wheel-made, gravel-tempered ware, archaic hand-made pottery, and Roman amphorae – two, three or even all four types of pottery are found in individual graves (cf. Ellis 1996 for summary in English). A variety of other items are also found in burials, such as fibulae, belt buckles, knives, jewelry, loomweights, needles, glass beads, bone combs, and glass drinking vessels, as well as food offerings as indicated by bones of sheep, pig, domestic birds (bones, whole eggs, and egg shells), and cattle. What is also noteworthy of third to fifth century graves is the widespread distribution (from Transylvania to the Ukraine) and substantial number of objects of Roman manufacture, in excellent condition, which must be indicative of an active system of exchange.

Another significant difference can be found in the funerary treatment of children, which reveals much about the nature of wealth and inherited social status in the post-colonial era. On burial grounds throughout the Sântana de Mureș–Černjakhov Culture, both children and adults show highly variable grave inventories. At Miorcani, northeast Romania, two examples (among many others) of children's grave inventories (nos. 48 and 129) contrast substantially with each other (Ioniță 1977: pls R 44 and R 50a–R 50b, respectively). Grave no. 48 of a very small child included relatively few offerings, most of which were damaged before burial: a pot with a broken rim, a small metallic fragment used as a pendant, a bronze fibula with an unraveled spiral wire base, and two glass beads. Grave no. 129 was endowed with five ceramic vessels, two bronze fibulae, a bronze pendant, bronze ring, clay spindle whorl, two amber beads, a boar's tusk pendant, a violet glass bead with fourteen facets, and sixty-eight additional glass beads of various colors. At Bîrlad-Valea Seacă, southeast Romania, children's burials again show significant contrasts (Palade 1986: pls R84 and R 91a–R 91b, respectively). Burial no. 417, for instance, contained ten blue glass beads, a ceramic bowl (which had been broken and repaired before final disposal), two other pots, and a bronze fibula. The burial of the other child (no. 541), however, has an abundance of goods which exceeded that of most adults and compares well with the wealthiest of adult graves: seventeen ceramics in excellent condition, a Roman amphora, a Roman glass vessel, two elaborate silver fibulae, a clay spindle whorl, a bone comb, animal bones, bird bones, egg shells, and an iron knife.

These necropolises are multigenerational, comprising many hundreds of burials, and certainly attest to a rich demographic history in the post-classical period. The social, economic, and demographic implications of these dramatic changes in burial custom have yet to be explained. Inhumation was long known and practiced among Dacians, albeit on a very limited scale, as well as among the Goths. Contributing to the population mosaic were the Sarmatians, who co-existed and collaborated with the Dacians in the Trajanic Wars and whose burials are found on many sites across Dacia. The explanation of cultural change in this region has been hesitant, since ethnic identity is invariably involved.

While it is still an unsettled issue, the shift to the use of inhumation coincided both with the Aurelian withdrawal from provincial Dacia and the movement of Goths into the Carpatho-Pontic-Danubian region. It is noteworthy that a contemporaneous and similar shift in burial ritual, from the native custom of cremation to the adoption of inhumation, was also occurring in Gaul (Nock 1932: 325–6). Furthermore, Roman society on the Italian peninsula was changing its burial practices from the use of cremation to inhumation, with burial gaining popularity during the reign of Trajan and becoming the exclusive rite by the end of the fourth century (Nock 1932: 322–4). Therefore, we may have to consider not only the effect of transitory populations such as the Sarmatians and Goths who practiced inhumation, but also the impact of Imperial withdrawal, changing frontiers, and contact with Romanized populations.

A valuable contribution for understanding the post-colonial period is the recently published archaeological survey for the Banat region (southwest Romania) which has recorded numerous settlements, storage pits, pottery kilns, glass furnaces, metallurgical production sites, and coins (both as hoards and found on sites) (Bejan 1995). These surveys indicate a continuation of both a sedentary population and maintenance of Roman military and economic interests via control of the left bank of the Danube as well as possible control over the Tisza and Mureș regions. The fortifications along the *limes* on the left bank of the Danube were strengthened after the third century. New fortifications appeared on both sides of the Danube at several locations. At Gornea, in particular, a castellum was constructed (294–300), where previously no Roman construction had existed. Coin circulation likewise continued in the Banat region after Roman withdrawal during the third and fourth centuries: 52 hoards and over 100 isolated discoveries of coins, the majority of which are bronze (Bejan 1995: 54 ff.). Coin finds for the third century are considerably fewer, but the monetary reform of 348 saw an influx of money from the Danube north to the Nera River in the mountainous region of the Banat. Exchange systems in general extended from south of the Danube to the north via river systems and may very well have been connected with the salt trade along the Mureş River (Bejan 1995: 91). A thorough study of post-Roman settlement patterns in Transylvania and the Banat regions, likewise, has revealed close associations with major salt reserves as well as metalliferous zones (Rusu 1977). Further research into the salt trade is merited when one considers that the mountainous regions of Romania have some of the richest salt deposits in Europe, which were exploited as early as the Neolithic (Ellis 1984: 205–6). Circulation of Roman and later Byzantine products was active throughout Late Antiquity on both sides of the Danube.

On the northernmost frontier of 'free' Dacia, another recent publication examines the cultural and economic transformations from the Iron Age to the fourth century in the upper Tisza region of Transcarpathia (Slovakian-Ukrainian-Romanian border) (Kotigoroško 1995). The archaeological inventory for the second to fourth centuries comprises 400 sites, 350 of which are settlements, others being necropolises, workshops, and coin hoards; to date, 21 coin hoards and 147 other isolated finds of coins, forming a total of 4,000 Roman coins (95 percent of silver, the rest of bronze, copper, or gold) with 97 percent of emissions from the first to fourth centuries and ending with Valens (364–72) (Kotigoroško 1995: 132 ff.). Since coins could remain in circulation for 100 or 200 years, precise dating is sometimes difficult. However, Kotigoroško was able to date ninety-two sites with coins independently of the emission date and estimates that coin circulation steadily grew in the first and second centuries with a decline in the third, and a rise again in the fourth century – the same frequency pattern as observed for the Banat region to the southwest. What is remarkable is the extent and increase in coin circulation even after Roman withdrawal from Dacia and as far north as Transcarpathia, which has no other analogy in neighboring provinces, nor in the rest of 'barbaricum'.

Population studies: future directions

Understanding of the population history of Dacia/Romania has been restricted largely by self-imposed limitations. The major issue discussed throughout is that archaeological research has focused on proving population and ethnic continuity in response to an agenda pre-determined by the Habsburg era. But yet another limitation is the 'culture' factor – the description of unifying blocks of material culture which is the legacy of archaeological methodology worldwide (Hodder 1978). The dangerous combination of culture = people = linguistic group = ethnicity forces one to examine archaeological data within a very narrow framework. Hodder's call to eliminate the culture paradigm has significant application here to population studies in the Balkans and Eastern Europe, where ethnic and political tensions have clouded archaeological research. By separating specific classes of objects, such as products of Roman and Byzantine manufacture, heretofore unrecognized patterns of commercial and social relations allow us to re-evaluate long-held hypotheses about cultural history in this region.

Archaeological data have shown that Romano-Byzantine commercial interests continued along river systems; the specific dynamics of these processes is only now beginning to emerge. The abundance of silver coins in the post-Aurelian period along the Danube may have been connected to east–west trade, especially with respect to Roman interests in slave procurement (Duncan 1993: 112–13). However, other economic issues, which would clarify population interaction and settlement, have yet to receive sufficient attention for this region, such as an analysis of natural resources (e.g. salt), local trade and products of local industries vs. long-distance trade and imported items (such as the use and distribution of Roman coinage, pottery and glass) across the entire territory (cf. comprehensive coin distribution maps in Butnariu 1987, 1988, 1991). Trade at towns along the Danube and the Black Sea coast vs. trade along tributary river systems should also be explored in connection with understanding settlement distributions beyond imperial borders.

The social and economic roles of the Roman legions, stationed along the *limes* during the colonial and post-colonial periods, merit investigation other than from the view of military history. Since most coins struck during the late empire were used to pay the military, the role of soldiers in the development of commercial activity along the Danube has been suggested (Duncan 1983). Social relations among the Danube legions and the issue of intermarriage (Benea 1983: 231) may also have had a significance in population dynamics.

Likewise concerning ethnic continuity, recent theoretical work in archaeology has forced the re-evaluation of long-held precepts about cultural identity (Shennan 1994). Ethnicity is a fluid category of human self-identification, subject to change, even during an individual's lifetime, under political, economic, or other cultural-historical circumstances. Equally important is that ethnicity is a behavioral strategy not only for self-identification but also for survival and for maintaining and crossing cultural, economic, and political boundaries. Unfortunately, throughout the Balkans and Eastern Europe, ethnicity continues to be a *cause célèbre*, defined in rigid terms and viewed as unchanging.

Perhaps pertinent here, in conclusion, is evaluating the Roman concept of 'citizenship' – first a privilege but eventually a universal right – as a legal and political paradigm designed to change one's self-identity and to unify a larger, multi-ethnic world. This new Roman order and its accompanying strategy for self-identification is quite apparent in the results of a recent statistical and linguistic analysis of personal names from the capital of Roman Dacia, Ulpia Traiana Sarmizegetusa (Alicu and Paki 1995). Although a majority of the colonists were of Italic origin, this study confirms Eutropius' statement that colonists derived *ex toto Orbe Romano* settled in this newly founded Roman urban center. However, what is intriguing is the absence of Dacian names in this city which appropriated the name of a Dacian citadel, while, concurrently, Dacian burial ritual continued under Roman occupation and into the post-Roman period (Diaconu 1965; Protase 1971, 1976). Rather than viewing the absence of epigraphic evidence as singular 'proof' of ethnic and population discontinuity, are we perhaps seeing a more complex rural–urban dichotomy with cultural as well as economic implications for Roman colonial frontier society?

Department of Classics and Classical Archaeology
San Francisco State University, USA

Note on spelling and names

Romanian orthography has undergone two changes. During the post-Second World War era, the vowel â was replaced with the identical vowel sound î. After December 1989, the letter â was restored. Hence, geographic names mentioned in this text are affected by these changes (e.g. Bîtca Doamnei is now Bâtca Doamnei, and Sîntana de Mureş Culture is now Sântana de Mureş Culture). The officially restored spelling is used here in text discussion, but the orthography of pre-1990 bibliographic items is preserved as originally published so that readers will be able to locate correctly the relevant archaeological literature.

References

Alicu, D. and Paki, A. 1995. *Town-planning and Population in Ulpia Traiana Sarmizegetusa*. Oxford: Tempus Reparatum, BAR International Series 605.

Andronic, M. 1997. *Evoluţia habitatului uman în bazinul hidrografic Soloneţ, din paleolitic pînă la sfîrşitul sec. al XVIII-lea*. Iaşi: Muzeul Naţional al Bucovinei.

Bejan, Adrian. 1995. *Banatul în secolele IV–XII*. Timişoara: Editura de Vest.

Benea, D. 1983. *Din istoria militară a Moesiei Superior şi a Daciei. Legiunea a VII-a Claudia şi legiunea a IIII-a Flavia*. Cluj-Napoca: Editura Dacia.

Bichir, G. 1973. *Cultura carpică*. Bucureşti: Editura Academiei Republicii Socialiste România.

Bichir, G. 1984. *Geto-dacii din Muntenia în epoca romană*. Bucureşti: Editura Academiei Republicii Socialiste România.

Butnariu, V. M. 1987. Monedele romane postaureliene în teritoriile carpato-dunăreano-pontice (anii 275–491). I. Perioada 275–324. *Arheologia Moldovei*, XI: 113–40.

Butnariu, V. M. 1988. Monedele romane postaureliene în teritoriile carpato-dunăreano-pontice (anii 275–491). II. Perioada 324–383. *Arheologia Moldovei*, XII: 131–96.

Butnariu, V. M. 1991. Monedele romane postaureliene în teritoriile carpato-dunăreano-pontice (anii 275–491). III. Perioada 383–491. *Arheologia Moldovei*, XIV: 67–107.

Chirica, V. and Tanasachi, M. 1984. *Repertoriul arheologic al judeţului Iaşi*. Iaşi: Institutul de istorie şi arheologie, Vol. 1.

Chirica, V. and Tanasachi, M. 1985. *Repertoriul arheologic al judeţului Iaşi*. Iaşi: Institutul de istorie şi arheologie, Vol. 2.

Coman, G. 1980. *Statornicie, continuitate. Repertoriul arheologic al judeţului Vaslui*. Bucharest: Editura Litera.

Costea, F. 1995. *Repertoriul arheologic al judeţului Braşov*. Braşov.

Cucoş, Ş: 1992. Contribuţii la repertoriul arheologic al judeţului Neamţ. *Memoria Antiquitatis*, 18: 5–61.

Deletant, D. 1991. Rewriting the past: trends in contemporary Romanian historiography. *Ethnic and Racial Studies*, 14(1): 64–86.

Diaconescu, T. 1993. Etnogeneza românilor. Revelaţia manuscriselor lui Eutropius. In *Antichitatea şi moştenirea ei spirituală* (eds T. Diaconescu and M. Alexianu). Iaşi: Editura Universităţii 'Al. I. Cuza', pp. 346–52. Actele sesiunii de comunicări a Societăţii de studii clasice din România, 1988.

Diaconu, G. 1965. *Tîrgşor. Necropola din secolele III-IV e.n.* Bucureşti: Editura Academiei Republicii Socialiste România.

Droysen, Hans. 1879. *Breviarium ab urbe condita cum versionibus graecis et Pauli Landolfique additamentis.* Berlin: Weidman.

Dumitraşcu, Sever. 1980. *Note privind descoperirile arheologice din Munţii Apuseni.* Oradea: Muzeul Ţării Crişurilor, Biblioteca Crisia VIII.

Dumitroaia, G. 1992. Materiale şi cercetări arheologice din nord-estul judeţului Neamţ. *Memoria Antiquitatis*, 18: 63–143.

Duncan, G. L. 1983. Coin circulation on the Danubian *limes*. In *Ancient Bulgaria* (ed. A. G. Poulter). Nottingham: University of Nottingham, part 2, pp. 165–254.

Duncan, G. L. 1993. *Coin Circulation in the Danubian and Balkan Provinces of the Roman Empire AD 294–578.* London: Royal Numismatic Society, Special Publication no. 26.

Ellis, L. 1984. *The Cucuteni-Tripolye Culture: A Study in Technology and the Origins of Complex Society.* Oxford: British Archaeological Reports, BAR International Series 217.

Ellis, L. 1996. Dacians, Sarmatians and Goths on the Roman-Carpathian frontier, 2nd–4th centuries. In *Shifting Frontiers in Late Antiquity* (eds R. Mathisen and H. Sivan). London: Variorum, pp. 105–25.

Fedorov, G. B. 1960. *Naselenie Prutsko-Dnestrovskogo meždureč'ja v I tysjačeletii n. è.* Moskva: Nauka, Materialy i issledovanija po arkheologija SSSR no. 89.

Gabinschi, M. 1997. Reconvergence of Moldavian towards Romanian. In *Undoing and Redoing Corpus Planning* (ed. Michael Clyne). Berlin and New York: Mouton de Gruyter, pp. 193–214.

Harţuche, N. 1980. Preliminarii la repertoriul arheologic al judeţului Brăila. *Istros*, 1: 281–354.

Hodder, I., ed. 1978. *The Spatial Organisation of Culture.* London: Duckworth.

Horaţiu, I. et al. 1992. *Repertoriul arheologic al judeţului Cluj.* Cluj: Muzeul de Istorie al Transilvaniei, Bibliotheca Musei Napocensis 5.

Horedt, K. 1974. Zur Frage der grossen Erdwälle an der mittleren und unteren Donau. In Actes du IXᵉ Congrès International d'Études sur les Frontières Romaines, 1972, pp. 207–14. Bucharest: Editura Academiei; Köln-Wien: Böhlau Verlag.

Ioniţă, I. 1961. Recunoaşteri arheologice în regiunea satelor Pogoraşti şi Rauseni. *Arheologia Moldovei*, 1: 295–306.

Ioniţă, I. 1966. Contribuţii cu privire la cultura Sîntana de Mureş-Cerneahov pe teritoriul Republicii Socialiste Românâ. *Arheologia Moldovei*, 4: 189–259.

Ioniţă, I. 1967. Cercetări arheologice în Podişul Sucevei. *Arheologia Moldovei*, 5: 309–25.

Ioniţă, I. 1977. La nécropole du IVᵉ siècle de n.è. à Miorcani. *Inventaria Archaeologica*, fasc. 8: R 42–R 51.

Ioniţă, I. 1982. *Din istoria şi civilizaţia dacilor liberi. Dacii din spaţiul est-carpatic în secolele II–IV e. n.* Iaşi: Editura Junimea.

Ioniţă, I. and Ursachi, V. 1988. *Văleni. O mare necropolă dacilor liberi.* Iaşi: Editura Junimea.

Kotigoroško, V. 1995. *Ţinuturile Tisei superioare în veacurile III î.e.n.-IV e.n. (Perioadele La Tène şi romană).* Bucharest: Ministerul Invăţământului, Institutul Român de Tracologie.

Köpeczi, Béla, ed. 1994. *History of Transylvania.* Budapest: Akadémiai Kiadó. Abridged English edition of 3–volume *Erdély története*, originally published in Hungarian in 1986.

Lazăr, V. 1995. *Repertoriul arheologic al judeţului Mureş.* Târgu Mureş: Casa de Editură 'Mureş'.

Magomedov, B. V. 1987. *Černjakhovskaja kul'tura Severo-Zapadnogo Pričërnomor'ja.* Kiev: Naukova Dumka.

Mihăilescu-Bîrliba, V. 1980. *La Monnaie romaine chez les Daces orientaux.* Bucureşti: Editura Academiei Republicii Socialiste Românâ.

Mihăilescu-Bîrliba, V. 1994. Römische Münzen östlich der Provinz Dazien im 2.-3. Jh. u.Z. *Arheologia Moldovei*, 17: 69–73.

Mihăilescu-Bîrliba, V. (1996–1997) Impact of political ideas on Romanian archaeology before 1989. *Studia Antiqua et Archaeologica*, 3–4: 157–60.

Moga, V. and Ciugudean, H. 1995. *Repertoriul arheologic al judeţului Alba*. Alba Iulia: Muzeul Naţional al Unirii Alba Iulia, Bibliotheca Musei Apulensis 2.

Nock, A. D. 1932. Cremation and burial in the Roman Empire. *Harvard Theological Review*, 25(4): 321–59.

Palade, V. 1986. Nécropole du IVᵉ et commencement du Vᵉ siècle de n.è. à Bîrlad-Valea Seacă. *Inventaria Archaeologica*, fasc. 12: R 72–R 92.

Pârvan, V. 1928. *Dacia: An Outline of the Early Civilizations of the Carpatho-Danubian Countries*. London: Cambridge University Press. Reprinted 1979, Greenwood Press, Westport, CT.

Păunescu, A. and Şadurschi, P. 1983. Repertoriul arheologic al României. Judeţul Botoşani. I. Comuna Albeşi. *Hierasus*, 5: 221–69.

Păunescu, A. and Şadurschi, P. 1989a. Repertoriul arheologic al României. Judeţul Botoşani. II. Comuna Avrămeni. *Hierasus*, 7–8: 299–336.

Păunescu, A. and Şadurschi, P. 1989b. Repertoriul arheologic al României. Judeţul Botoşani. III. Comuna Băluşeni. *Hierasus*, 7–8: 337–69.

Păunescu, A. and Şadurschi, P. 1994. Repertoriul arheologic al României. Judeţul Botoşani. Municipiul Botoşani. *Hierasus*, 9:11–48.

Păunescu, A., Şadurschi, P. and Chirica, V. 1976. *Repertoriul arheologic al judeţului Botoşani*. Bucharest: Institutul de arheologie Bucureşti.

Pop, I.-A. 1996. *Romanians and Hungarians from the 9th to the 14th Century: The Genesis of the Transylvanian Medieval State*. Cluj-Napoca: Centrul de Studii Transilvane, Fundaţia Culturală Română, Bibliotheca Rerum Transsilvaniæ XIII.

Protase, D. 1971. *Riturile funerare la daci şi daco-romani*. Bucureşti: Editura Academiei Republicii Socialiste România.

Protase, D. 1976. *Un cimitir dacic din epoca romană la Soporu de Cîmpie*. Bucureşti: Editura Academiei Republicii Socialiste România.

Rusu, Mircea. 1977. Transilvania şi Banatul în secolele VI–IX. *Banatica*, IV: 169–213.

Rybakov, B. A., ed. 1960. *Černjakhovskaja kul'tura*. Moskva: Nauka, Materialy i issledovanija po arkheologija SSSR, no. 82.

Santini, C. 1979. *Eutropii Breviarium ab urbe condita*. Leipzig: B. G. Teubner Verlagsgesellschaft, Bibliotheca Scriptorum Graecorum et Romanorum Teubneriana.

Şadurschi, P. and Ursulescu, N. 1989. Date istorico-arheologice privind dinamica locuirii în bazinul Miletinului (zona comunei Prăjeni, jud. Botoşani). *Hierasus*, 7–8: 281–98.

Shennan, S., ed. 1994. *Archaeological Approaches to Cultural Identity*. London: Routledge.

Teodor, D. 1997. *Descoperiri arheologiceşi numismatice la est de Carpaţi în secolele V–XI*. Bucureşti: Muzeul Naţional de Istorie a României.

Tudor, D. 1968. *Oraşe, tîrguri şi sate în Dacia romană*. Bucharest: Editura Ştiinţifică.

Ursachi, V., Hordilă, D., Alexianu, M. and Dumitroaia, G. 1992. Cercetări arheologice de suprafaţă pe valea Siretului, la nord de municipiul Roman. *Memoria Antiquitatis*, 18: 145–72.

Verdery, K. 1983. *Transylvanian Villagers: Three Centuries of Political, Economic, and Ethnic Change*. Berkeley and Los Angeles: University of California Press.

Vulpe, R. 1957. *Izvoare: Săpăturile din 1936–1948.* București: Editura Academiei Republicii Populare Romîne.

Vulpe, Radu. 1974. Les *valla* de la Valachie, de la Basse-Moldavie et du Boudjak. In Actes du IXe Congrès International d'Études sur les Frontières Romaines, 1972, pp. 267–76. Bucharest: Editura Academiei; Köln-Wien: Böhlau Verlag.

Zaharia, M., Petrescu-Dîmbovița and Zaharia, E. 1970. *Așezări din Moldova de la paleolitic pînă în sec. al XVIII-lea.* București: Editura Academiei Republicii Socialiste România.

Tiwanaku 'colonization': bioarchaeological implications for migration in the Moquegua Valley, Peru

Deborah E. Blom, Benedikt Hallgrímsson, Linda Keng, María C. Lozada C. and Jane E. Buikstra

Abstract

Nothing is more central to theories of prehispanic Andean state formation than the relationship between highland core areas and ecologically-distinct peripheral regions. Various models, ranging from direct colonization to trade relations have been proposed and are usually grounded in architectural and material cultural patterning. We examine the human biological implications of colonization from the perspective of Tiwanaku, primarily during the expansive Tiwanaku IV and V periods (*c.* AD 500–1000). Using inherited skeletal features and artificial cranial deformation, we explore community patterning within the Titicaca Basin in comparison to that for the Moquegua (Middle Osmore) Valley, a region known to have strong cultural ties with the highland altiplano. Based in a sample of over 500 individuals, we test archaeologically-derived models that posit mass migration into the Moquegua region. Our results are not inconsistent with a migration model.

Keywords

Andes; bioarchaeology; colonization; migration; identity; Tiwanaku.

Introduction

Throughout the second half of the first millennium AD, Tiwanaku flourished as the most prominent political and cultural influence in the south central Andes (Fig. 1). From its center near the shores of Lake Titicaca, Tiwanaku impacted regions throughout modern-day Bolivia, Peru, northern and central Chile, and northwestern Argentina (Berenguer 1978; Berenguer and Dauelsberg 1989; Caballero 1984; Kolata 1992; Mujica et al. 1983; Rivera 1985a; Thomas et al. 1985). Although archaeologists disagree about the reasons for the expansion of the Tiwanaku polity (based on the proliferation of Tiwanaku material culture), most concur that Tiwanaku was expanding its influence and using different

World Archaeology Vol. 30(2): 238–261 *Population and Demography*
© Routledge 1998 0043–8243

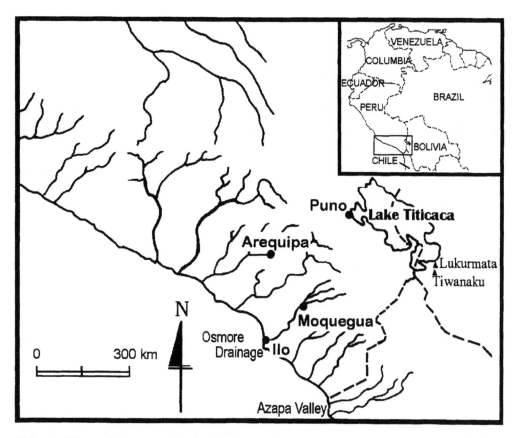

Figure 1 The study area.

methods to incorporate foreign areas, depending on such factors as the distance from the Tiwanaku core and local social, demographic, and ideological structures (Kolata 1993a, 1993b; Mujica 1985; Rivera 1985b). Specific proposed models for Tiwanaku's interaction with other areas include direct colonization and the development of a provincial center (Goldstein 1989), resident Tiwanaku living amongst local populations (Oakland Rodman 1992), and interregional exchange systems with autonomous or semi-autonomous groups (Browman 1978, 1980, 1984; Dillehay and Núñez 1988). Since each type of interaction would differentially impact demography, health, nutrition, and genetic and cultural aspects of group membership, human remains have implications for the study of core–periphery relations in the south central Andes.

The present study compares human skeletal samples from the Tiwanaku core in the Bolivian altiplano to those from the Moquegua Valley in southern Peru to test the most recently proposed model (Goldstein 1989, 1993a, 1993b; Moseley et al. 1991), which posits migration from the altiplano to Tiwanaku 'colonies' in the fertile, lowland region of Moquegua. The Moquegua region is ideal for studying the bioarchaeological implications of Tiwanaku interaction with the periphery because Tiwanaku's influence in the valley has been clearly established (Goldstein 1989), intensive archaeological investigations and ceramic chronologies allow for tight temporal control (Goldstein 1985), and a large collection of pre-Tiwanaku and Tiwanaku human skeletal remains is available. The present study uses inherited skeletal traits as a measure of genetic affinity between groups and cranial deformation as a marker of cultural group membership to test the archaeologically-derived model that Tiwanaku directly colonized and established a provincial center in the Moquegua Valley (Goldstein 1989, 1993a, 1993b; regarding colonization only, see Browman 1978: 335; Kolata 1992: 81; Moseley et al. 1991). While other studies have been based solely on the analysis of material culture, only the study of human skeletal remains in combination with the archaeological data can provide the data necessary to answer questions regarding actual population movement.

Archaeological and ethnohistorical models – Tiwanaku/Moquegua interaction

The urban settlement of Tiwanaku, at an altitude of approximately 3,800m a.s.l. (Fig. 2), was by AD 600 the most extensive and influential center in the south central Andean highlands (Kolata 1986, 1993a; Ponce 1972). Although earlier sources describe Tiwanaku as an unpopulated religious center (Bennett 1934; Squier 1877), recent work has revealed that Tiwanaku evolved into the densely populated capital of a centralized state (Janusek 1994; Kolata 1993a). By linking archaeological, ethnohistorical, and ethnographic data (e.g., Bastien 1978; Brush 1977; Platt 1982), researchers have constructed regional models for the specific ways in which Tiwanaku expanded its influence. Archaeological evidence

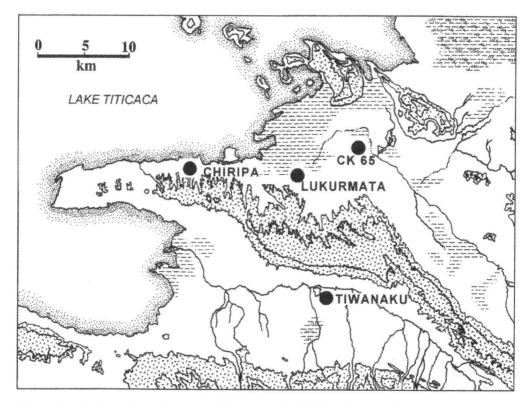

Figure 2   The Tiwanaku altiplano core (after Janusek 1994: figs 4.1 and 4.4).

indicates that Tiwanaku incorporated and directly controlled much of the southern Lake Titicaca basin, its political and demographic core, through hierarchically-organized regional centers such as Lukurmata (Bermann 1994; Janusek 1994; Kolata 1986; Stanish 1994). However, in settlements some distance from the core, such as the eastern valleys of Cochabamba and the western valleys of Azapa and Moquegua, archaeological data suggest that Tiwanaku employed mixed strategies ranging from economic exchange to direct colonization (e.g., Oakland Rodman 1992; Higueras-Hare 1996; Muñoz 1995/6).

John Murra (1968, 1972, 1985a, 1985b) greatly influenced the construction of socio-economic models for Tiwanaku interaction with lowland valleys such as Moquegua. Through the study of ethnohistoric documents on the Lupaqa, a large ethnic group in the Titicaca Basin during Inca and colonial times (Diez de San Miguel 1964 [1567]), Murra developed a model for highland groups' exploitation of resources from vertically-aligned ecological zones outside their immediate settlement area. He detailed different methods employed in gaining vertical control, which vary in intensity from day trips in neighboring regions to the establishment of permanent colonies in distant, foreign, and possibly multi-ethnic territories. Murra hypothesizes that people who lived in these colonies retained economic, ritual, and social rights and identities in their highland communities. By establishing vertical 'archipelagos', highland polities ensured a constant supply of lowland and coastal resources. Although it cannot be uncritically applied to the past (Murra 1972; Van Buren 1996), the verticality model continues to be valuable for explaining interactions between Tiwanaku and the lowlands.

Located approximately 300km southwest of the site of Tiwanaku, the settlements in the western lowland valley of Moquegua are clustered in the mid-valley region, between 1,000 and 2,000m a.s.l. (Fig. 3). This mid-valley region comprises the richest modern agricultural area in the Osmore drainage, a system of rivers running through the southern coastal desert of Peru (Rice 1989). The cultural ties between Moquegua and the altiplano were noted by earlier researchers (Disselhoff 1968; Ishida 1960; Pari 1987; Ponce 1972; Ravines 1969), and recent excavations have confirmed this affiliation existed during the Tiwanaku periods (Goldstein 1989, 1995; Owen 1997; Vargas 1988).

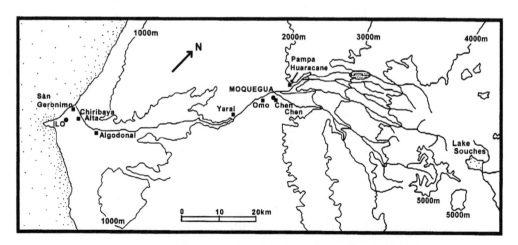

Figure 3   Osmore Drainage with detail of the Moquegua valley sites mentioned in the text.

Major archaeological investigations undertaken in the region have focused on two of the larger Tiwanaku-affiliated sites, Chen Chen and Omo. Each of these sites is known for its distinctive characteristics. Chen Chen is generally noted only for its vast cemeteries which cover approximately 11 hectares and have been estimated to contain over 12,000 burials (Owen 1997; Vargas 1988; Williams, pers. comm.). However, the area also included approximately 160 hectares of cultivation areas and another 18 to 30 hectares appears to have been used for the processing and storage of agricultural resources, and habitations and ceremonial areas for the 'support population' and a possible 'rotating population' (Bandy et al. 1996: 4,12; Goldstein 1995; Pari 1997; Williams 1997, pers. comm.). Omo is a multi-component site complex which consists of habitations and cemeteries but seems to have had a lesser focus on mortuary activities. Instead, Omo M10 is the site of a large Tiwanaku-type sunken temple (Goldstein 1989, 1993b). Goldstein's (1994) survey of the Moquegua Valley has also provided rich information on the prehistory of the area. These works provide the foundation for our study.

Goldstein developed a scenario for sociocultural changes in Moquegua from the pre-Tiwanaku, Huaracane Phase to the time of Tiwanaku collapse in the highlands (Fig. 4). According to Goldstein's (1990, n.d.; Cohen et al. 1995) interpretation, altiplano interaction with the Moquegua Valley before the fifth century AD was limited to the appearance of a

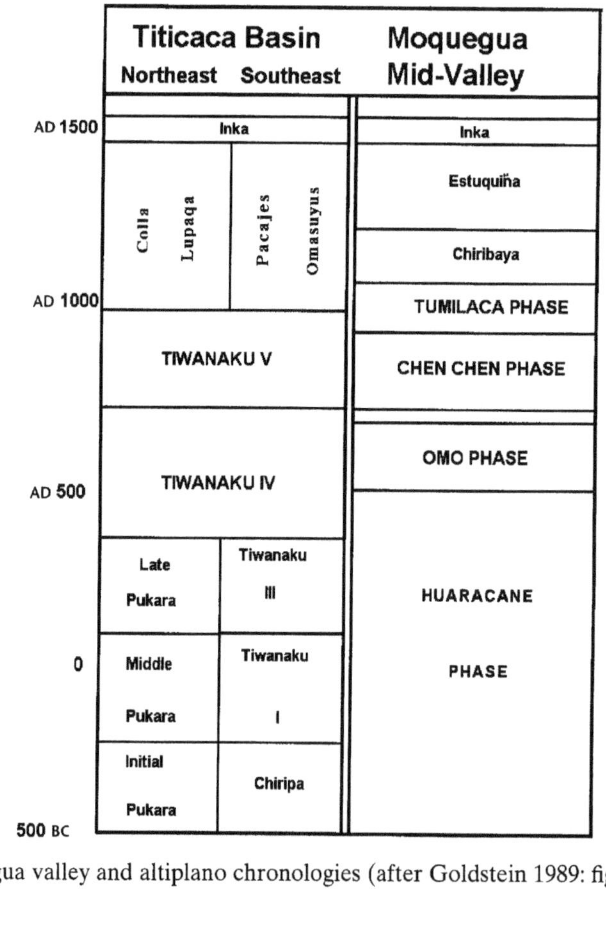

Figure 4 Moquegua valley and altiplano chronologies (after Goldstein 1989: fig. 3).

few exotic items. Sites during this period, labeled the Huaracane Phase in Moquegua, are characterized by distinct, overwhelmingly local (non-altiplano) settlement patterns, rituals, material culture, and burial patterns (Cohen 1995). Goldstein states that Tiwanaku expansion into the valley began during the fifth to eighth centuries AD. This time span is defined as the Omo Phase in Moquegua and corresponds to the latter half of the Tiwanaku IV Phase in the highlands (Goldstein 1993a). Based on a long history of maize cultivation in the region (Murra 1968) and archaeological correlates for agricultural production and large-scale storage (Bandy et al. 1996), it is almost certain that the Tiwanaku-affiliate settlements in Moquegua served as cultivation areas for maize, as well as other lowland products, to provide for local consumption as well as for export to the altiplano (Moseley et al. 1991). Maize, as well as providing dietary resources, was likely used to produce *chicha*, a beer important in Andean ceremony and corporate work reciprocities (Kolata 1992: 81; Morris 1985: 481–2; Murra 1968: 130; Sutherland 1992). During the subsequent three centuries, the settlements became more extensive as Tiwanaku strengthened its control over the valley (Goldstein 1993b). This period has been labeled the Chen Chen Phase in Moquegua and Tiwanaku V in the altiplano.

Goldstein (1989) suggests that at the point of greatest Tiwanaku presence in the valley, the situation exceeded that of a permanent colony and instead was a provincial center with the Tiwanaku being the sole inhabitants of the area. At this time, the residents of the Tiwanaku-affiliated sites in Moquegua were permanent settlers from the highlands who maintained their highland identity as members of the Tiwanaku polity at the level of the individual household. Although Goldstein's model is the currently accepted hypothesis for the nature of Tiwanaku occupations in the Moquegua mid-valley region, Goldstein and other Andeanists acknowledge that some aspects of his model require confirmation through the analysis of human skeletal remains. The goal of this research is to test the hypothesis that the inhabitants of Chen Chen were altiplano immigrants as opposed to local people who were incorporated into Tiwanaku.

Materials

The samples for the present study are derived from a larger analysis of more than 1,000 individuals from the Moquegua mid-valley and the altiplano (Blom 1997). The Moquegua sample (Table 1) consists of a large Chen Chen Phase sample from the site of Chen Chen (M1) (Owen 1997; Vargas 1988, 1994) and a much smaller number of the only available Huaracane Phase skeletons, from Omo (M10) Y and Pampa Huaracane (M29, M30) (Feldman 1989; Goldstein 1989, 1990). The altiplano sample is drawn from the urban sites of Tiwanaku, Lukurmata, and Chiripa and the rural site of Kirawi (CK65) (Bermann 1994; Hastorf et al. 1997; Janusek 1997; Kolata 1993a). The altiplano burials date from pre-Tiwanaku (known as Formative) to Tiwanaku phases. Only burials that could be securely placed into broad time categories – Early/Middle Formative (Chiripa) [N = 13]; Late Formative (Tiwanaku I and III) [N = 12]; Moquegua Formative (Huaracane) [N = 30] and Tiwanaku Phases (Tiwanaku IV and V) [N = 531] – were used. The Katari Basin (Lukurmata and CK65) and Moquegua Huaracane (M10, M29, and M30) contexts were combined for all analyses.

Table 1   The sample used in the study.

Moquegua Valley Tiwanaku sites:	**394**
Chen Chen (M1) [N = 394]	
Moquegua Valley Huaracane sites:	**30**
Pampa Huaracane (M29, M30) [N = 11]	
Omo (M10) Y [N = 19]	
Taraco Peninsula site:	**22**
Chiripa [N = 22]	
Katari Basin sites:	**45**
Lukurmata [N = 30]	
Kirawi (CK65) [N = 15]	
Tiwanaku capital:	**95**
Tiwanaku [N = 95]	
Total:	**586**

Methods

Population movement, ethnicity, and bioarchaeological studies

The primary issues discussed in this paper involve group membership or ethnicity. Unfortunately bioarchaeology cannot address ascription, the most critical aspect of ethnicity, in which members of an ethnic group recognize themselves and others as belonging to distinct groups holding different cultural values (Barth 1969; Chapman 1993). However, these values are frequently displayed in the 'cultural content' through overt signs or symbols such as clothing, textiles, house design, or life style, giving archaeologists an opportunity to distinguish ethnic groups through 'styles' in material culture (Aldenderfer and Stanish 1993; Conkey and Hastorf 1990; Jones 1997; Oakland Rodman 1992; Shennan 1989; Wiessner 1983). Bioarchaeologists can observe overt displays of group membership through cranial deformation styles and lifestyle as measured by diet and health (Buikstra 1995; Hoshower et al. 1995; Julien 1983: 42–5; Macbeth 1993). We recognize that the ways in which groups use and manipulate these types of cultural symbols is very flexible, depending on the physical and social environment in which they are operating (Barth 1969). Therefore, they must be interpreted within their larger contexts. Another way in which groups maintain boundaries is through rules about how individuals of two groups can interact. Boundaries to biological reproduction are often present through social means such as taboos and marriage rules or through geographic isolation (Macbeth 1993). Depending on the degree of endogamy in these groups, we can also address ethnicity through studies of genetic relationships. It should be recognized that social boundaries are the locus of interactions with others and can be flexible. An example of this flexibility is the construction of fictive kin ties in the Andes, where an outsider can be adopted as a full member of a group (Bastien 1978). Although this may cause mixing of gene pools and cultural material, interactions between ethnic groups are often quite rigidly controlled in order to maintain the boundaries.

In order to explore the degree of genetic relatedness between groups and test models regarding population movement, this study employs discrete, inherited skeletal and dental traits (also known as non-metric or epigenetic traits) to measure the genetic relatedness between samples. Cranial and dental morphology is genetically influenced and can be used to measure biological distance between groups (Berry and Berry 1967; Corrucini 1972; Finnegan 1978; Turner et al. 1991). The validity of using non-metric traits to measure biological affinity between groups was first established in studies of wild and laboratory rodents and later in human and non-human primates (Cheverud and Buikstra 1978, 1981a, 1981b, 1982; Hauser and De Stefano 1989; Saunders and Popovich 1978; Selby et al. 1955; Sjøvold 1984; Torgersen 1951). Analyses of these traits have been successful in discriminating between archaeologically-defined human groups (Buikstra 1976; Konigsberg 1987; Lane and Sublett 1972; Rothhammer and Silva 1989; Sutter 1997; Turner 1989; Verano 1987). The traits include small accessory bones (ossicles) within sutures; ossification of additional tissue (spurs or bridges); failures in ossification; and variation in the number and location of foramina and sulci, the bony pathways for vessels and nerves. Although differences in morphological data between populations may be in part attributable to environmental causes (Cavalli Sforza et al. 1994), this does not appear to be a problem in the present study, because groups which presumably share similar environmental conditions reveal large morphological distances and vice versa (see below). Future studies on genetic (using mitochondrial and microsatellite nuclear DNA sequence data) and morphological distance in the same populations are likely to clarify this issue to some degree. Because both sides were taken into account when scoring traits, the magnitude of the environmental variance to the total morphological variance was likely reduced.

To focus on the cultural aspects of group identity, we consider artificial cranial modification as a marker of group membership and/or ethnicity (Hoshower et al. 1995). The use of cranial deformation styles as overt signs of group membership is confirmed by ethnohistorical documents (de la Vega 1961[1609]; de las Casas 1892 [1561]). This permanent deformation was achieved by keeping cranial deformers made of boards, straps, and/or pads on children until they reached the age of 3 years. Various distinct cranial deformation types as well as unmodified skulls are often present in a population. The cranial deformation typology used for this analysis (Fig. 5) is a modified version of other typologies developed for collections from the Moquegua Valley (Hoshower et al. 1995; Lozada et al. 1996, 1997) and is similar to typologies used in other studies on Andean cranial deformation (Allison et al. 1981; Hrdlička 1912; Stewart 1950; Weiss 1972). Overall externally visible skull shape was considered in addition to the more technologically-based deformation apparati.

Expectations and hypotheses

Goldstein (n.d., 1989, 1993b) selected three archaeologically-visible conditions necessary to accept colonization under Murra's model: permanent residence, homeland identity, and multi-ethnicity. He observed evidence of permanent residence and architectural and artifactual characteristics corresponding with those in the altiplano core area, and therefore accepted the first two criteria as met. However, the lack of any indication of ethnic diversity and the presence of the Tiwanaku-type sunken-court temple complex at Omo, led

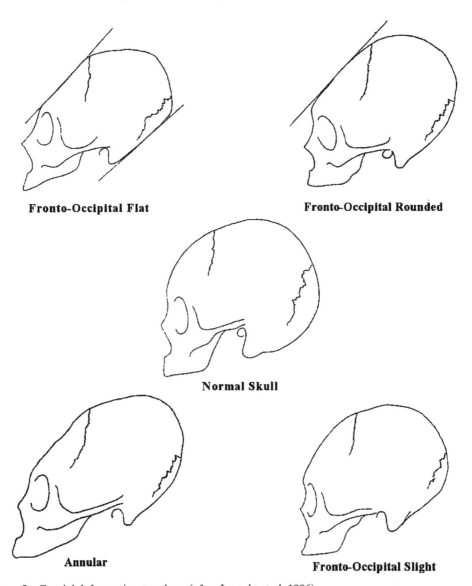

Figure 5   Cranial deformation typology (after Lozada et al. 1996).

Goldstein to posit instead the case of a Tiwanaku province in Moquegua. Bioarchaeological data can be used to further evaluate Goldstein's model for the Moquegua Tiwanaku-affiliated settlements.

If there was a Tiwanaku province in Moquegua composed of settlers from the altiplano, we would expect that those buried at Chen Chen would be more closely linked genetically to the inhabitants of the altiplano Tiwanaku sites as opposed to the pre-Tiwanaku Moquegua sample. The biological distance between the inhabitants of the Tiwanaku-affiliated sites of Moquegua and the pre-Tiwanaku, Huaracane Phase residents would be expected to be higher overall than that between the colonists and those from the Tiwanaku core. If solely local populations inhabited the settlements, the genetic affiliation of the highland and lowland groups should be quite different. This would still hold true if the pre-Tiwanaku Moquegua population had altiplano (pre-Tiwanaku) origins.

Because Goldstein's model also stipulates permanence, we also expect to see the presence of families occupying the settlements. This would contrast with, for example, temporary and specialized work groups or military outposts, which might be composed of only certain demographic segments of society (e.g., the absence of children, the elderly, males, or females), although this is not necessarily the case. Demographically, family structure will be reflected in the presence of both sexes and a mortality profile expected from an age-diverse population. Lastly, the cranial deformation types present in Moquegua should at least be represented in the altiplano sample.

Second, we can explore the question of cultural and ethnic diversity through within-site comparisons. Based on the presence of solely 'Tiwanaku-style' artifacts at the level of the individual household, Goldstein argues that the settlements were composed of one 'ethnic group' – meaning that all the inhabitants identified stylistically with Tiwanaku. After Goldstein completed his study, it was suggested that the Tiwanaku core was comprised of more than one ethnic group (Kolata 1993a), and Janusek (1994) has found subtle differences in the material culture in the core which likely indicate that it is not as homogenous as previously envisioned. Therefore, the Moquegua Tiwanaku sites may have been comprised of more than one group. If the settlements only contained one social group, we would expect to see little intergroup difference in cranial deformation style, and these groups should be drawn from a relatively homogenous genetic population. Alternatives that we will consider include Tiwanaku sending administrators to the lowland settlements to supervise locals (e.g., Kolata 1992; Mujica 1985; Oakland Rodman 1992) and that the initial Omo Phase settlers were of altiplano origin and then later, in the Chen Chen Phase, Moqueguan locals were incorporated into the Tiwanaku settlements (Kolata 1993a).

Biodistance analysis

The original list of non-metric traits used in this study includes ninety-four cranial, post-cranial, and dental traits (Table 2). The senior author collected non-metric and demographic data using published standards (Blom 1997; Buikstra and Ubelaker 1994; Turner et al. 1991). Because the biodistance analysis used gives undue weight to low frequency traits (Cavalli-Sforza et al. 1994), we first eliminated fifteen traits with overall present or absent frequencies below 5 per cent. Since our samples vary in their demographic profiles, we then used Chi square to distinguish traits that are linked to age or sex. Due to significant differences between age groups for several traits, we confined all further analysis to individuals older than 12 years. Seven traits that exhibited significant ($p < 0.05$) differences between males and females were eliminated from further analysis. Next, we removed five additional traits because two trials in an intra-observer error study were significantly different ($p < 0.20$) for those traits. Finally, to prevent artificial inflation in distance measures, we used Chi square to determine inter-trait correlations and eliminated twenty-seven traits that were significantly correlated with other traits. To make Bonferroni adjustment for multiple comparisons, significance was considered to be $p < 0.05$ within the skull, dental, and postcranial regions and $p < 0.01$ between regions. In

Table 2 Non-metric traits used in the study.

Cranial traits:	Post cranial traits:
Accessory lesser palatine foramen*	Allen's fossa*
Apical bone	Atlas lateral bridging
Asterionic bone	Atlas posterior bridge*
Auditory exostoses	Atlas retroarticular bridge
Bregmatic bone	Atlas transverse foramen bridge
Condylar canal	Circumflex sulcus*
Coronal ossicle	Poirier's facet
Divided hypoglossal canal–internal	Septal aperture**
Divided hypoglossal canal within canal	'Squatting facet' – lateral
Epiteric bone	'Squatting facet' – medial
Foramen ovale incomplete	Sternal foramen*
Foramen spinosum incomplete*	Suprascapular foramen/notch
Inca bone**	Supratrochlear spur
Infraorbital suture	Talar articulation shape*
Lambdoid ossicle**	Third trochanter*
Mandibular torus	Trochlear notch form
Mastoid foramen	Vastus notch*
Mental foramen*	
Metopic suture	**Dental traits:**
Multiple infraorbital foramina	Groove pattern–lower molars [M1*]
Mylohyoid bridge–centre of groove*	Cusp number–lower molars
Mylohyoid bridge–mandibular foramen*	Root number–lower molars [M2*]
Ossicle in occipito-mastoid suture**	Root number–upper 1st premolar
Palatine torus*	Protostylid–lower molars
Parietal foramen*	Cusp 5–lower molars [M3*]
Parietal notch bone	Cusp 6–lower molars [M1*]
Pterygo-alar bridge	Cusp 7–lower molars
Pterygo-spinous bridge*	Tome's root–lower 1st premolar
Rocker mandible	Shoveling–upper incisors [12*]
Sagittal ossicle	Double shoveling–upper incisors [I1*]
Superior sagittal sulcus turns left	Peg-shaped incisors–upper lateral incisor
Suprameatal pit	Winging–upper cental incisors
Supraorbital foramen	Hypocone–upper molars [M1*]
Supratrochlear foramen*	Cusp 5 (metaconule)–upper molars [M1*]
Tympanic dihiscence*	Carabelli's trait–upper molars [M2*]
Zygomatico-facial foramen*	Enamel extensions–upper molars

* Traits used in final analysis.
** Traits that may be affected by cultural practices.

contrast to others (e.g., Rothhammer et al. 1984; Sutter 1997), we did not eliminate traits that did not vary among the groups. In a large set of traits some differences between samples will appear at random. Therefore, selecting such traits for analysis will create artifactual differences between samples. Because we previously (Blom et al. 1997) determined that removing sutural bone traits, which may be affected by cranial deformation (Konigsberg et al. 1993), and septal apertures, which may be affected by activity patterns or sex (Hrdlička 1932), had a negligible effect on the results, we did not remove these traits.

Biodistance between each pair of sites was determined by using the mean difference of the trait frequencies:

$$D = \frac{\sum_{l=j}^{n} |f_{1i} - f_{2i}|}{n}$$

where D is biodistance, f_{1i} and f_{2i} are frequencies of the ith trait for populations 1 and 2, and n is the number of traits. To calculate the probability that each distance was obtained by chance in samples drawn from a homogenous population, we used a bootstrap method. In this method, the data set was subjected to a series of 1,000 randomizations in which each variable was independently sorted according to random numbers. This has the effect of randomizing the assignment of values to individuals while maintaining the probability distribution of trait values for the whole sample. This simulates the null hypothesis that the samples are drawn from the same population. Missing values were included in the randomization, but were excluded from the frequency calculations. That is to say that frequency was calculated as the number of times the trait was scored as 'present' divided by the sum of 'present' plus 'absent'. In cases where all individuals of a group had unobservable values for any trait, that trait was eliminated for all pair-wise comparisons with that group. This applies both to the calculation of the actual distance and to the distances generated at each iteration by the bootstrap. This procedure prevents the occurrence of biasing results in fragmentary data sets where many individuals have missing values. This test is, therefore, sensitive to missing values only in that missing values will tend to inflate the randomized variance of within sample trait frequencies, making significant p-values harder to obtain. We eliminated groups of less than eight individuals from the analysis because very small samples will not give useful results.

Results

We have said that we expect to see family groups present if the Moquegua Valley was a province or colony. Our data reveal that males and females (37/63 per cent male/female) of diverse age-at-deaths, as well as a significant number of children of all ages were buried at Chen Chen. Although looting and archaeological sampling strategy have not provided a sample suited to in-depth demographic analyses, these two observations lend support to the hypothesis that families inhabited the settlements. The predominance of females is suggestive. This could indicate that more women were living at Chen Chen and/or that the mortality for females was higher than that for males. This would necessitate the immigration of additional women into the population. However, it is also possible that the imbalance is due to differential burial treatment for men and women or the emigration of males. Further paleopathological and mortuary analyses may provide more information about this, but for now, it is out of the scope of this paper. The presence of families alone does not negate the possibility that the settlements also served a military function. Further support against an active military function for the settlements can be found in the lack of evidence for trauma associated with warfare in the Chen Chen sample (Isla et al. 1998).

Table 3 Cranial deformation type by area (F/O = Fronto-occipital. The 'Total F/O' and 'Total deformed' categories also include individuals that could not be placed in a sub-category).

Site(s)-Time	F/O flat	F/O round	F/O slight	Total F/O % of known broad style	Annular % of known broad style	Total deformed	Absent % vs deformed	Total
Moquegua-Tiwanaku	84	54	34	200 100%		241 84%	45 16%	286
Moquegua-Huaracane	2	1	1	4 100%		4 100%		4
Chiripa-Chiripa						1 25%	3 75%	4
Chiripa-Tiwanaku						1 25%	3 75%	4
Katari Basin-Formative					9 100%	11 100%		11
Katari Basin-Tiwanaku				1 13%	7 88%	11 69%	5 31%	16
Tiwanaku-Tiwanaku	6		4	15 60%	10 40%	30 83%	6 17%	36
Total						299 83%	62 17%	361

Before examining spatial patterns in cranial deformation styles, it is necessary to determine whether temporal distinctions exist. We found some temporal differences in cranial deformation within broad areas for these samples (Table 3). For example, of the individuals that had visible deformation types and known temporal context in the Katari Basin, the annular type of deformation was present in 100 per cent of the Formative and 88 per cent of the Tiwanaku period contexts. In contrast, the Moquegua Valley Tiwanaku and Huaracane periods samples are equivalent. This is consistent with what has been found in other samples in the area. Hoshower et al.'s (1995) analysis of the cranial deformation styles from six Huaracane Phase individuals from Omo revealed that their cranial deformation type was similar to that found in two of Omo's later, Chen Chen Phase cemeteries. Our previous analysis of Late Intermediate Period Moquegua sites indicated that some of the same deformation styles found in Chen Chen and Omo were present during post-Tiwanaku (Chiribaya and Tumilaca phase) times (Lozada et al. 1996).

The link between cranial deformation and spatial organization has long been of interest to researchers. For example, earlier researchers (e.g., Stewart 1950) asserted that annular deformation is present in the highlands while 'parallelo-fronto-occipital' deformation is found on the southern coast. Our results show that the distinction is not so simple. It does seem that fronto-occipital styles are solely present on the coast during Huaracane and Tiwanaku time periods (see Lozada et al. 1996 for Chiribaya samples). This holds true for the few other available specimens from Moquegua Valley Tiwanaku contexts (i.e., twelve individuals from the sites of M7, M43, and M1116, and those from Omo M10 discussed in Hoshower et al. 1995). However, in the highlands, annular types are present but in conjunction with fronto-occipital styles. We see a broad spatial pattern in cranial deformation with exclusively fronto-occipital types in Moquegua, annular types predominating (93 per cent) in the Katari Basin, and both roughly equally present at the site of Tiwanaku. Because the Moquegua Valley Tiwanaku cranial deformation styles are found in Tiwanaku, it is at least possible that the Moquegua Tiwanaku population consisted of immigrants from the altiplano.

In order to test multi-ethnicity within the sites, we analyzed within-site patterning of cranial deformation. Hoshower and colleagues (1995) studied cranial modification on a small sample from Tiwanaku period cemetery clusters at Omo and reported a relationship between spatial location of the burials and technological differences in cranial deformation. Distinct differences were found in the various cemeteries, based on number, shape and placement of the pads. After ruling out status differentiation through mortuary analyses, the researchers suggested that, if contemporaneous, the individual cemeteries at Omo may have represented residential descent groups (or *ayllu* clusters) whose corporate status was symbolized by unified cranial forms. Analyses on the cranial deformation in a sample from Chen Chen indicate that while the cranial deformation types at the two sites are similar, the distinct spatial patterning in Omo is absent in Chen Chen (Blom et al. 1995). Instead, at Chen Chen deformation types cross-cut all spatial boundaries.

Biological relationships can also add to this interpretation. To test the hypothesis that the different styles indicate different genetic groups that simply cannot be seen using burial location at Chen Chen, we measured the biodistance across cranial deformation types. We did not find appreciable distances (d=0.086–0.141) between these cranial deformation technology groups. Additionally, when comparing the genetic trait frequencies

Table 4   Distance measurements and p-values for Chen Chen broad mortuary areas.

	Hilltop	*Ridge*	*South*
Hilltop N = 57			
Ridge N = 107	d = .112 p = .043		
South N = 53	d = .154 p = .003	d = .121 p = .013	
Slope N = 119	d = .113 p = .025	d = .091 p = .040	d = .132 p = .000

between spatially distinct areas at Chen Chen (Table 4), the data indicate small distance measurements, suggesting that these areas are from a relatively homogeneous population.

The lack of spatial patterning at Chen Chen in deformation types and genetic affinity is not that surprising. Assuming that Hoshower et al. are correct in attributing cranial deformation style to ayllu identity, we do not necessarily expect ayllus to be endogamous, so we might expect individuals to be moving between them. This would result in gene flow and, because cranial deformation is permanent, a mixing of cranial deformation types. Therefore, it could be that in the Omo cemeteries, which were located around the temple, the population was creating a unique mortuary context where ayllu identity was being enforced and almost idealized. The data presented here on genetic affinity and spatial relations in Chen Chen suggest that there were few social or environmental boundaries to reproduction between these groups. This also seems to be the case for the broad cranial deformation styles (fronto-occipital vs. annular) in the entire study sample. We did not find large biological distances (d = 0.079–0.148) between these types, again indicating gene flow between the two groups.

Finally, when we analyzed biological distance between the broad temporal/spatial groups, a pattern emerges (Table 5). As we can see from the large p-values, the Katari Basin Formative sample, and to a lesser extent the Chiripa samples, have not produced many significant results. This is likely due to small sample sizes and fragmented remains. Nevertheless, we see a pattern of Chiripa being distinct from other sites in the altiplano area. Given the grossly high p-value, there is no reason to postulate that the Formative and Tiwanaku samples from Chiripa are not from a homogeneous population. Further, the Formative Chiripa and Huaracane samples are quite distant from one another. This is inconsistent with the suggested link based on ceramic styles between Huaracane and Chiripa (see Feldman 1989).

The statistically significant distances between Chen Chen and the other samples provide information about relationships during Tiwanaku time periods. The distance between the Tiwanaku site sample and Chen Chen is as small as that between mortuary areas within the Chen Chen site. Other distance values which approximate this distance are between Chen Chen and the Katari Basin-Tiwanaku sample and between Tiwanaku and the Katari Basin-Tiwanaku sample. Therefore, the three Tiwanaku period groups of Chen Chen, the Katari Basin, and Tiwanaku are closely linked, with small genetic distances. On the other hand, the Huaracane sample is approximately twice as distant

Table 5 Distance measurements and p-values for context by time (bold face indicates p-values less than 0.05).

Context/time Number of individuals	Chiripa/ Formative	Chiripa Tiwanaku	Katari Basin/ Formative	Katari Basin/ Tiwanaku	Tiwanaku/ Tiwanaku	Chen Chen
Chiripa/Formative N = 13						
Chiripa/Tiwanaku N = 8	d = 0.258 p = 0.667					
Katari Basin/Formative N = 12	**d = 0.331** **p = 0.033**	d = 0.313 p = 0.278				
Katari Basin/Tiwanaku N = 31	**d = 0.316** **p = 0.000**	d = 0.257 p = 0.511	d = 0.226 p = 0.381			
Tiwanaku/Tiwanaku N = 82	**d = 0.250** **p = 0.034**	d = 0.259 p = 0.395	d = 0.193 p = 0.600	**d = 0.167** **p = 0.025**		
Chen Chen/Tiwanaku N = 334	**d = 0.285** **p = 0.000**	d = 0.278 p = 0.176	d = 0.202 p = 0.419	**d = 0.147** **p = 0.042**	**d = 0.120** **p = 0.000**	
Huaracane N = 28	**d = 0.432** **p = 0.000**	d = 0.304 p = 0.148	d = 0.265 p = 0.087	**d = 0.287** **p = 0.000**	**d = 0.239** **p = 0.000**	**d = 0.225** **p = 0.000**

from these Tiwanaku samples. Therefore, the amount of gene flow was higher between Chen Chen and Tiwanaku than between Chen Chen and earlier Moquegua populations.

Various explanations may account for the small biodistance. As we have said, biological distance is a measure of gene flow between populations. In an archaeological mortuary population, gene flow happens in three different ways: through sexual relationships resulting in offspring, through permanent migration, or through the burial of individuals from one group in the area of the other. The first, sexual relationships resulting in offspring, could occur either through marriage or through sexual relations between locals or with foreign travelers. Possible circumstances of travel would include llama caravans, work parties, and pilgrimages. The second and third ways in which gene flow occurs, population migration and burial outside of one's natal community, could conceivably be in either direction, towards the altiplano or Moquegua. Until we have more information from such analyses as Sr isotopes studies which can detect a change of residence within the life of an individual, we will not be able to chose definitively between these possibilities. However, the overall context can provide a means of determining the more likely explanation. Given the large geographical distance between Moquegua and Tiwanaku, the small biological distance between the altiplano and Chen Chen and within Chen Chen areas, and the archaeological data presented by Goldstein, the data are not inconsistent with the migration hypothesis.

Conclusion

The data we have presented here indicate that during the Tiwanaku V phase, the Moquegua population was closely linked genetically to altiplano Tiwanaku populations, as opposed to the earlier, local population. Further, analyses of biological distance and cranial deformation technology within the Moquegua Tiwanaku sites show that, while residential descent groups may have been present (per Hoshower et al. 1995 for Omo), these groups were not endogamous and appear to have been part of a genetically homogeneous population. Our study has also shown that the Moquegua inhabitants were from a discrete segment of the 'Tiwanaku' population (possibly representing a group similar to a moiety or pseudo-moiety). The Moquegua lowland agriculturalists exhibited only fronto-occipital cranial deformation types, while the Katari Basin altiplano agriculturalists near Lake Titicaca almost exclusively displayed annular deformation. Both of these deformation types were found in significant proportions throughout the site of Tiwanaku, and biological distance analyses do not indicate that the deformation styles marked genetically distinct groups. Therefore, these groups appear to have been interacting biologically and socially in Tiwanaku if not elsewhere.

While we have suggested alternatives, these results are consistent with the model proposed by Goldstein that the Moquegua Tiwanaku-affiliated sites housed immigrants from the altiplano. The settlements in Moquegua might reflect a system such as the *mitmaq* colonies of the Inca, where large groups, often distinct ethnic groups, were sent to foreign lands to accomplish specific tasks (Morris 1985: 482; Murra 1968: 121–3; Rostworowski 1988: 221–4). The Moquegua colonies likely served to cultivate crops such as maize (used in making beer) and coca, as well as other lowland crops which could not be grown on a large scale in the altiplano. Because these crops are essential in the Andes to maintain ideals of hospitality, generosity, and reciprocity while organizing feasts, ceremonies, and labor parties, the products cultivated in Moquegua may have been a means of promoting authority and accessing labor.

Our research also indicates that while the individuals in Moquegua appear to be members of 'Tiwanaku' in all ways, they displayed differences from other Tiwanaku-affiliated sites in the altiplano in the ways in which they culturally-modified their head shapes. The implications of this are not entirely clear. Based on how the Inca organized *mitmaq* colonies we can propose some explanations. Although it is possible, we have no indication that the Moquegua group would have been sent there as a punishment or to dispel tensions in the highlands. Since the 'colonists' were engaged heavily in cultivation, we might expect that these individuals had some unique knowledge about lowland agricultural techniques or irrigation, which differ from those used in the altiplano. This group may have had prior ties to the Moquegua region. Because the products grown would have been valuable, access to Moquegua could have been protected by a group loyal to Tiwanaku or could have been granted to them as a reward. Lastly, it is possible that the individuals in Moquegua employed this distinct head form as a regional identity. Additional research in other areas of Tiwanaku influence, some of which is currently underway, may help in interpreting these results.

Artifactual information can reveal much about the sociopolitical structure of a particular group. However, human biological studies are often essential for the thorough testing of archaeological models and can add to and enhance data gained from more traditional analyses. To date, few bioarchaeological studies have dealt with the Tiwanaku core or its periphery. This paper provides the first analysis of the human skeletal collection of Tiwanaku and Chen Chen in the Moquegua Valley, and this study illustrates the importance of using human skeletal biology in conjunction with artifactual data in addressing archaeological questions.

Acknowledgments

We would like to thank the many who voluntarily helped the senior author in the field. They include Dale Yeatts, Liz Klarich, Carla Lee, Santiago Morales, Carrie Oehler, Ivonne Podestá, Henry Tantaleán, Bill Taylor, and Danilo Villamor. Access to collections and contextual information was generously supplied by Paul S. Goldstein, Christine Hastorf, Alan Kolata, Robert Feldman, Augusto Cardona, Antonio Oquiche, Bruce Owen, and Bertha Vargas. James Pokines reviewed several drafts of the manuscript. Clark Erickson provided invaluable comments and criticism, some of which could not be addressed in the present article but will influence future works. Funding was provided by a dissertation improvement grant from the Wenner-Gren Foundation for Anthropological Research which was awarded to Deborah E. Blom under the supervision of Jane E. Buikstra. Lee Blue assisted the second author in writing the statistical program used in this study. Finally, John W. Janusek helped in every stage of this research, and we are indebted to him. Of course, any errors are our own.

Deborah E. Blom and María C. Lozada C.
Department of Anthropology, University of Chicago
Chicago, IL 60637, USA
Benedikt Hallgrímsson
Department of Anatomy, University of Puerto Rico
San Juan, PR 00936–5067, USA
Linda Keng
Department of Anthropology, University of Houston
Houston, TX 77204-5882, USA
Jane E. Buikstra
Department of Anthropology, University of New Mexico
Albuquerque, NM 87131–1086, USA

References

Albarracín-Jordan, J. V. 1992. Prehispanic and Early Colonial settlement patterns in the Lower Tiwanaku Valley, Bolivia. Doctoral dissertation. Department of Anthropology, Southern Methodist University, Dallas, TX.

Aldenderfer, M. S. and Stanish, C. 1993. Domestic architecture, household archaeology, and the past in the South-Central Andes. In *Domestic Architecture, Ethnicity, and Complementarity in the South-Central Andes* (ed. M. S. Aldenderfer). Iowa City: University of Iowa Press, pp. 1–12.

Allison, M. J., Gerszten, E., Munizaga, J., Santoro, C. and Focacci, G. 1981. La práctica de la deformación craneana entre los pueblos andinos precolombinos. *Chungará*, 7: 238–60.

Bandy, M., Cohen, A. B., Goldstein, P. S., Cardona R., A. and Oquiche H., A. 1996. The Tiwanaku occupation of Chen Chen (M1): preliminary report on the 1995 salvage excavations. Paper presented to the 61st Annual Society for American Archaeology meetings, New Orleans, LA, 1996.

Barth, F. 1969. *Ethnic Groups and Boundaries: The Social Organization of Culture Difference.* Oslo, Norway: Johansen and Nielsen Boktrykkeri.

Bastien, J. W. 1978. *Mountain of the Condor: Metaphor and Ritual in an Andean Ayllu.* New York: West Publishing Company, American Ethnological Society, Monograph 64.

Bennett, W. C. 1934. Excavations at Tiahuanaco. *Anthropological Papers of the American Museum of Natural History*, 34: 359–494.

Berenguer, J. R. 1978. La problemática Tiwanaku en Chile: vision retrospectiva. *Revista Chilena de Antropología*, 1: 17–40.

Berenguer, J. R. and Dauelsberg H., P. 1989. El norte grande en la órbita de Tiwanaku (400 a 1,200 d.C). In *Culturas de Chile, Prehistoria desde sus Orígenes hasta los Albores de la Conquista* (eds J. Hidalgo L., V. Schiappacasse F., H. Niemeyer F., C. Aldunate Del S. and I. Solimano R). Santiago de Chile: Editorial Andres Bello, pp. 129–80.

Bermann, M. 1994. *Lukurmata: Household Archaeology in Prehispanic Bolivia.* Princeton: Princeton University Press.

Berry, A. C. and Berry, R. J. 1967. Epigenetic variation in the human cranium. *Journal of Anatomy*, 101: 361–79.

Blom, D. E. 1997. Final report submitted to the Wenner Gren Foundation for Anthropological Research, Grant # 5863 – to aid bioarchaeological research on Tiwanaku interaction with the Moquegua Valley, Peru. Wenner Gren Foundation for Anthropological Research, New York, NY. 3 March 1997.

Blom, D. E., Lozada C., M. C., Hallgrímsson, B., Keng, L. and Buikstra., J. E. 1997. Biology and culture in the prehispanic south-central Andes. Paper presented to the 62nd Annual Society for American Archaeology meetings, Nashville, TN, 1997.

Blom, D. E., Yeatts, D. J. and Buikstra, J. E. 1995. A bioanthropological approach to Tiwanaku-Moquegua Valley interaction. Paper presented to the 60th Annual Meeting of the Society for American Archaeology, Minneapolis, MN, 1995.

Browman, D. L. 1978. Toward the development of the Tiahuanaco (Tiwanaku) state. In *Advances in Andean Archaeology* (ed. D. L. Browman). The Hague: Mouton, pp. 327–49.

Browman, D. L. 1980. Tiwanaku expansion and altiplano economic pattern. *Estudios Arqueológicos (Museo Arqueológico de Cachi)*, 5: 107–20.

Browman, D. L. 1984. Tiwanaku: development of interzonal trade and economic expansion in the altiplano. In *Social and Economic Organization in the Prehispanic Andes* (eds D. L. Browman, R. L. Burger and M. A. Rivera). Oxford: British Archaeological Reports, BAR International Series 194 pp. 117–42.

Brush, S. 1977. *Mountain, Field, and Family.* Philadelphia: University of Pennsylvania Press.

Buikstra, J. E. 1976. *Hopewell in the Lower Illinois Valley: A Regional Approach to the Study of Human Biological Variability and Prehistoric Behavior.* Evanston, IL: Northwestern University Archeological Program, Scientific Papers, No. 2.

Buikstra, J. E. 1995. Tombs for the living . . . or . . . for the dead: the Osmore ancestors. In *Tombs for the Living: Andean Mortuary Practices* (ed. T. D. Dillehay). Washington, DC: Dumbarton Oaks Research Library and Collection, pp. 229–80.

Buikstra, J. and Ubelaker, D. (eds) 1994. *Standards for Data Collection from Human Skeletal Remains: Proceedings of a Seminar at the Field Museum of Natural History.* Fayetteville, AR: Arkansas Archeological Survey, Research Series No. 44.

Caballero, G. B. 1984. El Tiwanaku en Cochabamba. *Arqueología Boliviana*, 1: 67–72.

Cardona R., A. 1997. Rescate arqueológico en el sitio M 162 – Valle Medio de Moquegua – Peru. Report presented to the Instituto Nacional de Cultura, Lima, Peru.

Cavalli-Sforza, L. L., Menozzi, P. and Piazza, A. 1994. *The History and Geography of Human Genes.* Princeton, NJ: Princeton University Press.

Chapman, M. 1993. Social and biological aspects of ethnicity. In *Social and Biological Aspects of Ethnicity* (ed. M. Chapman). New York: Oxford University Press, pp. 1–46.

Cheverud, J. M. and Buikstra, J. E. 1978. A study of intragroup biological change induced by social group fission in Macaca mulatta using discrete cranial traits. *American Journal of Physical Anthropology*, 48: 41–76.

Cheverud, J. M. and Buikstra, J. E. 1981a. Quantitative genetics of skeletal non-metric traits in the rhesus macaques on Cayo Santiago I: single trait heritabilities. *American Journal of Physical Anthropology*, 54: 43–9.

Cheverud, J. M. and Buikstra, J. E. 1981b. Quantitative genetics of skeletal non-metric traits in the rhesus macaques on Cayo Santiago II: phenotypic genetic and environmental correlations between traits. *American Journal of Physical Anthropology*, 54: 51–8.

Cheverud, J. M. and Buikstra, J. E. 1982. Quantitative genetics of skeletal non-metric traits in the rhesus macaques on Cayo Santiago III: relative heritability of skeletal non-metric and metric traits. *American Journal of Physical Anthropology*, 59: 151–5.

Cohen, A. B. 1995. Ritual and landscape in the Moquegua Valley, Peru. Paper presented to the 60th Annual Meeting of the Society for American Archaeology, Minneapolis, MN, 1995.

Cohen, A. B., Bandy, M. and Goldstein, P. 1995. How old is that Archipelago: the Huaracane Tradition and the antiquity of vertical control in the South Andes. Paper presented to the 35th Annual Meeting of the Institute for Andean Studies, Berkeley, CA, 1995.

Conkey, M. W. and Hastorf, C. A. (eds) 1990. *The Uses of Style in Archaeology.* Cambridge: Cambridge University Press.

Corruccini, R. S. 1972. The biological relationships of some prehistoric and historic Pueblo populations. *American Journal of Physical Anthropology*, 37: 373–88.

de la Vega, G. 1961 [1609]. *The Incas: The Royal Commentaries of the Inca* (trans. Maria Jolas). New York: Orion Press, Inc.

de las Casas, F. B. 1892 [1561]. *De las Antiguas Gentes del Peru.* Madrid: Manuel G. Hernandes.

Diez de San Miquel, G. 1964 [1567]. *Visita Hecha a la Provincia de Chucuito por Garci Diez de San Míquel en el Año 1567).* Lima, Peru: Documentos Regionales para la Etnología y Etnohistoría Andinas. Ediciones de la Casa de La Cultura del Peru.

Dillehay, T. D. and Núñez A. L. 1988. Camelids, caravans, and complex societies in the south-central Andes. In *Recent Studies in Pre-Columbian Archeology* (eds N. J. Saunders and O. de Montmollin). Oxford: British Archeological Reports, BAR International Series 421, pp. 603–34.

Disselhoff, H. D. 1968. Huari und Tiahuanaco: Grabungen und Funde in süd-Peru. *Zeitschrift fur Ethnologie*, 93: 207–16.

Feldman, R. A. 1989. The early ceramic periods of Moquegua. In *Ecology, Settlement and History in the Osmore Drainage, Peru* (eds D. Rice, C. Stanish and P. Scarr). Oxford: British Archaeological Reports, p. 545.

Finnegan, M. 1978. Non-metric variation in the infracranial skeleton. *Journal of Anatomy*, 125(1): 23–37.

Goldstein, P. S. 1985. Tiwanaku ceramics of the Moquegua Valley, Peru. Masters thesis. Department of Anthropology, University of Chicago, Chicago, IL.

Goldstein, P. S. 1989. Omo, a Tiwanaku provincial center in Moquegua, Peru. Doctoral dissertation. Department of Anthropology, University of Chicago, Chicago, IL.

Goldstein, P. S. 1990. On the eve of empire: Moquegua before the Tiwanaku conquest, early altiplano control and the Paracas connection. Paper presented to the 18th Annual Midwest Conference on Andean and Amazonian Archaeology and Ethnohistory, Chicago, IL.

Goldstein, P. S. 1993a. House, community and state in the earliest Tiwanaku colony: domestic patterns and state integration at Omo M12, Moquegua. In *Domestic Architecture, Ethnicity, and Complementarity in the South-Central Andes* (ed. M. S. Aldenderfer). Iowa City: University of Iowa Press, pp. 25–41.

Goldstein, P. S. 1993b. Tiwanaku temples and state expansion: a Tiwanaku sunken-court temple in Moquegua, Peru. *Latin American Antiquity*, 4: 22–47.

Goldstein, P. S. 1994. Formative and Tiwanaku-contemporary settlement patterns in the Moquegua Valley, Peru: report of the Moquegua Archaeological Survey, 1993 season. Paper presented to the 59th Annual Society for American Archaeology meeting, Anaheim, FL.

Goldstein, P. S. 1995. *Informe de Campo, Rescate Chen Chen 1995: Investigaciones de los Sectores Habitacionales*. Museo Contisuyo, Moquegua, Peru. Internal Report.

Goldstein, P. S. n. d. Exotic goods and everyday chiefs: Paracas, Pukara and the Moquegua Valley Formative. Hanover, NH: Dartmouth University, manuscript.

Hastorf, C., Bandy, M., Blom, D., Dean, E., Goodman, M., Kojan, D., Montaño Aragón, M., Luis Paz, J., Steadman, D., Steadman, L. and Whitehead, W. 1997. Proyecto arqueológico Taraco: excavaciones de 1996 en Chiripa, Bolivia. Report presented to the Instituto Nacional de Arqueología, La Paz, Bolivia.

Hauser, G. and De-Stefano, G. F. 1989. *Epigenetic Variants of the Human Skull*. Stuttgart: Schweizerbart.

Higueras-Hare, A. 1996. Prehispanic settlement and land use in Cochabamba, Bolivia. Doctoral dissertation. Department of Anthropology, University of Pittsburgh, Pittsburgh, PA.

Hoshower, L. M., Buikstra, J. E., Goldstein, P. S. and Webster, A. D. 1995. Artificial cranial deformation in the Omo M10 site, a Tiwanaku complex from the Moquegua Valley, Peru. *Latin American Antiquity*, 6: 145–64.

Hrdlička, A. 1912. Artificial deformation of the human skull with especial reference to America. Actas del XVII Congreso Internacional de Americanistas, Buenos Aires, pp. 147–9.

Hrdlička, A. 1932. The principal dimension, absolute and relative, of the humerus in the white race. *American Journal of Physical Anthropology*, 16: 431–50.

Ishida, E. 1960. *Andes, The Report of the University of Tokyo Scientific Expedition to the Andes, 1958*. Tokyo: University of Tokyo.

Isla, C. J., Williams, P. R., Medina, L. and Blom, D. E. 1998. The nature of wari militarism at Cerro Baul. Paper presented to the 63rd Annual Meeting of the Society of American Archaeology, Seattle, WA, 1998.

Janusek, J. W. 1994. State and local power in a prehispanic Andean polity: changing patterns of urban residence in Tiwanaku and Lukurmata, Bolivia. Doctoral dissertation. Department of Anthropology, University of Chicago, Chicago, IL.

Janusek, J. W. 1997. Rural history and state formation in the Koani Pampa, Bolivia. Paper presented to the 62nd Annual Society for American Archaeology meetings, Nashville, TN, 1997.

Jones, S. 1997. *The Archaeology of Ethnicity: Constructing Identities in the Past and Present*. New York: Routledge.

Julien, C. J. 1983. *Hatungolla: A View of Inca Rule from the Lake Titicaca Region*. University of California Publications in Anthropology 15. Berkeley: University of California Press.

Julien, C. J. 1985. Guano and resource control in sixteenth-century Arequipa. In *Andean Ecology and Civilization* (eds S. Masuda, I. Shimada and C. Morris). Tokyo: University of Tokyo Press, pp. 185–231.

Kolata, A. L. 1986. The agricultural foundations of the Tiwanaku State: a view from the heartlands. *American Antiquity*, 51: 746–62.

Kolata, A. L. 1992. Economy, ideology, and imperialism in the south-central Andes. In *Ideology and Pre-Columbian Civilizations* (eds A. A. Demarest and G. W. Conrad). Santa Fe, NM: School of American Research, pp. 65–85.

Kolata, A. L. 1993a. *The Tiwanaku: Portrait of an Andean Civilization*. Oxford: Blackwell.

Kolata, A. L. 1993b. Understanding Tiwanaku: conquest, colonization, and clientage in the South Central Andes. In *Latin American Horizons* (ed. D. S. Rice). Washington, DC: Dumbarton Oaks Research Library and Collections, pp. 193–224.

Konigsberg, L. 1987. Population genetic models for interpreting prehistoric intra-cemetery biological variation. Doctoral dissertation. Department of Anthropology, Northwestern University, Evanston, IL.

Konigsberg, L., Kohn, L. A. P. and Cheverud, J. M. 1993. Cranial deformation and nonmetric variation. *American Journal of Physical Anthropology*, 90: 36–50.

Lane, R. A. and Sublett, A. J. 1972. Osteology of social organization: residence pattern. *American Antiquity*, 37: 186–201.

Lozada C., M. C., Blom, D. E. and Buikstra, J. E. 1996. Evaluating verticality through cranial deformation patterns in the south Andes. Paper presented to the 61st Annual Society for American Archaeology meetings, New Orleans, LA, 1996.

Lozada C., M. C., Blom, D. E. and Buikstra, J. E. 1997. La deformación craneana artificial: una práctica cultural entre los pobladores Chiribaya de Ilo, sur del Peru. Paper presented to the Seminario Sobre Arqueología de Ilo, Centro Cultural de la Pontificia Universidad Católica del Peru, Lima, Peru, 1997.

Macbeth, H. 1993. Ethnicity and human biology. In *Social and Biological Aspects of Ethnicity* (ed. M. Chapman). New York: Oxford University Press, pp. 47–91.

Mathews, J. E. 1992. Prehispanic settlement and agriculture in the Middle Tiwanaku Valley, Bolivia. Doctoral dissertation. Department of Anthropology, University of Chicago, Chicago, IL.

Morris, C. 1985. From principles of ecological complementarity to the organization and administration of Tawantinsuyu. In *Andean Ecology and Civilization* (eds S. Masuda, I. Shimada, and C. Morris). Tokyo: University of Tokyo, pp. 477–90.

Moseley, M. E., Feldman, R. A., Goldstein, P. S. and Watanabe, L. 1991. Colonies and conquest: Tiahuanaco and Huari in Moquegua. In *Huari Administrative Structure: Prehistoric Monumental Architecture and State Government* (eds W. H. Isbell and G. F. McEwan). Washington, DC: Dumbarton Oaks, pp. 121–40.

Mujica, E. 1985. Altiplano-coast relationships in the south-central Andes: from indirect to direct complementarity. In *Andean Ecology and Civilization* (eds S. Masuda, I. Shimada and C. Morris). Tokyo: University of Tokyo, pp. 103–40.

Mujica, E., Rivera, M. and Lynch, T. 1983. Proyecto de estudio sobre la complemenariedad económica Tiwanaku en los valles occidentales del centro-sur Andino, Arcia, Chile. *Chungará*, 11: 85–109.

Muñoz, O. I. 1995–6. Poblamiento humano y relaciones interculturales en el valle de Azapa: nuevos hallazgos en torno al Período Formativo y Tiwanaku. *Diálogo Andino*, 14/15: 241–76.

Murra, J. V. 1968. An Aymara kingdom in 1567. *Ethnohistory*, 15: 115–51.

Murra, J. V. 1972. El 'control vertical' de un máximo de pisos ecológicos en la economía de las sociedades andinas. In *Visita de la Provincia de León de Huánuco en 1562* (ed. J. V. Murra). Huánuco: Universidad Nacional Hermilio Valdizán, pp. 429–76.

Murra, J. V. 1985a. The limits and limitations of the 'vertical archipelago' in the Andes. In *Andean Ecology and Civilization: An Interdisciplinary Perspective on Andean Ecological Complementarity* (eds S. Masuda, I. Shimada and C. Morris). Tokyo: University of Tokyo Press, pp. 15–20.

Murra, J. V. 1985b. 'El archipielago vertical' revisited. In *Andean Ecology and Civilization* (eds S. Masuda, I. Shimada and C. Morris). Tokyo: University of Tokyo Press, pp. 3–14.

Oakland Rodman, A. 1992. Textiles and ethnicity: Tiwanaku in San Pedro de Atacama, North Chile. *Latin American Antiquity*, 3: 316–40.

Owen, B. 1997. Informe de excavaciones en los sectores mortuarios de Chen Chen. Museo Contisuyo, Moquegua, Peru. Internal report.

Pari F., R. 1987. El proceso histórico social de los Tiwanaku y su implicancia en el Valle de Moquegua. Tesis de licenciado. Departmento de Arqueología, UCSM Arequipa, Arequipa, Peru.

Pari F., R. 1997. Chen Chen: un sitio Tiwanaku. Paper presented to the VII Congreso Nacional de Estudiantes de Arqueología 'Máximo Neira Avendaño', Arequipa, 1997.

Pease G. Y., F. 1985. Cases and variations of verticality in the southern Andes. In *Andean Ecology and Civilization* (eds S. Masuda, I. Shimada and C. Morris). Tokyo: University of Tokyo, pp. 141–60.

Platt, T. 1982. *Estado Boliviano y Ayllu Andino: Tierra y Tributo en el norte de Potosí*. Lima, Peru: Instituto de Estudios Peruanos.

Ponce Sangines, C. 1972. *Tiwanaku: Espacio, Tiempo y Cultura: Ensayo de Síntesis Arqueológica*. La Paz, Bolivia: Academia Nacional de Ciencias, Publicación 30.

Ravines, R. 1969. Investigaciones arqueológicos en el Peru: 1965–1966. *Revista del Museo Nacional, Lima*, 34: 247–54.

Rice, D. S. 1989. Osmore Drainage, Peru: The ecological setting. In *Ecology, Settlement and History in the Osmore Drainage, Peru* (eds D. S. Rice, C. Stanish and P. R. Scarr). Oxford: British Archaeological Reports, pp. 17–34.

Rivera, M. A. 1985a. Alto Ramírez y Tiwanaku, un caso de interpretación simbólica a través de datos arqueológicos en al área de los valles occidentales, sur del Peru y norte de Chile. In *La Problemática Tiwanaku Huari en el Contexto Panandino del Desarrollo Cultural* (ed. M. A. Rivera). Arica: Universidad de Tarapacá, Departamento de Historia y Geografía, Diálogo Andino No. 4. Congreso Internacional de Americanistas No. 45, Bogotá pp. 39–58.

Rivera, M. A. (ed.) 1985b. *La Problemática Tiwanaku Huari en el Contexto Panandino del Desarrollo Cultural*. Arica: Universidad de Tarapacá, Diálogo Andino No. 4.

Rostworowski de Diez Canseco, M. (ed.) 1988. *Historia del Tahuantinsuyu*. Lima, Peru: Instituto de Estudios Peruanos.

Rothhammer, F. and Silva, C. 1989. Peopling of Andean South-America. *American Journal of Physical Anthropology*, 78: 403–10.

Rothhammer, F., Quevedo, S., Cocilovo, J. A. and Llop, E. 1984. Microevolution in prehistoric Andean populations: chronologic nonmetrical cranial variation in Northern Chile. *American Journal of Physical Anthropology*, 65: 157–62.

Saunders, S. R. and Popovich, F. 1978. A family study of two skeletal variants: atlas bridging and clinoid bridging. *American Journal of Physical Anthropology*, 49: 193–204.

Selby, S., Garn, S. M. and Kanareff, V. 1955. The incidence and familial nature of a bony bridge on the first cervical vertebrae. *American Journal of Physical Anthropology*, 13: 129–41.

Shennan, S. 1989. Introduction: Archaeological approaches to cultural identity. In *Archaeological Approaches to Cultural Identity* (ed. S. Shennan). London: Unwin Hyman, pp. 1–32.

Sjøvold, T. 1984. A report on the heritability of some cranial measurements and non-metric traits. In *Multivariate Statistics in Physical Anthropology*. Dordrecht, The Netherlands: D. Reidl, pp. 223–46.

Squier, E. 1877. *Peru, Incidents of Travel and Exploration in the Land of the Incas*. London: Macmillan.

Stanish, C. 1994. The hydraulic hypothesis revisited: Lake Titicaca Basin raised fields in theoretical perspective. *Latin American Antiquity*, 5: 312–32.

Stewart, T. D. 1950. Deformity, trephining, and mutilation in South American Indian skeletal remains. In *Handbook of South American Indians*, Vol. 6 *Physical Anthropology, Linguistics and Cultural Geography of South American Indians* (ed. J. H. Steward). Washington, DC: Smithsonian Institution, Bureau of American Ethnology Bulletin 143, pp. 43–8.

Sutherland, C. A. 1992. Ritual drinking in the Andes: the Akapana kero smash. Paper presented at the 58th Annual Meetings of the Society for American Archaeology, New Orleans, LA, 1992.

Sutter, R. C. 1997. Dental variation and biocultural affinities among prehistoric populations from the coastal valleys of Moquegua, Peru and Azapa, Chile. Doctoral dissertation. Department of Anthropology, University of Missouri, Columbia, MO.

Thomas, C., Benavente, M. A. and Massone, C. 1985. Algunos efectos de Tiwanaku en la cultura de San Pedro de Atacama. In *La Problemática Tiwanaku Huari en el Contexto Panandino del Desarrollo Cultural* (ed. M. A. Rivera). Arica: Universidad de Tarapacá, Diálogo Andino No. 4, pp. 259–76.

Torgersen, J. H. 1951. Heritability factors in the sutural patterns of the skull. *Acta Radiologica*, 36: 521–3.

Torres P., E. 1992. *Inventario y reorganización de los restos oseos de Chen Chen*. Report.

Turner, C. G., II. 1989. Teeth and prehistory in Asia. *Scientific American*, 260: 88–96.

Turner, C. G., II, Nichol, C. R. and Scott, G. R. 1991. Scoring procedures for key morphological traits of the permanent dentition: the Arizona State University Dental Anthropology System. In *Advances in Dental Anthropology* (eds M.A. Kelley and C. S. Larsen). New York: Wiley Liss, pp. 13–31.

Van Buren, M. 1996. Rethinking the vertical archipelago: ethnicity, exchange, and history in the South Central Andes. *American Anthropologist*, 98: 338–51.

Vargas V., B. 1988. Informe final del proyecto: 'Rescate arqueológico del cementerio de Chen Chen'. Final report presented to the Instituto Nacional de Cultura, Departmental Moquegua, Peru.

Vargas V., B. 1994. Informe sobre tumbas intactas (334) excavadas durante el proyecto 'Rescate arqueológico en el cementerio de Chen Chen – Moquegua.' Report.

Verano, J. W. 1987. Cranial microvariation at Pacatnamú: a study of cemetery population variability. Doctoral dissertation. Department of Anthropology, University of California, Los Angeles, CA.

Weiss H., P. 1972. Las deformaciones intencionales como factores de la arqueología. In XXXIX Congreso Internacional de Americanistas, 1970. Actas, Documentos y Memorias Volumen 1. Lima, pp. 165–80.

Wiessner, P. 1983. Style and social information in Kalahari San projectile points. *American Antiquity*, 48: 253–76.

Williams, P. R. 1997. The role of disaster in the development of agriculture and the evolution of social complexity in the south-central Andean sierra. Doctoral dissertation. Department of Anthropology, University of Florida, Gainesville, FL.

Colonization and microevolution in Formative Oaxaca, Mexico

Alexander F. Christensen

Abstract

Linguistic evidence indicates that the Zapotecan languages spread from the Central Valleys of Oaxaca to the southwest during the Middle and Late Formative (800 BC–AD 250), and to the north and east during the Classic and Postclassic (AD 250–1521). The archaeological record of the lower Río Verde Valley, on the western coast of Oaxaca, supports this model of linguistic differentiation. The earliest significant settlement in the valley dates to the late Middle Formative, and this population probably spoke an ancestral form of Chatino, a Zapotecan language. Cranial non-metric and odontometric analyses of biological distance demonstrate that the skeletal remains from the Verde are more similar to those from the Early and Middle Formative Valley of Oaxaca than to those from the Late Formative Mixteca Alta and Valley of Oaxaca. This follows the predictions of the model of linguistic divergence. Despite this similarity, the teeth of the coastal series are dramatically smaller than those of any highland sample. This suggests rapid adaptation in response to the different selective pressures exerted by the lowland environment.

Keywords

Mesoamerica; odontometrics; cranial non-metrics; dental reduction.

Introduction

Mesoamerica is one of the more linguistically diverse areas of the world. When the Spanish arrived in 1519, its 1,300,000km² contained an estimated 22,000,000 inhabitants speaking at least sixty-nine languages, which belonged to fourteen different linguistic stocks (Campbell et al. 1986; Nichols 1992). These languages were (and are) distributed very unevenly across the landscape, with some restricted to a single village and others spanning thousands of kilometers. This complicated linguistic patchwork had evolved over the 12,000 years of documented human habitation of the region. Little work has been done in Mesoamerica on the correlation of language, archaeology, and human biology, especially compared to the slightly larger region of Western Europe (e.g., Sokal 1991; Cavalli-Sforza 1997). This paper examines the archaeological and biological evidence for the spread of one particular language family, Zapotecan, which is largely restricted to the modern state of Oaxaca, Mexico.

At the Spanish Conquest, Oaxaca was inhabited by speakers of a minimum of sixteen languages, belonging to five different families. The two largest language families were Mixtecan and Zapotecan, belonging to the Otomanguean phylum. Each contained a series of dialects of varying degrees of divergence. Within Zapotecan, two linguistic communities, Chatino and Papabuco, are generally considered distinct languages (Rendón 1995; Hopkins 1984). Each is presently located on the western border of the Zapotecan distribution (Fig. 1). Glottochronological estimates place the divergence of these languages at around 500 BC; even if the exact date is not accepted, the split can reasonably be placed within the first millennium BC (Hopkins 1984: 42–3). The remaining dialects are grouped under the name Zapotec, although by some estimates this 'language' contains as many as thirty-eight mutually unintelligible forms (Egland et al. 1978). The Zapotec dialects are grouped into three broad sublanguages, Northern, Central, and Southern (Urcid 1992). Chatino is closest to the Miahuatlan dialect of Southern Zapotec, which is its immediate neighbor (Swadesh 1967: 95). The Northern group can in turn be split into Nexitzo and Villalteco, while Central divides into Main and Smaller Valley forms, as well as the eastern, Tehuano extension. These dialects probably began to diverge during the first millennium AD, with the process intensifying in the second (Rendón 1995). Historical reconstruction of the Otomanguean languages generally puts their centre of origin in the highlands, with their few coastal extensions considered recent expansions (Josserand et

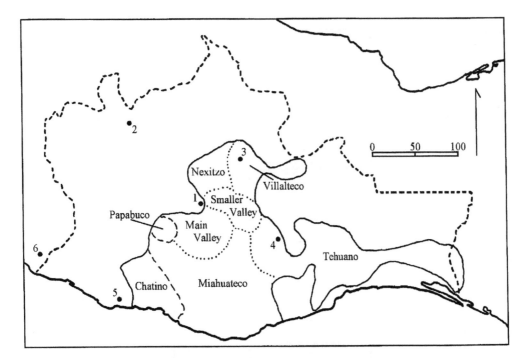

Figure 1 Distribution of Zapotecan languages (after Urcid 1992: figs 1.17, 1.21). Numbers indicate the known extent of Zapotec inscriptions: 1 Monte Albán; 2 Magdalena Jicotlan; 3 Yaguila; 4 Nejapa; 5 Río Viejo; 6 Piedra Labrada.

al. 1984b: 8). Given the archaeological evidence for long occupation and cultural continuity in the Central Valleys of Oaxaca (on which see below), it is logical to see them as
the hearth of the Zapotecan family. How did Zapotec spread from this center over such
a wide area?

In the case of Tehuano, there is ethnohistorical evidence for the spread of Zapotec by
a process of extensive migration in the Postclassic period (AD 900–1521; for the chronology of Oaxaca see Table 1). In response to the military expansion of the Mexica Aztec,

Table 1 Chronology of Oaxaca. All dates are calibrated after Christensen (1998b). For the Valley
of Oaxaca, phase names on the left refer to the traditional chronology, those on the right to that of
Lind (1991–2). *Sources*: Valley of Oaxaca (Lind 1991–2); Mixteca (Winter 1989); Río Verde (Joyce
1993). While general phase correspondences are reliable, temporal boundaries are arbitrary and
probably do not align quite as well in reality.

Date	Period	Valley of Oaxaca	Mixteca Alta	Mixteca Baja	Río Verde
AD 1500	Postclassic	Chila Monte Albán V Liobaa	Natividad	Nuyoo	Yucudzaa
AD 1000					
	Classic	Monte Albán IIIb–IV Xoo	Las Flores	Ñuiñe	Yuta Tiyoo
AD 500					Coyuche
		Monte Albán IIIa Pitao			
AD 1	Late Formative	Monte Albán II Niza	Ramos	Ñudée	Chacahua
					Miniyua
		Monte Albán Ic Pe			Minizundo
		Monte Albán Ia/Danibaan			Charco
500 BC	Middle Formative	Rosario			
		Guadalupe	Late Cruz		
1000 BC	Early Formative	San José			
		Tierras Largas	Early Cruz		
1500 BC		Espiridión			

the last Prehispanic rulers of Zaachila, a city-state in the Valley of Oaxaca, moved their capital east to Tehuantepec (Marcus 1983b). The date of this shift correlates well with a glottochronological estimation of the separation of Tehuano from the other Central dialects (Winter et al. 1984: 94). For the remainder of the family, however, the spread occurred long enough ago that historical sources are silent, and we must rely upon archaeological and biological data. Of the archaeological data, by far the most useful for tracing language spread are inscribed monuments. Some of the earliest examples of writing in Mesoamerica occur in the Valley of Oaxaca, and although the linguistic content of this script remains hard to interpret, it is generally assumed that it represents a form of Zapotec speech (Urcid 1992). The distribution of inscriptions in this script correlates well with the current distribution of Zapotec: the majority come from the Central Valleys, with others from the northern Sierra, Nejapa to the east, and the Pacific coast (Fig. 1). There are a handful of texts from the Mixteca, but the later epigraphic developments in that region (the Classic Ñuiñe and Postclassic Mixtec styles) are quite distinct. On the coast, Zapotec-style texts occur considerably to the west of the modern distribution of Chatino, even reaching into Guerrero at the site of Piedra Labrada (Urcid 1993). There are other grounds for suspecting the ancient presence of Zapotecans to the west of their current distribution. Early Colonial accounts describe one Zapotec community on the coast of Guerrero at Quahuçapotla (Cuauhtzapotlan), more than 50km further west than any inscriptions (Barlow 1943, 1944).

The writing system used on the Pacific coast in the Classic is a distinct variant of that found in the Valley of Oaxaca. Such regional variation could easily correlate, whether as a direct effect or parallel development, with the beginnings of a linguistic divergence between the two regions. However, most of these texts contain little other than names and dates, and thus their linguistic significance is not assured. Evidence of borrowed stress patterns in Pochutec, a Nahua language preserved until early this century in a small pocket on the coast, suggest that Chatino was the status language in the region when Pochutec speakers arrived, probably during the Classic period (Bartholomew 1980). Ethnohistoric accounts date the Mixtec conquest of the western coast to the tenth or eleventh century, which corre- lates well with the divergence of the coastal dialect of Mixtec from that of the Alta (Josserand et al. 1984a: 154). It has been argued that Tututepec, the great Postclassic polity that resulted from this conquest, was multiethnic, containing Mixtecs, Chatinos, and smaller groups of speakers of several other languages under Mixtec rulership (Spores 1993).

Thus epigraphic and linguistic data suggest that proto-Zapotecan-speakers had spread onto the Pacific coast by the Classic period (AD 250–900), while glottochronological esti- mates indicate that the coastal Zapotecan language, Chatino, diverged from its relatives by the Late Formative (300 BC–AD 250). How well does this correlate with the archaeo- logical evidence? Archaeological work within Oaxaca has been concentrated in four areas of the highlands (Fig. 2; Winter (1989) provides a summary). The primary focus has been the Valley of Oaxaca, the locus of both the modern capital and the largest and best known Precolumbian site, Monte Albán. A lesser amount of work, primarily survey, has been conducted in the Valleys of Ejutla, Miahuatlan, and Sola de Vega, which adjoin the Valley of Oaxaca to the south. Both surveys and excavations have also been conducted in the Mixteca, to the west of the Central Valleys, and in the Cuicatlan Cañada, to the north- west. Although there has been some reconnaissance in the remainder of the highlands,

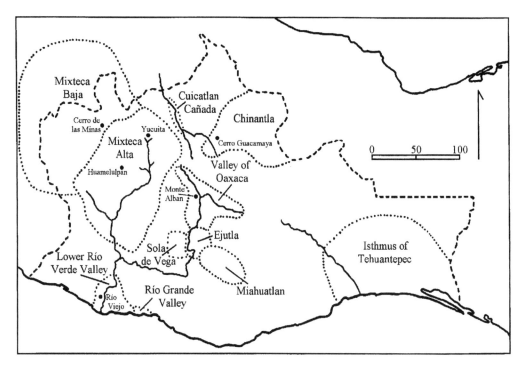

Figure 2   Archaeological map of Oaxaca.

the areas to the north and east of the Central Valleys remain practically unknown archaeologically. Along the coast, the only places where extensive work has been done are the
Isthmus of Tehuantepec and the lower Río Verde Valley.

While the Mixteca Alta and the Valley of Oaxaca have traces of settlement reaching back
into the Archaic, and certainly had extensive Early Formative settlements in at least some
regions, the early history of the coast appears quite different (Zeitlin 1979; Joyce 1993).
The Isthmus of Tehuantepec, where the majority of Zapotec speakers now live, had closer
ties to the modern state of Chiapas to the east than to the rest of Oaxaca at this time. No
Zapotec-style texts occur in the region, which confirms the linguistic and ethnohistoric
evidence that speakers of the language did not arrive in the area until the Postclassic, by
which time the writing system had fallen out of use (at least on stone monuments; it may
have continued to be used on perishable materials which do not survive). On the western
coast, the largest and most fertile river valley, that of the lower Río Verde, does not seem
to have had any significant settlement until the Late Formative period. The earliest defined
ceramics in the Verde belong to the Charco phase, which dates to the fifth century BC,
although a few redeposited Early Formative sherds have been found at the site of Charco
Redondo (Joyce 1991a). Prior to the Late Formative the floodplain of the Verde may have
been less productive, and therefore not attractive for dense human occupation (Joyce and
Mueller 1997; research on this subject is ongoing). This Middle Formative phase shows
some ceramic ties to the Valley of Oaxaca (Joyce 1991b: 128), a pattern suggesting that the
initial settlers came from the Proto-Zapotec-speaking region of central Oaxaca. The south-
ernmost of the Central Valleys, those of Sola and Miahuatlan, also do not show any traces
of settlement prior to the Late Formative (Balkansky 1997; Markman 1981). The Ejutla

Valley does have some earlier settlement, as does the southern arm of the Valley of Oaxaca, but both show dramatic population increases in the Middle–Late Formative (Feinman and Nicholas 1990; Kowalewski et al. 1989). Some Early and Middle Formative remains have been found in the Río Grande Valley, adjacent to the lower Río Verde, but the population history of this area is still quite poorly known. This suggests that the appearance of settlers in the lower Río Verde may have been the leading edge of a general southwards expansion of Zapotecan populations.

If the earliest known inhabitants of the lower Río Verde were Zapotecan migrants, either from the Central Valleys or from the mountain periphery, their skeletal remains should be more similar to Early and Middle Formative series from the Valley of Oaxaca than to their Late Formative neighbors and contemporaries in the Mixteca. If local population continuity with some contact between neighbors is the rule throughout western Oaxaca, then each region should be distinct, with the coastal sample most similar to its neighbors in the Mixteca Alta. Unfortunately, no skeletal samples are available from the area in between the coast and the Central Valleys, or from earlier occupations in the Mixteca, which would help provide a more detailed understanding of the population history of the lower Río Verde.

Materials and methods

The skeletal remains of approximately 1,500 individuals recovered from archaeological excavations throughout Oaxaca were examined in the spring and summer of 1996 (for full details see Christensen 1998a). Two sets of data were used to assess population affinities among these individuals, cranial non-metrics and dental metrics. Both have been used in previous studies of biological relationships in Mesoamerica (e.g., Case 1976; Christensen 1997a; Salas 1982; Spence 1994) and elsewhere (e.g., Berry and Berry 1967; Hemphill et al. 1991; Jacobs 1994). It appears likely that each system is subject to different genetic and environmental controls. In conjunction they provide a broader view of population relationships than any one system of variation could, and whatever patterns appear in both analyses are likely to reflect biological reality.

The relevant skeletal series for this analysis are that from the lower Río Verde and the Formative remains from the Valley of Oaxaca and the Mixteca Alta (more detailed accounts of these remains and of the Classic and Postclassic materials examined appear in Christensen 1998a). Due to small sample size, all of the remains from the Río Verde had to be lumped together (sample RVE). The majority of these come from the site of Cerro de la Cruz and date to the Minizundo and Miniyua phases (300 BC–AD 150). Others from both the same period and later ones come from the sites of Río Viejo, Barra Quebrada, and Charco Redondo. Most of the later burials date to the Coyuche phase (AD 300–600), but a handful may derive from Late Classic or Postclassic contexts. The Valley of Oaxaca materials were divided into Early, Middle, and Late Formative samples (VEF, VMF, and VLF, respectively), while the single Mixtec sample (MF) comes primarily from the Late Formative, with limited Middle Formative remains from Etlatongo. Both odontometric and cranial non-metric data were collected from each individual. Because the former data could only be collected from those individuals with extant permanent

Table 2   Skeletal samples used. Abbreviations as follows: VEF = Valley Early Formative; VMF = Valley Middle Formative; VLF = Valley Late Formative; MF = Mixteca Formative; RVE = Río Verde.

Sample	Mean date	Cranial N	Dental N	Sites
VEF	1200 BC	90	126	Hacienda Blanca, San José Mogote, Santo Domingo Tomaltepec, Tierras Largas
VMF	550 BC	47	50	Fábrica San Jose, Hacienda Blanca, Huitzo, Monte Albán, San José Mogote, Santo Domingo Tomaltepec, Tierras Largas
VLF	25 BC	63	60	Caballito Blanco, Dainzu, Fábrica San Jose, Hacienda Blanca, Monte Albán, Nazareno Etla, San José Mogote, Santo Domingo Tomaltepec, Tierras Largas, Yagul
MF	25 BC	115	124	Cerro de las Minas, Etlatongo, Huamelulpan, Monte Negro, Yucuita, Yucunama
RVE	AD 250	69	98	Barra Quebrada, Cerro de la Cruz, Charco Redondo, Río Viejo
ARB	650 BC	29	na	El Arbolillo
TIC	400 BC	17	na	Ticoman
BAS	550 BC	56	na	El Arbolillo, Ticoman, Zacatenco

teeth, while the latter required preserved adult crania, sample sizes for each data set differ slightly. Table 2 lists the dates, sites, and respective numbers of individuals for each sample used. In addition, previously published Formative samples from the Basin of Mexico, including remains from El Arbolillo, Ticoman, and Zacatenco, were considered in the non-metric analyses. They were initially lumped together as one sample (BAS); in a second analysis El Arbolillo (ARB) and Ticoman (TIC) were considered separately. The archaeological context of much of this central Mexican sample is unsure, but it is predominantly Middle Formative (Christensen 1997a). Inclusion of these series provides some insight into the external connections of Oaxacan populations.

Fifty-five cranial non-metric traits were scored on each individual, but only twenty-four were used in the analyses. The others were either too rare or poorly preserved to be of use, or appeared to be strongly correlated with other traits, sex, or the environment (for methodological details, see Christensen 1998a). The traits were scored by side, and frequencies were summed for each series. These traits were analyzed in two manners. First, a dissimilarity matrix was constructed using the Mean Measure of Divergence (Berry and Berry 1967; Constandse-Westermann 1972:119). The MMD values were standardized by dividing them by their standard deviation (Sofaer et al. 1986). This provides some indication of statistical significance, as an MMD of greater than twice its SD is generally taken to be significant (Sjøvold 1977). Although both sets of distances are provided here, the non-standardized values were used in the multivariate analysis, in which the dissimilarity matrix was multidimensionally scaled into two dimensions. Secondly, a correlation matrix was constructed from angular-transforms of trait frequencies and subjected to principal components analysis. The populations were ordinated along the resulting dimensions and principal components, with a minimum-spanning tree superimposed upon each ordination.

The mesiodistal (length) and buccolingual (breadth) diameters of each tooth were measured to 0.05mm after the method of Moorrees (1957). Because of antimeric symmetry, only left-hand values were used in the analysis, unless they were missing, in which case right-hand values were substituted. Mean values of each measurement were corrected for size by dividing each by the geometric mean of all the measurements of that sample (Darroch and Mosimann 1985; Jungers et al. 1995). These corrected means were subjected to principal components analysis of a correlation matrix, and the resulting component scores ordinated. In addition, crown areas were calculated for each tooth by multiplying length and breadth. These facilitated a comparison of overall tooth size between samples. Summary measurements were calculated by adding the means from the anterior (incisor and canine) and posterior (premolar and molar) teeth in each jaw.

Results

Cranial non-metrics

Table 3 lists the frequencies of the twenty-four traits used in the non-metric analysis. The dissimilarity matrix (Table 4) indicates that none of the samples diverge wildly from the others. The Early and Middle Formative Valley of Oaxaca series are the most divergent from all others. Standardized values exhibit similar patterning. The only distances found to be insignificant (that is, with standardized MMDs < 2) are those between VLF and MF, ARB, and BAS, and those between BAS and MF, ARB, and TIC. The minuscule distances between BAS and its two constituent series ARB and TIC are understandable, as is the one negative value (which is a logical impossibility as two series cannot be less dissimilar than absolute identity, or an MMD of zero). The other low values suggest a close relationship between the Late Formative series from the Mixteca and Central Valley and the slightly earlier series from Central Mexico.

Principal components analysis produced five components with eigenvalues greater than one, explaining a total of 100 per cent of the variance (Table 5). The first component is heavily weighted for several temporal and facial traits, the second for cranial vault and basal traits, and the third for the mastoid foramen. They thus appear to have some biological significance, perhaps indicating the effects of different genes. When the first three principal components, explaining 81 per cent of the variance, are ordinated, BAS is central, with VLF and MF as its nearest neighbors (Fig. 3). The Early and Middle Formative Central Valley samples are widely spread around the periphery; RVE is intermediate to VEF, VMF, and MF. Although it is closer to MF, this is due largely to its score on the less explanatory third component. On the first two components, it is far closer to VEF, including practically identical scores on the second component.

The central placement of BAS was so counterintuitive that it was replaced by two of its constituent series, ARB and TIC, for the next analysis. Multidimensional scaling of this new data set into two dimensions using Kruskal's method had a stress of 0.014 and explained

Table 3 Cranial non-metric trait frequencies, by side. Traits defined in Christensen (1998a).

Trait		VEF	VMF	VLF	RVE	MF	ARB	TIC	BAS
MET	Metopic suture	0/35	1/27	2/31	0/37	1/74	1/29	0/15	1/56
AST	Asterionic ossicle	1/21	0/16	4/18	1/20	7/70	10/48	5/30	16/100
MFS	Mastoid foramen sutural	5/20	14/24	7/21	24/35	36/83	18/46	10/29	33/97
MFT	Mastoid foramen temporal	22/29	19/28	19/33	14/37	67/112	29/47	23/30	67/99
PNB	Parietal notch bone	0/17	2/19	2/23	2/24	10/74	9/48	2/30	12/99
PPR	Parietal process	0/22	5/14	1/18	1/20	5/84	2/50	1/27	4/97
ATR	Auditory torus	23/98	3/51	0/64	3/67	2/142	4/50	2/30	6/102
PFRA	Parietal foramen absent	4/17	5/20	11/23	5/17	33/81	23/57	7/30	37/109
FGR	Frontal grooves	2/14	10/22	6/19	3/17	18/72	15/50	10/28	39/100
SFO	Supraorbital foramen	17/43	14/38	15/35	19/40	43/97	19/48	16/30	48/102
ZFFA	Zygomaticofacial foramen absent	3/45	2/36	1/46	1/34	1/81	4/50	1/27	7/99
OJP	Os japonicum	0/20	0/23	2/29	1/22	8/55	2/46	2/27	5/93
IOS	Infraorbital suture	2/12	6/17	12/22	6/14	23/52	41/47	15/27	67/97
AIF	Accessory infraorbital foramen	4/10	4/16	4/18	5/15	14/47	8/43	1/26	20/92
PBR	Palatine bridging	0/30	1/25	2/30	0/25	1/76	0/48	0/26	0/95
FOV	Foramen ovale incomplete	0/23	0/19	2/31	0/24	3/62	0/44	5/27	5/91
FSI	Foramen spinosum incomplete	0/27	1/23	2/31	6/23	14/79	5/43	7/28	16/92
PSB	Pterygospinous bridging	2/32	4/29	3/35	3/21	2/82	3/47	1/28	4/98
PAB	Pterygoalar bridging	1/31	0/28	5/34	0/19	7/79	3/47	0/28	3/98
BHC	Bifid hypoglossal canal	3/48	6/23	4/33	1/25	13/80	7/43	4/28	16/93
FHS	Foramen of Huschke	17/67	10/39	11/51	14/44	64/125	8/50	14/30	28/102
TMF	Tympanic marginal foramen	14/64	2/37	7/45	5/36	17/113	9/49	2/28	18/99
MHB	Mylohyoid bridge	6/51	3/39	6/46	4/49	6/93	6/47	4/33	15/99
MEN	Accessory mental foramen	5/78	2/56	3/64	5/67	7/124	2/48	2/33	5/101

Table 4 Cranial non-metric dissimilarity matrix. Values below the diagonal are raw MMDs; those above have been standardized by dividing them by their standard deviation.

	VEF	*VMF*	*VLF*	*RVE*	*MF*	*ARB*	*TIC*	*BAS*
VEF		4.75	4.83	4.30	6.14	9.35	7.19	4.84
VMF	0.13		4.06	2.45	5.23	6.89	5.56	4.13
VLF	0.14	0.10		3.23	0.35	1.27	2.95	0.42
RVE	0.10	0.06	0.07		2.20	4.18	3.28	3.80
MF	0.14	0.10	0.01	0.03		7.07	2.77	1.50
ARB	0.17	0.13	0.02	0.07	0.07		4.66	−0.08
TIC	0.16	0.12	0.06	0.07	0.04	0.08		0.50
BAS	0.13	0.10	0.01	0.06	0.03	0.00	0.07	

Table 5 Cranial non-metric principal component loadings. Most heavily weighted component for each trait is in boldface.

	PC1	*PC2*	*PC3*	*PC4*	*PC5*
MET	0.54	**−0.71**	0.31	−0.15	−0.30
AST	**0.76**	0.38	0.45	0.12	−0.24
MFS	−0.08	−0.27	**−0.93**	0.13	−0.19
MFT	−0.31	−0.26	**0.77**	−0.11	0.48
PNB	**0.73**	−0.42	−0.47	0.17	0.20
PPR	−0.04	**−0.93**	−0.36	−0.07	−0.03
ATR	**−0.94**	−0.17	0.19	0.09	0.21
PFRA	**0.93**	0.13	0.13	−0.25	−0.20
FGR	0.34	**−0.87**	0.12	0.30	0.15
SFO	0.52	**0.62**	−0.30	0.51	−0.02
ZFFA	**−0.66**	−0.24	0.40	0.58	0.06
OJP	**0.83**	0.41	−0.28	−0.20	0.17
IOS	**0.81**	−0.09	0.00	0.57	0.04
AIF	**−0.74**	0.55	−0.14	−0.36	−0.02
PBR	0.30	**−0.63**	0.08	−0.52	−0.49
FOV	**0.92**	0.04	0.38	−0.01	0.10
FSI	0.52	0.24	**−0.71**	0.40	0.08
PSB	−0.42	−0.39	−0.41	0.11	**−0.70**
PAB	**0.66**	0.26	0.48	−0.49	−0.15
BHC	0.27	**−0.86**	0.07	−0.02	0.44
FHS	0.28	0.32	−0.53	−0.36	**0.64**
TMF	0.01	**0.86**	0.50	0.10	0.01
MHB	0.10	0.10	**0.78**	0.54	−0.27
MEN	−0.29	**0.85**	−0.35	0.04	−0.23
Eigenvalue	8.04	6.55	4.85	2.47	2.09
% variance	33.50	27.36	20.20	10.29	8.71

99.9 per cent of the variance. When the series are ordinated along these two dimensions, the VEF and VMF samples are most peripheral, as might be expected from the underlying dissimilarity matrix (Fig. 4). The VLF and MF samples are superimposed. The two Central Mexican series are not quite as close to them as the lumped BAS series was, but are still their nearest neighbors, one on either side. RVE occupies an intermediate position,

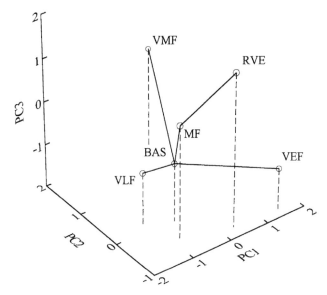

Figure 3 Ordination of first three cranial non-metric principal components. Percent variance explained: PC1 33.5, PC2 27.3, PC3 20.2.

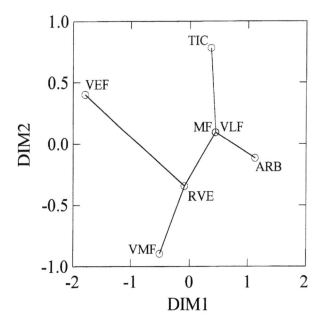

Figure 4 Ordination of cranial non-metric Kruskal dimensions.

connecting the earlier Central Valley samples to the Late Formative and central Mexican series. A comparison of this figure with the MMDs themselves shows that the close relationship of the VLF and RVE samples in this depiction is a result of the former's proximity to the Mixtec sample, rather than an indication of close kinship between the two series themselves (Table 4).

Odontometrics

Table 6 shows the mean tooth lengths and breadths of all five series considered (no data was available from the Central Mexican samples), and Table 7 the summary measures. Odontometric data were first compared by a simple plotting of crown area profiles (Fig. 5). In this plot, it is clear that the coast is quite distinct from all the highland series. Practically every tooth in this profile is smaller than all the other examples. In fact, the total crown area of the RVE series is far smaller than even the Postclassic sample from the Valley of Oaxaca, which is the smallest known from elsewhere in the state (Christensen 1998b). At the opposite end of the range, the Mixtec series is significantly larger than its Late Formative contemporaries.

Principal components analysis of size-corrected means yielded only four components (Table 8). The first component explains almost 55 per cent of the variance, and is the most heavily weighted component for twenty measurements. When the first three components, explaining 92.6 per cent of the total sample variance, are ordinated, the VEF sample occupies a central position (Fig. 6). All four other series radiate out from it, with RVE the furthest. There is no clear pattern to the relationships of the later series. The separation between the lower Río Verde and the other series occurs largely along the first component, which suggests that this component still largely reflects overall size, despite the correction of the measurements.

Dental microevolution in the lower Río Verde

The cranial non-metric and odontometric analyses both indicate that the Río Verde sample is more closely related to the Valley Early and Middle Formative samples than to either the Late Formative Valley or the Basin of Mexico. It demonstrates reduced affinities with its nearest neighbors in both space and time, the Formative Mixtec sample. This suggests that the coastal population may well be descended from Archaic or Early Formative inhabitants of the Central Valleys. While it is possible that the affinities between the Río Verde and Early and Middle Formative samples reflect an evolutionary convergence rather than a descent relationship, the linguistic and archaeological data support the latter model. While the Late Formative populations of the Central Valley and the Mixteca appear to be closely intertwined genetically, and are linked to earlier series from the Basin of Mexico, the largely contemporary coastal sample stands apart. There are some ties between the lower Río Verde and the Mixteca, which are geographically adjacent. These probably indicate a degree of gene flow across the cultural boundary between them.

Given the affinities revealed by the multivariate analyses, the large difference in tooth size between the coastal sample and all those from the highlands stands out. An earlier study demonstrated a steady reduction in tooth size within the Valley of Oaxaca from the Early Formative through the Postclassic (Christensen 1998b). In Figure 7, the crown areas of the five Valley samples considered in that study as well as those from the Mixteca and Coast are plotted against time. For the lower Río Verde sample, AD 250 was used as the mean date. If anything, this date is too late, as the coastal sample is weighted towards the Late Formative. Use of such a late date minimizes the size difference between the Verde and its highland contemporaries. The first regression line was fitted to just the five Valley

Table 6 Odontometric means (in mm²)

		VEF Mean	N	S	CV	VMF Mean	N	S	CV	VLF Mean	N	S	CV	RVE Mean	N	SD	CV	MF Mean	N	SD	CV
I¹	L	8.83	52	0.42	4.7	8.75	15	0.47	5.3	8.98	23	0.55	6.1	8.72	29	0.43	4.9	8.76	39	0.56	6.4
	B	7.56	68	0.49	6.4	7.54	21	0.50	6.7	7.45	29	0.54	7.3	7.31	32	0.82	11.2	7.35	42	0.48	6.5
I²	L	7.37	50	0.62	8.4	7.30	16	0.65	8.9	7.37	26	0.52	7.1	6.83	27	0.55	8.0	7.35	35	0.45	6.2
	B	6.73	63	0.64	9.5	6.46	21	0.66	10.2	6.69	28	0.56	8.4	6.25	31	0.43	6.9	6.67	39	0.58	8.7
C¹	L	8.27	57	0.45	5.4	8.14	20	0.44	5.4	8.17	32	0.48	5.9	7.99	41	0.56	7.0	8.22	51	0.38	4.6
	B	8.79	67	0.62	7.1	8.64	23	0.61	7.0	8.71	34	0.63	7.3	8.27	44	0.70	8.5	8.68	62	0.60	6.9
P³	L	7.57	64	0.52	6.8	7.41	22	0.36	4.9	7.38	30	0.54	7.4	7.10	38	0.47	6.6	7.60	53	0.54	7.1
	B	9.66	67	0.63	6.5	9.46	23	0.67	7.1	9.45	31	0.63	6.6	8.99	39	0.56	6.2	9.70	56	0.66	6.8
P⁴	L	7.08	62	0.45	6.4	7.30	21	0.69	9.4	7.13	31	0.54	7.6	6.87	44	0.57	8.2	7.27	54	0.44	6.1
	B	9.50	65	0.66	7.0	9.37	22	0.65	6.9	9.31	33	0.80	8.6	9.08	45	0.64	7.0	9.54	56	0.63	6.6
M¹	L	11.15	63	0.69	6.2	11.00	26	0.50	4.6	11.16	30	0.88	7.8	10.71	52	0.58	5.4	11.13	55	0.66	5.9
	B	11.98	68	0.57	4.8	11.72	29	0.51	4.3	11.92	34	0.75	6.3	11.49	54	0.58	5.1	11.89	56	0.60	5.1
M²	L	10.63	75	0.53	5.0	10.34	23	0.48	4.7	10.44	31	0.43	4.1	10.01	39	0.75	7.4	10.65	54	0.66	6.2
	B	11.69	75	0.62	5.3	11.54	21	0.46	4.0	11.57	33	0.61	5.2	10.93	37	0.67	6.1	11.63	54	0.76	6.5
M³	L	9.52	60	0.90	9.4	9.47	25	0.73	7.7	9.08	29	0.92	10.1	9.49	32	0.76	8.0	9.22	41	0.92	9.9
	B	10.85	60	1.00	9.2	10.94	25	0.95	8.7	10.66	29	0.81	7.6	10.52	32	0.58	5.5	10.62	41	1.05	9.9
I₁	L	5.46	34	0.37	6.7	5.48	18	0.25	4.6	5.44	18	0.38	7.0	5.67	27	0.70	12.3	5.62	29	0.46	8.3
	B	5.92	47	0.35	6.0	5.91	26	0.34	5.8	5.83	25	0.31	5.3	5.80	27	0.56	9.7	5.89	33	0.32	5.4
I₂	L	6.34	53	0.41	6.5	6.32	20	0.39	6.2	6.31	25	0.33	5.3	6.28	36	0.53	8.4	6.30	46	0.45	7.2
	B	6.38	66	0.36	5.6	6.33	31	0.35	5.6	6.26	28	0.29	4.6	6.28	41	0.51	8.1	6.28	55	0.43	6.9
C₁	L	7.36	75	0.43	5.8	7.18	37	0.44	6.1	7.33	36	0.55	7.5	7.11	49	0.58	8.2	7.33	71	0.41	5.5
	B	7.98	86	0.56	7.0	7.80	39	0.58	7.5	7.91	41	0.63	7.9	7.55	51	0.68	9.0	7.96	75	0.60	7.5
P₃	L	7.27	80	0.43	5.9	7.25	31	0.44	6.1	7.18	36	0.54	7.5	6.81	44	0.57	8.3	7.27	70	0.49	6.7
	B	8.05	82	0.53	6.6	7.99	31	0.51	6.4	7.79	39	0.45	5.7	7.77	47	0.59	7.6	7.98	70	0.48	6.1
P₄	L	7.41	80	0.48	6.4	7.31	28	0.54	7.3	7.31	28	0.51	6.9	6.79	35	0.56	8.3	7.40	61	0.54	7.3
	B	8.47	80	0.51	6.0	8.29	29	0.41	5.0	8.16	28	0.55	6.7	7.87	35	0.65	8.3	8.24	63	0.50	6.0
M₁	L	11.95	72	0.59	4.9	12.01	31	0.57	4.7	11.90	29	0.73	6.2	11.75	44	0.74	6.3	11.96	57	0.63	5.3
	B	11.09	80	0.47	4.2	10.95	33	0.49	4.4	11.15	31	0.73	6.5	10.80	45	0.62	5.8	11.05	59	0.47	4.2
M₂	L	11.45	78	0.60	5.2	11.34	26	0.66	5.8	11.27	27	0.72	6.4	10.78	37	0.84	7.8	11.53	53	0.65	5.6
	B	10.69	79	0.58	5.4	10.48	28	0.64	6.2	10.46	27	0.55	5.2	10.34	39	0.63	6.0	10.52	49	0.58	5.5
M₃	L	11.34	65	0.84	7.4	11.22	23	0.84	7.5	10.78	21	1.25	11.6	10.97	37	0.91	8.3	11.29	44	1.01	8.9
	B	10.50	66	0.64	6.1	10.37	23	0.79	7.6	10.17	21	0.64	6.3	10.23	37	0.58	5.7	10.51	44	0.86	8.2

Table 7 Odontometric summary measures (in mm²).

Summary measurement	VEF	VMF	VLF	RVE	MF
Maxillary anterior length	24.46	24.19	24.51	23.55	24.33
Maxillary posterior length	45.96	45.53	45.18	44.18	45.87
Mandibular anterior length	19.17	18.98	19.08	19.06	19.25
Mandibular posterior length	49.42	49.12	48.45	47.09	49.46
Maxillary length	70.43	69.71	69.69	67.73	70.20
Mandibular length	68.59	68.10	67.53	66.15	68.71
Maxillary anterior breadth	23.07	22.64	22.85	21.82	22.70
Maxillary posterior breadth	53.67	53.04	52.91	51.00	53.39
Mandibular anterior breadth	20.29	20.04	20.00	19.63	20.14
Mandibular posterior breadth	48.80	48.07	47.72	47.00	48.30
Maxillary breadth	76.74	75.68	75.76	72.83	76.08
Mandibular breadth	69.09	68.11	67.72	66.63	68.44
Maxillary anterior area	189.06	185.12	188.00	172.47	186.69
Maxillary posterior area	503.46	489.64	488.81	459.63	498.90
Mandibular anterior area	131.68	128.56	129.57	126.08	130.79
Mandibular posterior area	495.91	485.27	476.98	458.58	492.91
Anterior area	320.74	313.68	317.57	298.55	317.47
Posterior area	999.38	974.91	965.79	918.21	991.81
Maxillary area	692.52	674.76	676.81	632.10	685.59
Mandibular area	627.60	613.83	606.55	584.66	623.70
Total area	1320.12	1288.58	1283.36	1216.77	1309.29

series, the second to all seven series. This shows that, compared to their contemporaries from the Valley of Oaxaca, the coastal population exhibits a greater reduction in tooth size, and the Mixtec sample a lesser. The inclusion of the coast sample also provokes a sharp departure from linearity, as demonstrated by the lower r^2 and higher p values of the second regression.

How can these disparate lines of evidence be reconciled? One possible interpretation is that the population of the lower Río Verde did not originate in the highlands at all, but rather came from some unexplored area of the coast, perhaps in the neighboring state of Guerrero. This would fit with other bioarchaeological studies, which have used discrepancies in tooth size as evidence for migration from outside the study region (Brace 1980; Jacobs 1994). The archaeological evidence from other coastal areas is limited, but what there is does not appear to bear this theory out. It is possible that there were slightly earlier settlements in the Río Grande Valley, just east of the Verde, but these too show ceramic affinities with the Valley of Oaxaca (Zárate 1995). Similarly, the only linguistic evidence for significant contacts between the Oaxaca coast and Guerrero consists of the epigraphically and ethnohistorically attested presence of a few Zapotecan settlements in the latter state. Another interpretation is that the odontometrics, but not the cranial non-metrics, reflect the action of natural selection. By this theory, the reduction in tooth size observed in the Río Verde can be seen as the result of the great environmental change between the highlands and the coast. Supporting evidence for this contention comes from studies of the different systems of biological variation observed on Bougainville (Rogers

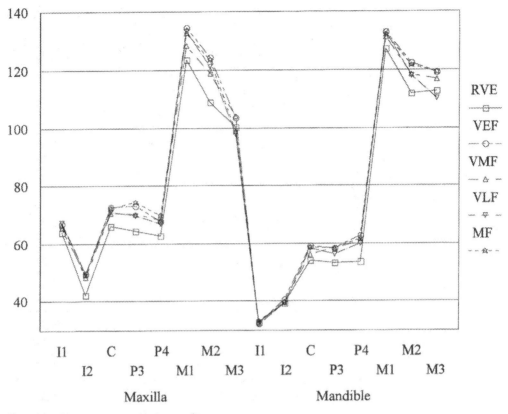

Figure 5 Crown area profile (in mm²).

and Harpending 1983). There, anthropometric eigenvalues exhibited far more asymmetry than dermatoglyphic ones. Rogers and Harpending argued that this divergence from symmetrical weighting indicated that the observed anthropometric differentiation was not due to drift alone, while the dermatoglyphic change may have been. In the case considered here, cranial non-metric eigenvalues were far more symmetrical than odontometric ones. While size-correction reduced the asymmetry (a principal components analysis of uncorrected means produced a first component that explained 70.9 per cent of the sample variance), it did not eliminate it, perhaps because of size-related allometry that cannot easily be corrected for. This suggests that natural selection is still visible in the corrected odontometric data, but not the cranial non-metric data.

Previous studies of biological affinities have attempted to attach historical or biological meanings to each principal component produced in their analysis (e.g., Cavalli-Sforza et al. 1994). In this case, it is possible that the first odontometric component is an environmental gradient, with the sample from the lowest altitude (RVE) having a very negative value (−1.69), the three from the Valley of Oaxaca grouped in the middle (−0.09 to 0.56), and the highest altitude series (MF) exhibiting the highest value (0.80). None of the cranial non-metric components are as easy to interpret.

The first step in testing the selective interpretation is to compare the rate of reduction observed on the coast with that found in the Valley of Oaxaca, which probably was

Table 8 Odontometric principal component loadings. Most heavily weighted component for each trait is in boldface.

Measurement		PC1	PC2	PC3	PC4
I^1	L	−0.50	**0.83**	0.18	−0.14
	B	−0.61	0.05	**0.71**	0.31
I^2	L	**0.92**	0.14	0.35	−0.05
	B	**0.81**	0.51	−0.15	0.22
C^1	L	**−0.61**	0.61	−0.46	0.16
	B	**0.82**	0.35	0.36	0.24
P^3	L	**0.83**	−0.35	−0.40	0.04
	B	**0.94**	−0.24	−0.21	0.00
P^4	L	0.24	−0.37	0.37	**−0.81**
	B	0.50	−0.48	**−0.67**	−0.22
M^1	L	0.33	**0.91**	0.10	−0.20
	B	0.21	**0.95**	−0.17	0.15
M^2	L	**0.83**	0.07	−0.52	0.10
	B	**0.95**	0.00	0.30	0.04
M^3	L	**−0.92**	−0.30	0.01	0.24
	B	−0.61	−0.29	**0.72**	0.09
I_1	L	**−0.81**	0.05	−0.44	−0.35
	B	**−0.97**	−0.18	0.07	−0.11
I_2	L	**−0.94**	0.30	0.06	−0.12
	B	**−0.98**	0.03	0.05	0.15
C_1	L	−0.09	**0.89**	−0.43	0.07
	B	**0.87**	0.42	−0.23	0.06
P_3	L	**0.87**	−0.29	0.36	−0.11
	B	−0.58	**−0.78**	−0.12	0.15
P_4	L	**0.97**	−0.12	0.17	0.02
	B	0.47	−0.45	0.32	**0.68**
M_1	L	**−0.85**	0.08	0.24	−0.45
	B	−0.32	**0.93**	0.02	−0.16
M_2	L	**0.91**	−0.34	−0.09	−0.20
	B	**−0.81**	0.19	−0.22	0.50
M_3	L	−0.46	**−0.78**	−0.38	0.12
	B	**−0.64**	−0.50	−0.57	−0.02
Eigenvalue		17.59	7.91	4.14	2.36
% variance		54.96	24.72	12.95	7.37

produced by natural selection (Christensen 1998b). For these purposes, the evolutionary rate was calculated in darwins, or proportional units of change per million years (Haldane 1949). These calculations assume that the lower Río Verde population derived from the Early Formative population of the Central Valleys. If there was any significant gene flow from the Mixteca, the actual rate of reduction would be even greater, given the larger teeth of the Alta sample. Similarly, any genetic contribution from a substrate coastal population which had already adapted to the local environment might reduce tooth size without the need for evolutionary change – although such a substrate, if pre-agricultural, might have had larger teeth than highland farmers did.

The evolutionary rates of individual measurements (Table 9) show how much more

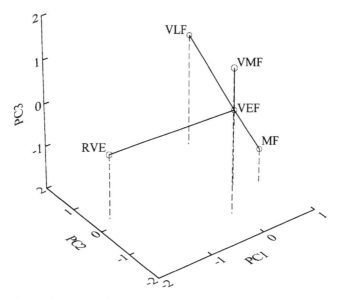

Figure 6   Ordination of first three odontometric principal components. Percent variance explained: PC1 54.96, PC2 24.72, PC3 12.95.

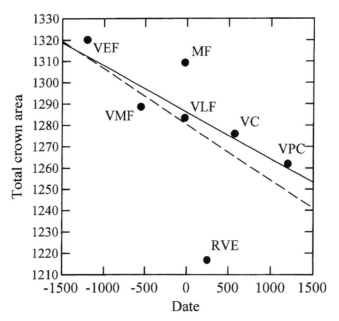

Figure 7   Summed tooth size (in mm^2) against time. Solid line is the regression of only the Valley of Oaxaca samples (y = 1286.00 - 0.022x, r^2 = 0.907, p = 0.012), dashed line is the regression of all seven samples (y = 1280.276 - 0.026x, r^2 = 0.354, p = 0.159).

pronounced the coastal diminution is than that found in the Valley of Oaxaca, where the average rate of reduction over the entire time span was 8.95d. The only increases are in I_1L and I_1A. The former measurement also increased steadily in the Valley of Oaxaca between the Early Formative and the Postclassic (Christensen 1998b: table 12). Given that

Table 9 Odontometric evolutionary rates (in darwins). Areal values are divided by two for comparability with linear values (Brace et al. 1987).

		Maxilla	Mandible
I1	L	−8.41	25.31
	B	−23.18	−14.87
	A	−14.74	4.13
I2	L	−51.80	−6.92
	B	−51.19	−11.78
	A	−53.80	−11.17
C	L	−23.73	−23.93
	B	−41.96	−37.90
	A	−33.01	−28.60
P3	L	−44.42	−45.43
	B	−49.39	−24.51
	A	−44.65	−32.07
P4	L	−20.95	−60.33
	B	−31.17	−50.82
	A	−26.59	−54.41
M1	L	−27.56	−11.54
	B	−28.84	−18.37
	A	−29.11	−14.97
M2	L	−41.57	−41.71
	B	−46.35	−23.03
	A	−45.89	−30.74
M3	L	−2.65	−23.04
	B	−21.05	−17.97
	A	−11.93	−20.52

even imperceptible amounts of dental wear can reduce the observable length of any incisor, it is possible that what this increase really reflects is not a genetic change, but rather a reduction in dental attrition. Measurements of other teeth, whose maximum diameters are located below the occlusal plane, are not as sensitive to wear. The remainder of the rates are far higher than those observed in the Valley, with a maximum reduction of 60.3d for P_4L. The summary measurements which reduced the least were anterior mandibular length (4.0d) and area (15.0d). Every other summary value reduced by more than 20 darwins. By comparison, half of the summary evolutionary rates observed between the Early Formative and Postclassic in the Valley of Oaxaca are less than 10d, and the other half fall between 10d and 17.2d. The only transition in the Valley over which comparable rates were observed was that between the Early and Middle Formative, but even those were slightly lower than those found on the coast.

The primary advantage of using darwins to measure diachronic change is that rates can be compared to those reported from other animal species. Gingerich (1983) and Kurtén (1959) have divided rates into several discrete categories. All of the Río Verde evolutionary rates fit well within Gingerich's Domain II, Colonization. While many do fit within Domain III, Post- Pleistocene Mammalia (equivalent to Kurtén's 'tachytelic' rate A), they tend towards the high end of that range (32d). Domain II rates have been reported in cases where a species expanded into a previously unoccupied area, probably due both to rapid adaptation to new circumstances and to exponential population expansion from a small founding group. The high rates found in the Valley of Oaxaca between the Early and Middle Formative can be explained similarly, as they reflect the rapid adaptation and growth of Archaic populations with the adoption of sedentism and an increased dependence upon agriculture. The degree of change found on the coast is comparable in magnitude to this transition, but spread over an even longer time. This suggests two possibilities. The slower evolutionary rates found after the Middle Formative in the Valley may reflect a natural lessening of selective pressure as teeth reduced, while the constant or increasing rates in the Verde reflect an environmental change that increased the selective pressure. It is also possible that the rates found on the coast are a continuation of the initial rates from the highlands under the same pressure, while the lower rates in the highlands reflect some cultural or technological change that occurred in the Middle or Late Formative in the highlands but not prior to the Classic on the coast. Given the obvious environmental difference between the highlands and lowlands, and the clear difference in tooth size between the coastal samples and all those from the highlands, it seems more logical to investigate the first hypothesis.

How easy is it to explain such high rates of evolution by either random genetic drift or natural selection? Lande (1976) provides equations to determine, for a given phenetic change and time span, both the minimum effective population to rule out random genetic drift as a cause (N_E^*) and the selective mortality necessary for natural selection to have caused the change. Use of these equations in subsequent studies of human dental evolution (Sciulli and Mahaney 1991; Christensen 1998b) has confirmed the value of natural selection as an explanation of the observed change. Assuming a heritability value (h^2) of 0.5 for tooth dimensions, most of the rates of change observable on the Verde have only a minuscule chance of being due to random genetic drift: a bottleneck in effective breeding population down to a handful of people would be required to offer even a 5 per cent chance of such an occurrence. Natural selection, on the other hand, would only require five extra deaths per thousand to cause this change. Given the extent of dental pathology observed (but not yet quantified) in many of these specimens, this mortality does not seem unreasonable. A change in selective pressures on the dentition is most likely to be caused by a dietary shift. The evidence for prehistoric Oaxacan subsistence is not yet fine-grained enough to identify such a change, but it does appear that coastal populations were consuming more fish than their highland cousins (Joyce 1991a). A more likely selective force than seafood would be added consumption of maize, which is quite cariogenic. Paleodietary studies of the Monte Albán skeletal series indicate that consumption of maize, as opposed to other, wild plants, increased over time (Blitz 1995). It is possible that the rich agricultural setting of the Verde encouraged a greater dependence on maize throughout the archaeological sequence. As a corollary to this, it is possible that the larger teeth of the Mixtec sample indicate either the later adoption of agriculture or a lesser dependence upon maize, and it is certainly noteworthy that the relative tooth-size of the three regions mirrors their agricultural productivity, with the richest area (the Río Verde) having the smallest teeth and the poorest (the Mixteca) the largest. The one Oaxacan skeletal sample available from an area higher than and agriculturally inferior to the

Mixteca Alta, the Chinantec site of Cerro Guacamaya, has still larger teeth, despite its Postclassic date (Christensen 1997b, 1998a). Testing of this hypothesized relationship between tooth-size and environment, however, must await future studies of both dental pathology and paleodiet throughout Oaxaca.

Discussion

To understand the biological affinities revealed by skeletal remains, one needs to understand the social structures that pattern genetic change. These include the rate of population growth or decrease, the degree of endogamy and exogamy and the size of the resulting breeding populations, and the extent of gene flow between these populations. For any ancient society, many of these parameters can only be studied indirectly, with a healthy dose of ethnographic analogy.

The origins of the various Mesoamerican language families can be placed in the Archaic period (8000–2000 BC), when Mesoamerica was ranged by many small bands of hunters and collectors who were beginning to experiment with agriculture. Population densities were low enough to require obtaining a mate from outside the immediate social group, maintaining a network of biological and cultural ties. The best archaeological evidence for this period comes from the Valleys of Tehuacan and Oaxaca, which appear to have been linked into such a network, with limited differentiation in material culture (Flannery 1983, 1986). Each language family is presumably descended from a single language community which spanned the several bands needed to constitute a breeding population; the bearers of the Tehuacan Archaic Tradition may have been speakers of proto-Otomanguean (Winter et al. 1984).

With the domestication of maize and consequent sedentism population levels began to increase in the third millennium BC. Linguistic and biological fragmentation probably increased simultaneously. The Yanomama of Brazil and Venezuela provide perhaps the best modern, well-studied parallel to this transitional, semi-agricultural stage (Neel 1978a). Among the Yanomama, there is a high level of genetic variation between villages that are linguistically and historically linked, and an even higher degree of variation between those speaking different languages. Intervillage genetic variation accounts for approximately 80 per cent of that between linguistically-differentiated tribes. Villages are small, and regularly split to form two new communities; those which are unsuccessful due to warfare, disease, or any other reason may well be reabsorbed by a parent or cousin community. There is a high differential fertility rate: it is estimated that over half of all males (47/86) leave no grandchildren, while the other half may leave as many as 33 each (Neel 1978b). The factors of founder effect, genetic drift, and natural selection thus alter gene frequencies far more rapidly than they might in a more densely settled and stable environment. These effects can be hypothesized to have caused a similar level of genetic variation within Mesoamerica during the Early and Middle Formative. In particular, the high rates of evolutionary change observed in the lower Río Verde may reflect a colonization similar to those observed among the Yanomama and Makiritari, where strongly differential reproduction and kin-structured community fission and migration cause rapid natural selection and divergence of related populations. The reduction in evolutionary rates observed in the Valley of Oaxaca after the Middle Formative (Christensen 1998b) may be due to increases in total population and in community exogamy as the Central Valleys were integrated into a single state, as both of these processes would reduce selection and drift.

The data also indicate that there is no clear link between language and biology in Formative Mesoamerica. If such a correlation were the dominant structure behind the phenetic data, one would expect all of the Valley samples to cluster together, with the lower Río Verde an outlier, the Mixtec Formative still more distant, and the Basin of Mexico on the far periphery. The cluster of the Late Formative Valley and Mixteca materials with the Basin samples suggests some degree of gene flow, but the cultures of the Formative Basin of Mexico are quite distinct from those of Oaxaca, and there is no evidence that either Mixtecan or Zapotecan languages were ever spoken in the Basin. This tight grouping may also reflect sample composition: when two single-site samples are substituted for the Basin series, they appear more divergent. Preliminary results of a similar division of the Mixtec data exhibit the same pattern (Christensen 1998a). This indicates that the situation may be similar to the Yanomama case, with variability within each local, ethnolinguistically connected region outweighing that between lumped regional groupings. Unfortunately, no earlier series from the Mixteca Alta is available to examine the affinities of the earliest agricultural populations in the area. These data are therefore insufficient to test the phylogenetic model of Oaxacan cultural development (Marcus 1983a), by which the Mixtecan and Zapotecan traditions developed in distinct paths from a common Archaic origin, with a limited degree of contact and, presumably, gene flow.

While the available data fit the proposed model of Zapotecan expansion in the Middle Formative, they are insufficient to confirm it. For such a proof, more skeletal series from the intervening area are necessary. This example does, however, provide a case study of colonization and subsequent adaptation that can inform on-going archaeological research in both the Río Verde and elsewhere in the state.

Acknowledgments

This paper grew out of a dissertation in the Department of Anthropology at Vanderbilt University, and I thank the members of my committee, John Monaghan, Alice Harris, Brian Hemphill, Arthur Joyce, and Javier Urcid, for their advice on that larger work. In addition, Chris Beekman, Steve Houston, Arthur Joyce, and two anonymous reviewers provided useful suggestions on this paper itself.

Department of History and Anthropology
Augusta State University
Augusta, GA 30904
USA

References

Balkansky, A. K. 1997. Archaeological settlement patterns of the Sola Valley, Oaxaca, Mexico. *Mexicon*, 19: 12–18.

Barlow, R. H. 1943. A western extension of Zapotec. *Tlalocan*, 1: 267–8.

Barlow, R. H. 1944. A western extension of Zapotec: further remarks. *Tlalocan*, 1: 359–61.

Bartholomew, D. 1980. Otomanguean influence on Pochutla Aztec. *International Journal of American Linguistics*, 46: 106–16.

Berry, A. C. and Berry, R. J. 1967. Epigenetic variation in the human cranium. *Journal of Anatomy*, 101: 361–79.

Blitz, J. A. 1995. Dietary variability and social inequality at Monte Albán, Oaxaca, Mexico. Doctoral dissertation. Department of Anthropology, University of Wisconsin, Madison.

Brace, C. L. 1980. Australian tooth-size clines and the death of a stereotype. *Current Anthropology*, 21: 141–64.

Brace, C. L., Rosenberg, K. R. and Hunt, K. D. 1987. Gradual change in human tooth size in the late Pleistocene and post Pleistocene. *Evolution*, 41: 705–20.

Campbell, L., Kaufman, T. and Smith-Stark, T. C. 1986. Meso-America as a linguistic area. *Language*, 62: 530–70.

Case, H. W. 1976. Odontometrics and taxonomy of prehistoric inhabitants of the Marismas Nacionales, Sinaloa and Nayarit, Mexico. Master's thesis. Department of Anthropology, University of Wyming, Laramie.

Cavalli-Sforza, L. L. 1997. Genetic and cultural diversity in Europe. *Journal of Anthropological Research*, 53: 383–404.

Cavalli-Sforza, L. L., Piazza, A. and Menozzi, P. 1994. *The History and Geography of Human Genes*. Princeton, NJ: Princeton University Press.

Christensen, A. F. 1997a. Cranial non-metric variation in North and Central Mexico. *Anthropologischer Anzeiger*, 55: 15–32.

Christensen, A. F. 1997b. La microevolución odontométrica en Oazaxa. Paper presented at the 9th Coloquio Internacional Antropología Física 'Juan Comas', Queretaro, Mexico, and submitted to *Estudios de Antropología Biológica* 9.

Christensen, A.F. 1998a. Biological affinity in Prehispanic Oaxaca. Doctoral dissertation. Department of Anthropology, Vanderbilt University.

Christensen, A. F. 1998b. Odontometric microevolution in the Valley of Oaxaca, Mexico. *Journal of Human Evolution*, 34: 333–60.

Constandse-Westermann, T.S. 1972. *Coefficients of Biological Distance: An Introduction to the Various Methods of Assessment of Biological Distance between Populations, with Special Reference to Human Biological Problems*. Oosterhout N.B.: Anthropological Publications.

Darroch, J, N. and Mosimann, J. E. 1985. Canonical and principal components of shape. *Biometrika*, 72: 241–52.

Egland, S., Bartholomew, D. and Cruz R., S. 1978. *La intelegibilidad interdialectal en México: Resultados de algunos sondeos*. Mexico, DF: Summer Institute of Linguistics.

Feinman, G. M. and Nicholas, L. M. 1990. At the margins of the Monte Albán state: settlement patterns in the Ejutla Valley, Oaxaca. *Latin American Antiquity*, 1: 216–46.

Flannery, K. V. 1983. Settlement, subsistence, and social organization of the Proto-Otomangueans. In *The Cloud People: Divergent Evolution of the Zapotec and Mixtec Civilizations* (eds K. V. Flannery and J. Marcus). New York: Academic Press, pp. 32–6.

Flannery, K. V., Ed. 1986. *Guilá Naquitz*. New York: Academic Press.

Gingerich, P. D. 1983. Rates of evolution: effects of time and temporal scaling. *Science*, 222: 159–61.

Haldane, J. B. S. 1949. Suggestions as to quantitative measurements of rates of evolution. *Evolution*, 3: 51–6.

Hemphill, B. E., Lukacs, J. R. and Kennedy, K. A. R. 1991. Biological adaptations and affinities of Bronze Age Harappans. In *Harappa Excavations 1986–1990: A Multidisciplinary Approach to Third Millennium Urbanism* (ed. R. Meadows). Madison, WI: Prehistory Press, pp. 137–82.

Hopkins, N. A. 1984. Otomanguean linguistic prehistory. In *Essays in Otomanguean Culture History* (eds J. K. Josserand, M. Winter and N. Hopkins). Nashville, TN: Vanderbilt University Publications in Anthropology 31, pp. 25–64.

Jacobs, K. 1994. Human dento-gnathic metric variation in Mesolithic/Neolithic Ukraine: possible evidence of demic diffusion in the Dnieper rapids region. *American Journal of Physical Anthropology*, 95: 335–56.

Josserand, J. K., Jansen, M. E. R. G. N. and Romero, M. de los Á. 1984a. Mixtec dialectology: inferences from linguistics and ethnohistory. In *Essays in Otomanguean Culture History* (eds J. K. Josserand, M. Winter and N. Hopkins). Nashville, TN: Vanderbilt University Publications in Anthropology 31, pp. 141–63.

Josserand, J. K., Winter, M. and Hopkins, N. A. 1984b. Introduction. In *Essays in Otomanguean Culture History* (eds J. K. Josserand, M. Winter and N. Hopkins). Nashville, TN: Vanderbilt University Publications in Anthropology 31, pp. 1–24.

Joyce, A. A. 1991a. Formative period social change in the lower Río Verde Valley, Oaxaca, Mexico. *Latin American Antiquity*, 2: 126–50.

Joyce, A. A. 1991b. Formative period occupation in the lower Río Verde Valley, Oaxaca, Mexico: interregional interaction and social change. Doctoral dissertation. Department of Anthropology, Rutgers University.

Joyce, A. A, 1993. Interregional interaction and social development on the Oaxaca coast. *Ancient Mesoamerica*, 4: 67–84.

Joyce, A. A. and Mueller, R. G. 1997. Prehispanic human ecology of the Río Verde drainage basin, Oaxaca. *World Archaeology*, 29: 75–94

Jungers, W. L., Falsetti, A. B. and Wall, C. E. 1995. Shape, relative size, and size-adjustments in morphometrics. *Yearbook of Physical Anthropology*, 38: 137–61.

Kowalewski, S. A., Feinman, G. M., Finsten, L., Blanton, R. E. and Nicholas, L. M. 1989. *Monte Albán's Hinterland, Part II: Prehispanic Settlement Patterns in Tlacolula, Etla, and Ocotlán, the Valley of Oaxaca, Mexico*. Ann Arbor: Memoirs of the Museum of Anthropology 23, University of Michigan.

Kurtén, B. 1959. Rates of evolution in fossil mammals. *Cold Spring Harbor Symposium in Quantitative Biology*, 24: 205–14.

Lande, R. 1976. Natural selection and random genetic drift in phenotypic evolution. *Evolution*, 30: 314–34.

Lind, M. 1991–2. Unos problemas con la cronología de Monte Albán y una nueva serie de nombres para las fases. *Notas Mesoamericanas*, 13: 177–92.

Marcus, J. 1983a. The genetic model and the linguistic divergence of the Otomangueans. In *The Cloud People: Divergent Evolution of the Zapotec and Mixtec Civilizations* (eds K. V. Flannery and J. Marcus). New York: Academic Press, pp. 4–9.

Marcus, J. 1983b. The reconstructed chronology of the later Zapotec rulers, A.D. 1415–1563 . In *The Cloud People: Divergent Evolution of the Zapotec and Mixtec Civilizations* (eds K. V. Flannery and J. Marcus). New York: Academic Press, pp. 301–8.

Markman, C. W. 1981. *Prehispanic Settlement Dynamics in Central Oaxaca, Mexico: A View from the Miahuatlan Valley*. Nashville: Vanderbilt University Publications in Anthropology 26.

Moorrees, C. F. A. 1957. *The Aleut Dentition: A Correlative Study of Dental Characteristics in an Eskimoid People*. Cambridge: Harvard University Press.

Neel, J. V. 1978a. The population structure of an Amerindian tribe, the Yanomama. *Annual Review of Genetics*, 12: 365–413.

Neel, J. V. 1978b. On being headman. *Perspectives in Biology and Medicine*, 23: 277–94.

Nichols, J. 1992. *Linguistic Diversity in Space and Time*. Chicago: The University of Chicago Press.

Rendón, J. J. 1995. *Diversificación de las lenguas zapotecas*. Oaxaca: Instituto Oaxaqueño de las Culturas.

Rogers, A. R. and Harpending, H. C. 1983. Population structure and quantitative characters. *Genetics*, 105: 985–1002.

Salas C., M. E. 1982. *La Población de México-Tenochtitlan: Estudio de osteología antropológica*. Mexico City: Departamento de Antropología Física, Instituto Nacional de Antropología e Historia.

Sciulli, P. W. and Mahaney, M. C. 1991. Phenotypic evolution in prehistoric Ohio Amerindians: natural selection versus random genetic drift in tooth size reduction. *Human Biology*, 63: 499–511.

Sjøvold, T. 1977. Non-metrical divergence between skeletal populations. *Ossa*, 4: 1–133.

Sofaer, J. A., Smith, P. and Kaye, E. 1986. Affinities between contemporary and skeletal Jewish and non-Jewish populations. *American Journal of Physical Anthropology*, 70: 265–75.

Sokal, R. R. 1991. The continental population structure of Europe. *Annual Review of Anthropology*, 20: 119–40.

Spence, M. 1994. Human skeletal material from Teotihuacan. In *Mortuary Practises and Skeletal Remains at Teotihuacan* (ed. R. Millon). Salt Lake City: University of Utah, pp. 315–427.

Spores, R. 1993. Tututepec: a Postclassic-period Mixtec conquest state. *Ancient Mesoamerica*, 4: 167–74.

Swadesh, M. 1967. Lexicostatistic classification. In *Handbook of Middle American Indians*, Vol. 5, *Linguistics* (ed. N. A. McQuown). Austin: University of Texas Press, pp. 79–115.

Urcid S., J. 1992. Zapotec hieroglyphic writing. Doctoral dissertation. Department of Anthropology, Yale University.

Urcid S., J. 1993. The pacific coast of Oaxaca and Guerrero: the westernmost extent of Zapotec script. *Ancient Mesoamerica*, 4: 141–65.

Winter, M. 1989. *Oaxaca: The Archaeological Record*. Mexico, DF: Minutiae Mexicana.

Winter, M., Gaxiola G., M. and Hernández D., G. 1984. Archeology of the Otomanguean area. In *Essays in Otomanguean Culture History* (eds J. K. Josserand, M. Winter and N. Hopkins). Nashville, TN: Vanderbilt University Publications in Anthropology 31, pp. 65–108.

Zárate M., R. 1995. El Corozal, un sitio arqueológico en la costa del Pacífico de Oaxaca. *Cuadernos del Sur*, 10: 9–36.

Zeitlin, R. N. 1979. Prehistoric long distance exchange on the southern Isthmus of Tehuantepec, Mexico. Doctoral dissertation. Department of Anthropology, Yale University.

Modelling Paleoindian dispersals

James Steele, Jonathan Adams and Tim Sluckin

Abstract

It is reasonable to expect that the global dispersal of modern humans was influenced by habitat variation in space and time; but many simulation models average such variation into a single, homogeneous surface across which the dispersal process is modelled. We present a demographic simulation model in which rates of spatial range expansion can be modified by local habitat values. The broad-scale vegetation cover of North America during the late last glacial is reconstructed and mapped at thousand-year intervals, 13,000–10,000 radiocarbon years BP. Results of the simulation of human dispersal into North America during the late last glacial are presented; output appears to match observed variation in occupancy of habitats during this period (as assessed from discard rates of diagnostic artefacts), if we assume that intrinsic population growth rates were fairly high and that local population densities varied as a function of environmental carrying capacity. Finally, a number of issues are raised relating to present limitations and possible future extensions of the simulation model.

Keywords

Demographic modelling; paleoecology; human dispersals; Fisher-Skellam; Paleoindian; Clovis; fluted point.

Introduction

Expansion of the hominid geographical range into high latitudes came late. It may only be within the last 20,000 years that humans colonized the tundra to the northeast of the Verkhoyansk Range in eastern Siberia (Hoffecker et al. 1993). But once this had occurred, there was little other impediment than glacial ice to the spread of humans into eastern Beringia, and thence southward into the rest of the Americas. What is surprising is the apparent rapidity of this subsequent southward expansion. A number of terminal Pleistocene sites in southern South America appear to be contemporary with, or to predate, the best-dated North American Clovis sites (e.g. Steele, Gamble and Sluckin in press). Demographically, such a rapid spread implies a high intrinsic reproductive rate – and this has been seen by some as inconsistent with observed demographics of extant hunter-gatherer populations (Whitley and Dorn 1993). This puzzling situation has led some workers to suggest that humans were already present in South America before the last glacial maximum – despite the lack of clear traces of such a long-lasting population. Thus we are faced with two startlingly different scenarios. In the prevailing scenario, there were one or more late glacial dispersals, characterized by high rates of dispersal and rapid population growth rates. This scenario implies an archaeological signature of a sudden appearance of a cultural record and a rapid increase in artefact densities across the whole colonized surface of the Americas, with a compressed time range for the dates of earliest occupation at different locations on that surface. Alternatively there is another, less widely-favoured scenario which states that there were one or more much earlier (pre-last glacial maximum) colonization events characterized by low rates of dispersal and population growth. This scenario implies gradual increase in the visibility of a cultural record, and a clearer gradient in dates of earliest occupation at progressively greater distances from the origin of the dispersal.

Overall, the archaeological data appear to support some version of the first scenario over its competitor (for judicious reviews of the evidence and arguments, see Meltzer 1993, 1995). In either scenario, taphonomic and sampling effects make it hard to identify the earliest occupation remains. None the less, in all of the Americas no candidate for a site with occupation predating the last glacial maximum (LGM) has yet been verified to conventional standards of proof. The earliest sites with securely-dated Paleoindian associations appear quite abruptly during approximately the 12,500–11,000 BP period, with little clear contrast between the dates of the more southerly sites and those nearer the origin of the dispersals in the north. It may well be that earliest occupation will prove to predate this efflorescence, while still being post-LGM. Following the dates of earliest occupation in most regions surveyed, there is generally a rapid increase in recorded artefact densities. However, there are also conflicting data. In North America, the greatest densities of Early and Middle Paleoindian fluted points appear to be in the south and east, although dispersal is assumed to have originated in the northwest (Faught et al. 1994). In South America, the earliest securely-dated sites are somewhat earlier than the best-dated North American Clovis sites, implying not just gaps in the North American radiocarbon record, but also an initial phase of long-distance exploratory dispersal by some proportion of the colonizing populations. On the face of it, neither of these observations seem consistent with existing 'wave of advance' models of rapid late glacial Paleoindian dispersals. In this paper we propose that the answer lies not in rejecting the prevailing scenario of a late glacial Beringian colonization of the Americas, but in making refinements to existing demographic expansion models to make them more realistic.

Spatial range expansion: the standard model

For our own first phase of simulation work, we have been using a discrete approximation of R.A. Fisher's classic equation for the 'wave of advance' of advantageous genes (Fisher 1937), which has already been generalized to the case of animal range expansion and is widely used for this purpose in biogeography (Williamson 1996; Shigesada and Kawasaki 1997; cf. Young and Bettinger 1995).

The Fisher equation describes the rate of growth of a population at a given location as a function of the intrinsic growth rate, the environmental carrying capacity, and the mean individual dispersal rate, and is:

$$\frac{dn}{dt} = f(n;K) + D\nabla^2 n \tag{1}$$

where $n(\mathbf{r},t)$ denotes the local human population density (number per unit area) at time t and position $\mathbf{r} = (x,y)$. The diffusion constant D (in km^2 yr^{-1}) and the carrying capacity K are functions of position. The function $f(n) = \alpha n(1-\frac{n}{k})$ describes the rate of density-dependent population increase, and is the logistic function widely used in theoretical ecology (Murray 1990); the quantity α denotes the intrinsic maximum population growth rate.

At this point, some mathematical details may be useful for specialists. In order to work with discrete time (in iterated steps) and discrete space (in a lattice of cells), we approximate time differentials at particular sites by finite differences (Press et al. 1986):

$$\frac{dn(\mathbf{r},t)}{dt} \approx \frac{n(\mathbf{r},t + \Delta_t) - n(\mathbf{r},t)}{\Delta t} \tag{2}$$

Typically we use $\Delta t = 1$ year.

Space differentials are similarly approximated by finite differences:

$$D\nabla^2(\mathbf{r}_0) = h^{-2} \sum_\alpha w_\alpha D'_\alpha [n(\mathbf{r}_\alpha) - n(\mathbf{r})], \tag{3}$$

where for a given position $\mathbf{r}_0$ the sum is taken over nearest neighbour sites $\mathbf{r}_\alpha$ on the lattice, and where the lattice size is h. There are two types of neighbour sites: those along the lattice axes and those along the diagonals. The sum is weighted appropriately with parameters w_α; this parameter is typically $\frac{2}{3}$ for sites α along the lattice axes and $\frac{1}{6}$ along the diagonals. The effective diffusion parameter D'_α, appropriate to motion between the sites $\mathbf{r}_0$ and $\mathbf{r}_\alpha$, is given by $D'_\alpha = \sqrt{D(\mathbf{r}_\alpha)D(\mathbf{r}_0)}$. In practice in any given simulation, only two values of D are used: $D = D_0$ and $D = 0$, the latter representing the fact that the particular cell is inaccessible.

The crucial input parameters for the model are then the carrying capacity K, the so-called Malthusian parameter α and the diffusion constant D. D represents the degree of mobility of an individual (e.g. Ammerman and Cavalli-Sforza 1984). In general individuals will move from their birth place a distance λ during their generation time τ. The square of this distance will in general be proportional to the time available; the constant of proportionality is the diffusion constant D:

$$D = \frac{\lambda^2}{4\tau} \tag{4}$$

It is an assumption of the standard model that individual dispersal is equally likely in all directions.

The differential equation (1) in the case of constant D and K, and for populations which can only move in one rather than two, dimensions, predicts that there will be a population wave of advance, with the frontier traveling with velocity (v) :

$$v = 2\sqrt{D\alpha} \tag{5}$$

A more detailed account of our methodology is given elsewhere (Steele et al. 1995).

We obtain estimates of realistic values of α, K and D from the ethnographic and archaeological literatures. α we take conservatively to be in the range 0.003–0.03/yr, since ethnographic evidence suggests that human populations can expand at rates of up to 4 per cent per year when colonizing new habitat (Birdsell 1957). We note, contra Hassan (1981), that this is consistent with the much lower observed rates of increase in contemporary hunter-gatherer populations which are close to carrying capacity – the density-dependent logistic growth function implies that a population at 95 per cent of its carrying capacity K will be growing at a rate of 0.05α (or 0.15 per cent per year, assuming α = 0.03). K, in turn, we estimate for different habitats from observed hunter-gatherer population densities, on the assumption that ethnographic populations are usually observed at or close to their equilibrium limit. D we estimate from archaeological evidence for raw material transport distances, which we take to be indicators of mean individual lifetime mobility during the colonization phase. We return to the question of realistic values for D in a later section.

Paleovegetation reconstruction

Because observed hunter-gatherer densities vary greatly according to habitat, it is neces-sary to take account of paleohabitat distribution in order to simulate accurately popu-lation densities at different locations on the surface of the Americas during the Paleoindian dispersal phase. Many different sources of evidence can be used to contribute towards reconstructing past broadscale vegetation cover. The most direct and useful evidence comes from the fossil remains of plant types characteristic of each vegetation zone, indicating for example prairie or temperate forest. Unfortunately, plant fossils are normally only preserved in lakes, swamps and river deposits, and if the climate in an area was dry then such preservation sites would have been an infrequent component in the landscape. Often, a shortage of plant fossil data means that the vegetation cover can only be reconstructed indirectly using other indicators to 'fill in' the large spatial gaps between sites. Even at those sites where plant fossil evidence has been obtained, natural transport processes or decay could have selectively concentrated certain plant remains to give a misleading impression of what the local vegetation was actually like. Thus it is always desirable to cross check the picture from plant fossil evidence against other indicators of past vegetation coverage.

These additional sources of data include sedimentological indicators such as particular buried soil types or buried sand dunes, which can indicate the general nature of the vege-tation cover which once existed there. Animal fossils can also suggest the existence of a vegetation habitat that suited them; for example, the presence of the extinct American horses (which closely resembled Eurasian species) may be taken to indicate that open grassy vegetation was an important part of the landscape in the past.

In the present study, all these various sources of evidence have been combined to produce an overall picture. Because many palaeovegetation sites are ambiguously dated (due to problems, for example, of 'age plateaus' in the radiocarbon record), it is only poss-ible to put forward fairly tentative time scenarios for the time course of vegetation change. The general timing of broadscale environmental changes shown in the maps is based on extrapolation from particular well-dated sites, assuming that climates at other less

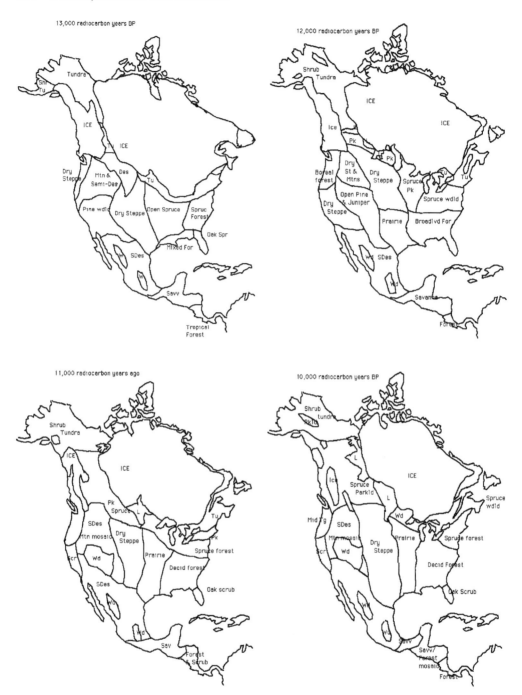

Figures 1–4   Paleovegetation maps of North America at 13,000 BP, 12,000 BP, 11,000 BP and 10,000 BP (¹⁴C years). *Key*: Tu = grassy tundra; Des = extreme desert; Sdes = semi-desert; ShrTu = shrub tundra; Pk = parkland; L = lake; Wd = woodland; Scr = scrub.

well-dated sites changed roughly in synchrony with these. Even the background of events at the best-dated sites is to some extent ambiguous because the radiocarbon chronology that most of them are based on is often subject to uncertainties of thousands of years.

In general, the greatest uncertainty exists for the older timeframes. For the more recent timeslices, especially after about 11,000 years ago, the large number of dated pollen sites makes vegetation reconstruction much easier. For North America, the task has been greatly aided by graphical display packages such as ShowTime, which illustrates the percentage of each pollen type at sites across North America for progressive time intervals. The maps reproduced here are part of a larger series in preparation depicting the evolution of vegetation cover of the Americas since the last glacial maximum (Adams 1998).

Due to restrictions on space, neither a full range of literature sources nor a full list of sites is given here. Only some general comments are given, together with a few key papers and the names of some of the most important sites. A broader range of relevant literature sources can be obtained by accessing the QEN atlas site of the World Wide Web.

Figure 1. 13,000 radiocarbon years ago. In the aftermath of the last glacial maximum, indicators of a significant warming and moistening of climate begin to appear by around 14,000 BP, but only in some areas. In Alaska, a widespread change from herb-dominated to moist shrub-dominated tundra had occurred at around 14,000 BP, suggesting moister and slightly warmer conditions (Anderson and Brubaker 1993). A similar trend towards moister and warmer conditions is seen in the changing tundra flora and insect fauna on the eastern part of the Beringian land bridge (Elias et al. 1996). Elsewhere in North America, conditions seem to have remained dry and cold. In the High Plains of the Midwest, desert conditions remained widespread, with continuing dune activity and the absence of mammal fossils from this time (Wells 1992). Further west, across Washington State, pollen diagrams suggest that dry and very cold conditions dominated the Cordilleran region, with a sparse parkland existing on the coastal plain and polar desert inland and at higher altitudes (Thompson et al. 1993). In the central Mexican uplands, an increase in woodlands and a reduction in grasslands after 15,000 ^{14}C y.a. suggests a switch to more humid – but still cooler – conditions than had occurred previously (Lozano-Garcia et al. 1993). Cooler conditions may have lasted up until about 9,000 y.a. (Lozano-Garcia et al. 1993).

However, continuing glacial retreat was exposing new surfaces in North America. At around this time, according to the mapping chronology of Dyke and Prest (1987a, b), a continuous ice-free corridor opened for the first time between Alaska and the contiguous USA. However, for a considerable part of its length (about 750km) it would have been less than 50km wide, and further obstructed in several places by large meltwater lakes. The chronology of the first appearance of the ice free corridor is not completely settled however; Bobrowsky and Rutter (1992) conclude that although the southern and northern ends were open by this time, it is quite possible that the central region was still closed.

Conditions at the southern end of the ice-free corridor (e.g. in the area around 50°–52° N and 110°–115° W, reviewed in detail by Beaudoin et al. 1996) still seem to have been very arid. Burns et al. (1993) note the absence of radiocarbon dates on faunal remains between about 21,300 and 11,600 ^{14}C y.a. in the Edmonton area, suggesting that the landscape was incapable of supporting fauna during this interval.

Figure 2. 12,000 radiocarbon years ago. By around 12,000 radiocarbon years ago, boreal forest had spread through the western lowlands of Washington State (northwest USA), indicating the continued effects of warming and moistening of climate as the ice sheets retreated (Thompson et al. 1993; and ShowTime database). On the eastern part of the Beringian land bridge, insect communities suggest that present-day temperatures had been reached (Elias et al. 1996).

The ice-free corridor through Canada had by this time widened considerably, though it remained wholly or partly obstructed by large meltwater lakes (Dyke and Prest 1987a, b). To the north, birch shrub-tundra had suddenly became widespread throughout deglaciated areas of Alaska and northwest Canada.

The desert area which had occupied much of the the High Plains of the Midwestern USA began to show signs of moister conditions, with dune stabilization and the spread of shortgrass prairie vegetation and its associated grazing mammals (Wells 1992). At the southern and western fringes of the High Plains, pine and spruce woodland seems to have begun to spread in at around this time (Wells 1992).

Temperate tree species began to spread and increase in abundance through the forests and open woodlands of the eastern USA, although the vegetation remained dominated by boreal conifers (Overpeck et al. 1992; ShowTime database). A map of vegetation distribution for 12,000 y.a. has been assembled by Overpeck et al. (1992) for the eastern USA, using pollen data.

Through much of the southern and central Cordilleran area of the USA, conditions may have been slightly moister than at present (although generally semi-arid), with greater woodland and scrub cover than at present. The same appears to have been the case for the lowland American and Mexican deserts to the south (Thompson et al. 1993; Benson et al. 1997).

Figure 3. 11,000 Radiocarbon years ago. The picture of climate and vegetation change at around 11,000 radiocarbon years ago is complicated by the fact that in many areas there was a cold and arid event that correlates with the 'Younger Dryas' cold event in Europe. Changes in pollen spectra from the eastern seaboard, the midwest and the northwest Pacific coast suggest colder, drier conditions, with a mean annual temperature decline of about 3°–4° C across these areas (Anderson 1997). A relatively dry phase in the Great Basin (comparable in aridity with the present-day) – following on from the previous initial moist phase – also corresponds in age to the Younger Dryas (Benson et al. 1997).

However in most regions of North America the Younger Dryas interval was apparently a time of continuing colonization by interglacial-type vegetation, quite unlike the major setback that it represented for European and Eurasian forests. In fact, insect assemblages from the Beringian land bridge suggest that summer temperatures were several degrees warmer than today's around 11,000 [14]C y.a. (Elias et al. 1996), though this might hypothetically have been just before a cooling event.

Rising sea levels seem to have finally cut off the land bridge of Beringia at around this time (rather later than was previously thought), according to recent studies by Elias et al. (1996).

The retreating North American ice sheets had by now exposed an ice-free corridor that was some 500km or more wide along much of its length (Dyke and Prest 1987). Animal remains start to appear at the southern end of the corridor about this time. Tree species began to colonize deglaciated parts of Canada, with conifer parkland appearing in the Rocky Mountains at about 11,000 years ago (Thompson et al. 1993). A number of pollen sites have been obtained from this general area, and the summarized 'ShowTime' pollen abundances appear to suggest that spruce (*Picea*) parkland was also widespread at the southern end of the ice-free corridor. However, this picture may be based on poor radio-carbon dates. In a review of the environmental history of the southern end of the corri-dor, Beaudoin et al. (1996) suggest that most of the vegetation was in fact non-arboreal, with birch shrubs. They note that earlier studies suggested spruce woodland already important in the landscape by this time, but that this is now in doubt because the radio-carbon-dated materials were contaminated by coal and carbonates.

Shrub tundra, and not parkland, also seems to have remained the main vegetation type across most of Alaska and in the northern part of the deglaciated corridor.

In southeastern Alaska, a short-term climate cooling that coincides with the Younger Dryas age occurred between about 10,600 and 9,900 ^{14}C years ago and was marked by expansion of tundra elements and deposition of inorganic sediments (Hansen and Engstrom 1996). To the south of the southern entrance to the ice-free corridor, both dune and zoological evidence suggest a temporary return of desert conditions to the High Plains of the American Midwest (Wells 1992), although the timing and relative severity of this event remains highly uncertain. The parkland and conifer woodland that had covered the eastern prairie zone during the full glacial period had by now mainly disappeared, being replaced by treeless grassland, although from the high conifer pollen percentages it seems that a band of conifer parkland may still have existed across the northern part of the prairie zone (ShowTime database).

In the eastern USA, deciduous forest species continued to increase in abundance. In the deglaciated areas of the northeast, however, the predominant vegetation remained tundra and spruce parkland (ShowTime database).

Figure 4. 10,000 radiocarbon years ago. The colder, relatively arid phase associated with the Younger Dryas seems to have ended shortly before this time slice (around 10,200 radiocarbon years ago), in those areas which it had affected. In many areas of North America, forest vegetation continued to spread in, although it had not yet attained its Holocene coverage and remained an open parkland or forest-grassland mosaic in many areas, especially in Canada (ShowTime database).

The ice sheets of North America were by this time greatly reduced in size. Large lake systems had formed around the fringes of the Laurentide ice sheet but the retreat of the western Cordilleran ice sheet had left a broad area of lowland which was gradually becom-ing colonized by conifer parkland or open forest (ShowTime database). Beaudoin et al. (1996) suggest that conifer forest was present in the southeastern foothills of the Rocky Mountains in Canada by around this time. Note that the parkland was probably much sparser towards the ice sheet margins, with a treeless zone of several hundred kilometres resulting from lags in tree colonization in the areas exposed by the rapidly-retreating ice sheets. For example, pollen ecological studies by Ritchie in southern Canada suggest a lag of 2000 ^{14}C years at many sites between deglaciation of a site and subsequent colonization by spruce and other boreal trees.

However, in the northeastern USA/southeastern Canada, colonization by trees had progressed up to the stage of giving boreal conifer forest in many areas. Deciduous tree species continued to increase in range and abundance through the eastern USA (Show-Time database).

In the western USA, such as the Owens Lake site in the Great Basin, earliest Holocene conditions may have been moister than present (with open juniper scrub vegetation replacing the more open semi-desert) between about 10,000 and 9,000 ^{14}C y.a., followed by dessication to conditions similar to those of today (Benson et al. 1997).

It is necessary to emphasize again that these vegetation map reconstructions and the accompanying text descriptions must be regarded as a preliminary and incomplete view of the environmental changes which took place in the Americas during deglaciation. More information is continually becoming available, and no doubt significant changes to these maps will be needed when a more complete picture becomes possible. Nevertheless, most of the broad vegetation trends and the general timing of events appear well supported at present.

Results

Our simulation model allows us to use these paleovegetation maps as input data. We can observe the effect of variation in this evolving continental landscape on predicted occupancy rates by Paleoindians during the initial settlement phase.

In our simulations, we have studied the effects of habitat on dispersals by varying K (carrying capacity) across the grid, taking median observed hunter-gatherer population densities in different habitats as the source for our carrying capacity values. Table 1 gives the relevant data from Kelly (1995), and the paleovegetation categories which we have assimilated to Kelly's broader habitat types for this study. We might also expect that in reality, D (the diffusion constant) would be inversely correlated with K across habitat types: relevant ethnographic data is too sparse to enable us to assign habitat-specific values of D in this way, although we will return to this in a later paper (Steele, Adams and Sluckin, in prep.).

We have assumed that the Early and Middle Paleoindian phase lasted 2,000 years, from approximately 12,000 to approximately 10,000 ^{14}C years BP. Figures 5–10 give cumulated population density plots (in person-years) for the first 1,000 years and also for the first 2,000 years after dispersal from the southern end of the ice free corridor, for each location on the surface of North America south of the ice sheets. We located the origin of the simulated dispersal at the southern end of the 'ice-free corridor'; certainly other scenarios such as that of a coastal migration route might be considered, and we shall also return to this in a later paper (Steele, Adams and Sluckin, in prep.). We held D as a global constant in all experiments, with the value $D = 900$ (implying a mean individual mobility of 250–300km between birth and reproduction, a figure consistent with observed raw material transport distances from this period – e.g. Tankersley 1992). Direct empirical data on initial population growth rates is lacking. Powell and Steele (1994) report a mean age of 3.5 years for formation of linear enamel hypoplasias in the teeth of Late Paleoindian skeletons, which may imply late

Table 1 Hunter-gatherer population densities (p.p. 100km^2) in different broad habitat classes (derived from Kelly 1995: 222).

Class	N	Mean	Median	Range	Adams equivalents
Arctic	18	9.7	3.0	0.2–65	tundra, shrub tundra
Subarctic/cold forest	37	4.0	1.4	0.2–23.5	boreal forest, spruce woodland, mid taiga, open pine and juniper, coniferous forest, park, spruce parkland
Temperate deserts	16	7.3	4.7	1–19	semi-desert, semi-desert/montane mosaic
Temperate forests	14	12.4	7.2	1.3–38	deciduous forest, broadleaved forest, scrub, oak scrub
Plains	9	3.2	3	1.4–5.8	dry steppe, dry steppe/montane, prairies
Tropical/subtropical deserts	31	28.5	7.6	0.2–200	savanna, savanna/forest mosaic
Seasonal/wet tropical forests	19	31.7	18.7	3–86	tropical forest, tropical forest and scrub

weaning and thus decreased fertility rates: but these skeletons are Early Holocene in date. Between our simulation runs we varied the value of α, which was treated as a global constant. In some simulations we took K to be uniform for all locations on the colonizable surface, while in others we used the inferred habitat-specific values of K (see above, Table 1), using as our basemaps the paleovegetation reconstructions for the 12, 11 and 10 kyr intervals. In the latter case, we used the 12 kyr map for the first 500 years of the simulation, the 11 kyr map for the next 1,000 years, and the 10 kyr map for the final 500 years.

As our control data, we use the distribution map of fluted point densities for the contiguous United States compiled by Faught, Anderson and Gisiger (1994), based on a database of 10,198 points (Figs 11–12 below; see Anderson (1990: 168; 1995: 148) for comments on problems in its compilation). We make the grossly simplifying assumptions that the variation in artefact densities in this map reflects variation in Paleoindian discard rates and not just variation in recent recovery rates (cf. Anderson 1990: 171), and that the rate of discard was a simple function of the number of person-years lived at any location. For our limited purposes here – comparing mean densities across biomes at the continental scale – such assumptions are more likely to be reasonable than they would be at finer scales, where variation in discard behaviour and in recovery rates will be most significant.

Figures 5–10 are each shaded to best represent variation across the colonized surface in cumulated person-years: we are interested in matching simulated gradients of cumulated occupancy to observed gradients in discard rates. There is enormous variation in the absolute numbers of occupants in the grid at the end of the different simulations (see Table 2); we might compare these figures with estimates of total population size for North America at time of first European contact, which range from one to two million (excluding Mexico and the Caribbean (Crawford 1998)). There is also enormous variation in the

$\alpha = 0.003$, K constant, irrespective of habitat.

$\alpha = 0.01$, K constant, irrespective of habitat.

$\alpha = 0.03$, K constant, irrespective of habitat.

$\alpha = 0.003$, K varies with habitat.

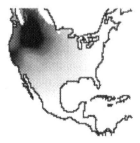 

$\alpha = 0.01$, K varies with habitat.

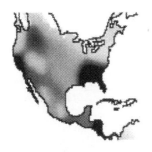 

α = 0.03, K varies with habitat.

Figures 5–10 Cumulated occupancy of North America by a colonizing population over the first 1,000 years (left hand maps) and over the first 2,000 years (right hand maps), under different assumptions about intrinsic rates of increase (α) and carrying capacity (*K*). All experiments assumed an initial population of 100 individuals originating at the southern end of the ice-free corridor. Grey scale values are autoscaled within each map to maximize contrast, and do not conform to a single absolute scale of values across the series.

Figures 11–12 Early and Middle Paleoindian fluted point densities for the contiguous United States, with overlays of the paleovegetation maps for 11,000 ^{14}C years BP (top) and 10,000 ^{14}C years BP (bottom). Artefact plot after Faught et al. (1994).

cumulated number of person-years of occupancy of the colonized cells of the grid in different conditions: and this variation is also summarized in Table 2, which would be relevant for predictions of absolute discard rates. For example, if we assume arbitrarily that the plotted sample of recovered fluted points represents 0.1 per cent of the total number originally discarded (thus total discards = *c*. 10 million), and that only men in the later third

Table 2   Final population sizes and cumulated total occupancy for the simulation runs represented in Figures 5–10.

1,000-year runs

Experimental condition	Final population size	Cumulated total occupancy (millions of person/years)
$\alpha = 0.003$, K constant, irrespective of habitat.	1,941	0.7
$\alpha = 0.01$, K constant, irrespective of habitat.	199,085	53.2
$\alpha = 0.03$, K constant, irrespective of habitat.	401,278	234.9
$\alpha = 0.003$, K varies with habitat.	1,831	0.7
$\alpha = 0.01$, K varies with habitat.	173,033	44.6
$\alpha = 0.03$, K varies with habitat.	554,301	265.8

2,000-year runs

Experimental condition	Final population size	Cumulated total occupancy (millions of person/years)
$\alpha = 0.003$, K constant, irrespective of habitat.	33,568	13.7
$\alpha = 0.01$, K constant, irrespective of habitat.	418,910	364.6
$\alpha = 0.03$, K constant, irrespective of habitat.	426,320 (= K for entire grid)	420.5
$\alpha = 0.003$, K varies with habitat.	29,936	12.5
$\alpha = 0.01$, K varies with habitat.	533,478	407.6
$\alpha = 0.03$, K varies with habitat.	635,718 (= K for entire grid)	638.1

of their life used and discarded these artefacts (so that the number of person-years of the discarders among the cumulated experimental population is one sixth of the cumulated total occupancy), and also that only 80 per cent of the simulated colonization surface is included in the fluted point dataset, then estimated rates of discard per fluted point user range from six points every year, to one point every eight years. But the assumptions made in this example are arbitrary and for illustration only.

It is clear from the Figures that certain conditions must be met for our simulated population histories to match the observed variation in fluted point densities. In those simulations in which *K* was held as a global constant (with a value equivalent to 0.03 persons per square kilometre), the simulated population history inevitably shows a greater cumulated density of person-years at the assumed northwestern origin of the dispersals. This conflicts with the fluted point data, which suggest greatest density of occupation in the eastern woodland habitats (Figs 11–12). In those simulations in which *K* was varied in accordance with observed habitat-specific variation in hunter-gatherer population densities in the ethnographic record, the simulated population history best matched the observed fluted point data when α was set at a relatively high value in the range 0.01–0.03 (which is also the range which best matches observed natural rates of increase in human populations far from carrying capacity). This is because with D held constant, only high values of α enable the travelling wave to diffuse across the surface fast enough for the higher carrying capacity of the southern and eastern areas to affect the cumulated population plot within the 2,000-year span of the simulation. Even with $\alpha = 0.01$, the greatest density of cumulated occupancy after the initial 1,000 years is still in the dry steppe/montane region of the Rockies to the south of the ice free corridor, whereas when $\alpha = 0.03$ the predicted densest cumulated occupancy is already found by that time to be in the eastern woodlands. With lower values of α (e.g. $\alpha = 0.003$), v (the velocity of expansion) is low, and the travelling wave does not reach the eastern woodlands soon enough to show an effect of varying K with habitat. Thus in our simulations, where the standard demic expansion model is used and realistic values selected for D, α and K, there is no conflict between a late glacial dispersal scenario and the North American data which suggests a greater density of late glacial occupation in the eastern woodlands.

Dispersal and mobility: constraints of the standard model

Our experiments with the Fisher–Skellam model have demonstrated that realistic dispersal models must, at the very least, recognize both the density-dependent nature of population growth and the constraining role of vegetation structure on maximum equilibrium population density (or carrying capacity). Paradoxically, the assumption of the late glacial colonization scenario that is most often called into question in this context – namely, that there is a high natural rate of increase of human hunter-gatherer populations, $\alpha \geq 0.03$/yr – seems to us to be the most secure and uncontroversial. The reason for this confusion appears to lie in the low observed rates of increase of ethnographic hunter-gatherer populations close to carrying capacity. As we have shown, these low observed rates are in fact consistent with far higher natural rates of increase, since we may assume that growth rates are density dependent. That is, we assume that as a population approaches carrying capacity so mortality increases relative to fertility, due to pressures on resources and to diseases of crowding. It is well known that human hunter-gatherer populations adapt to these constraints by cultural mechanisms of fertility regulation, such as infanticide, delayed weaning and lactation-induced amenorrhea. Confusion has arisen when it has implicitly been assumed that growth rates are density-independent, and that observed ethnographic rates must therefore represent realistic maxima for a past colonizing population.

There are, however, other aspects of the North American Paleoindian data which remain in conflict with this standard model of demic expansion. Our experiments assumed that Early Paleoindian population expansions into new habitats were constrained by carrying capacity values analogous to those seen in ethnographic hunter-gatherer societies. This assumes, in turn, that the Early Paleoindian populations were initially already fully adapted to exploit the resources of each new habitat zone: and this is in conflict with a common assumption of the prevailing scenario, which is that Early Paleoindian mobility reflected a big game focus and that only later did populations adapt to more generalist foraging strategies exploiting the full resource base of each habitat zone. Of course, that assumption may be mistaken: we do not really know how quickly a human forager population was capable of adapting to the resource structure of a new habitat zone to the degree seen in the ethnographic record. But another, related observation is that there appears to have been an increase in population density in the later part of this period, as indicated by increases in numbers of sites and in artefact frequencies in higher layers of sites with more than one episode of occupation (Anderson 1990: 199). This would also suggest an increase in the carrying capacity of habitats as Paleoindian populations became culturally adapted to their particular resource opportunities.

In fact, it may be that while dispersal velocities were high, the initial colonization of the surface of the Americas remained patchy and tethered to key resources or landmarks while initial populations accumulated knowledge of their new environments. Anderson (1990) has argued that initial dispersals may have followed major river valleys, with aggre-gation sites located close to dramatic and easily relocatable natural landmarks. Compared with the random movement assumption of the standard demic expansion model, Anderson's account places far greater weight on the ways in which spatial dispersal patterns may have been constrained by the information requirements of a colonizing population during the initial settlement phase.

When we consider the South American data, the limitations of the standard model become even more apparent. If we assume that the terminal Pleistocene sites with clear Paleoindian occupation represent a demic expansion from an origin in North America after the last glacial maximum, then it becomes necessary to assume extremely high rates of exploratory mobility through the more productive open South American habitats (including the open montane habitats of the Andean chain) if we are to account for the presence of very early dates from sites in the southern cone. These rates of exploratory dispersal are inconsistent with the standard model of range expansion, in terms of which such velocities would imply mean lifetime dispersal distances of the order of thousands of kilometres, random with respect to direction. Such extremely rapid dispersal velocities are more consistent with more qualitative models of exploratory dispersal such as Beaton's (1991) 'transient explorers', highly mobile foragers with narrow diet breadth and generalized, conservative toolkits who repeatedly relocate (in preference to settling and learning to adapt to a more specialized exploitation of the spectrum of resources avail-able in a given habitat).

One feature which is often associated with hypotheses of extremely rapid dispersal is movement along linear habitats, seen as dispersal corridors. With regard to the initial entry into the Americas south of the ice sheets, it has been demonstrated by Aoki that coloniz-ation of an inhospitable ice free corridor by a standard demic expansion process is highly unlikely, due to the probability of stochastic extinction of local groups. This does not mean that such a route of entry is implausible, merely that successful entry via such a route requires it to be treated as a corridor connecting preferred habitat patches. We can envis-age a simple decision rule for mobility along such corridors, in which a given resource threshold must be exceeded for the decision to be made to continue exploratory move-ment outwards, but in which a further, higher resource threshold must be crossed before the decision is made to settle in a home range. It is a property of successful dis-persal corri-dors that resource availability is such that the first of these thresholds should be exceeded, but not the second. The ice-free corridor between the receding Cordilleran and Lauren-tide ice sheets is not the only linear habitat which may have served as such a corridor to early Paleoindian populations. Other candidates include parts of the western coastal margin, the major river systems, and the open montane habitat of the Andean chain. Perhaps part of the reason for the cluster of early sites at the furthest reaches of the southern cone is simply that colonists followed such a decision rule, treating the Andes as a corridor, until they reached the point beyond which further outward movement was impossible.

It would therefore be far more productive, in our view, to question the assumption of the standard demic expansion model that dispersal can be represented by a single constant representing a mean distance travelled between birth and reproduction, with an equal probability that that distance will be travelled in any given direction. It is well established that travelling wave velocities in demic expansions are more influenced by the shape of the distribution of dispersal distances than by other, demographic parameters (van den Bosch et al. 1992). Although the standard model assumes a single value for D, derived from an underlying assumption of a two-dimensionally symmetric and normal distribution of dispersal distances, it is clear that this does not always match the empirical realities of animal movement even in the simplest invertebrate cases. To take the case of the observed distribution of dispersal distances in *Drosophila*, redistribution kernels with better empirical fit than the normal distribution have been shown to generate travelling waves with velocities as much as an order of magnitude greater than those predicted by the standard model (equation 5, above) (Kot et al. 1996). Moreover, in some cases these velocities may be accelerating rather than constant (Kot et al. 1996).

The assumption of symmetry in the distribution of dispersal distances in two dimensions can also be called into question. It is a feature of the logistic model of density-dependent growth that as a population approaches carrying capacity, so there is a linear decline in the net rate of increase. Consequently if we assume a colonizing population of fitness-maximizers seeking to maximize their individual reproductive rate, we will predict that people will disperse preferentially into those areas of adjacent habitat in which human occupancy is furthest from carrying capacity. However, positive density-dependent dispersal may not of itself imply accelerated rates of range expansion. Newman (1980) found that when the diffusion coefficient has the density-dependent form $D(\frac{n}{K})^b$, the velocity of range expansion can be expressed in the form $\upsilon \sqrt{(2D\alpha)}$, with υ a function of b. When $b = 0$, $\upsilon = \sqrt{2}$, consistent with the standard model's solution (equation 5, above). When $b > 0$, and people move further as population approaches carrying capacity, then it seems that $\upsilon \approx (b + 1)^{-1}$; from which it follows that if $b = 1$, then individual dispersal distances when $n = K$ (and dispersal distance is assumed to be greatest due to crowding) must be at least 3 times the value taken for mean lifetime dispersal distance in the standard model, for range expansion to be *faster and not slower* than in the standard model. By contrast, when $b < 0$ (such that dispersal distances are greatest at low densities, due for instance to mate searching), then υ assumes any value. We might then expect that density-dependent dispersal will accelerate range expansion when it is negatively density-dependent and driven by mate searching, and when α is low – such that at a given location, n is slow to approach K. MacDonald (1997) suggests that ethnographic and archaeological data imply such a pattern for Early Paleoindian mobility.

In raising such questions about the standard model's assumption about individual mobility – which is that, in aggregate, dispersal can be approximated as rotationally symmetric, density-independent, and proportional to the mean squared individual displacement distance per generation time – we are identifying a key philosophical issue of ecological modelling. On the one hand whatever the redistribution kernel used, the random movement assumption remains appropriate if it adequately predicts observed rates of population expansion, even if individuals are known to have used complex and intelligent navigational behaviour relying on environmental cues. This is because models of population-level processes should aim to suppress any such detail which is irrelevant to the simulation of spatial patterns at the population scale (Andow et al. 1990). On the other hand, such 'behavioural minimalism' may be inappropriate where the complex navigational decisions of many individuals follow common rules such that their movements are correlated, leading to population-level deviation from the simple random dispersal pattern. Lima and Zollner (1996: 132) have emphasized the importance for understanding animal movement and dispersal of the perceptual range, defined as 'the distance from which a particular landscape element can be perceived as such (or detected) by a given animal'. An extended perceptual range decreases the risks of mortality of a dispersing animal searching for a suitable habitat patch, and can thus act as a determinant of landscape connectivity. At the initial phase of colonization, learning the distribution of patches at large spatial scales may have been risky if it required repeated abandonment and relocation of potentially widely spaced patches (ibid.). It is plausible to assume that one of the main priorities of the early Paleoindian settlers of the Americas was balancing the risks and potential benefits of exploratory dispersal as local groups extended their perceptual range.

As we have seen, such information-based approaches to animal movement and habitat selection are implied by accounts of Early Paleoindian dispersal patterns such as Anderson's, with its emphasis on the importance of rivers as dispersal corridors and on clearly-recognizable places as aggregation sites in the initial colonization phase. They may also be necessary to explain dispersal through inhospitable habitat corridors, and for explaining the apparent rapidity of Paleoindian dispersal into the southern cone of South America, when the standard model would entail populations of individuals dispersing hundreds or thousands of kilometres in every direction during their lifetimes, while simultaneously maintaining high natural reproductive rates. Beaton's 'transient explorer' strategy is an example of a qualitative model of foraging decision-making which would lead to such rapid, long-distance mobility. Standard dispersal models which assume random movement at the population level may need to be modified to take account of foragers' decisions and their perceptual basis, when these are correlated among individuals – leading to non-random dispersals which deviate from the rotationally symmetric assumption of the 'information-free' approach. One good reason for examining such 'information-based' approaches in more detail is that we do not yet understand their implications for the velocity of range expansion.

We have demonstrated in this paper that the United States fluted point distribution is consistent with a late glacial colonization from the northwest, given realistic assumptions about population growth rates, about mobility, and about equilibrium population densities as they vary between biomes. This has been demonstrated by a series of computer simulations using the standard demic expansion model derived from animal ecology. It is very likely that understanding may be further improved by more sophisticated treatments of the information-seeking and decision-making processes affecting individual dispersal distances in a colonizing population.

Acknowledgements

We thank David Meltzer and Cheryl Ross for constructively commenting on an earlier draft, and David Anderson for permission to use a version of the US Fluted Point distribution map (after Faught et al. 1994). This project has been developed as part of a wider programme of collaboration between the Departments of Archaeology and of Mathematics at the University of Southampton, and we are very grateful to Clive Gamble for his continuing support for that endeavour.

James Steele
Department of Archaeology, University of Southampton
Highfield, Southampton SO17 1BJ, UK

Jonathan Adams
Environmental Sciences Division, Oak Ridge National Laboratory
Oak Ridge, TN 37831, USA

Tim Sluckin
Department of Mathematics, University of Southampton
Highfield, Southampton SO17 1BJ, UK

References

Adams, J. 1998. North America During the Last 150,000 Years. http://www.esd.ornl.gov/ern/qen/nercNORTHAMERICA.html

Ammerman, A. J. and Cavalli-Sforza, L. L. 1984. *The Neolithic Transition and the Genetics of Populations in Europe*. Princeton: Princeton University Press.

Anderson, D. E. 1997. Younger Dryas research and its implications for understanding abrupt climatic change. *Progress in Physical Geography*, 21: 230–49.

Anderson, D. G. 1990. The Paleoindian colonization of Eastern North America: a view from the southeastern United States. In *Early Paleoindian Economies of Eastern North America* (eds K. B. Tankersley and B. L. Isaac). *Research in Economic Anthropology*, Supplement 5: 163–216.

Anderson, D. G. 1995. Recent advances in Paleoindian and Archaic Period research in the southeastern United States. *Archaeology of Eastern North America*, 23: 145–76.

Anderson, P. M. and Brubaker, L. B. 1993. Holocene vegetation and climate histories of Alaska. In *Global Climates Since the Last Glacial Maximum* (eds H. E. Wright Jr, J. E. Kutzbach, T. Webb III, W. F. Ruddiman, F. A. Street-Perrott and P. J. Bartlein). Minneapolis: University of Minnesota Press, pp. 385–400.

Andow, D., Kareiva, P., Levin, S. and Okubo, A. 1990. Spread of invading organisms. *Landscape Ecology*, 4: 177–88.

Aoki, K. 1993. Modeling the dispersal of the 1st Americans through an inhospitable ice-free corridor. *Anthropological Science*, 101: 79–89.

Beaton, J. M. 1991. Colonizing continents: some problems from Australia and the Americas. In *The*

First Americas: Search and Research (eds T. D. Dillehay and D. J. Meltzer). Boca Raton, FL: CRC, pp. 209–30.

Beaudoin, A. B., Wright, M. and Ronaghan, B. 1996. Late Quaternary landscape history and archaeology in the 'ice-free corridor': some recent results from Alberta. *Quaternary International*, 22: 113–26.

Benson, L., Burdett, J., Lund, S., Kashgarian, M. and Mensing, S. 1997. Nearly synchronous climate change in the Northern Hemisphere during the last glacial termination. *Nature*, 388: 263–5.

Birdsell, J. B. 1957. Some population problems involving Pleistocene man. *Cold Spring Harbor Symposium on Quantitative Biology*, 22: 47–69.

Bobrowsky, P. T. and Rutter, N. W. 1992. Quaternary geologic history of the Canadian Rocky Mountains. *Geographie Physique et Quaternaire*, 46: 5–15.

Burns, J. A., Young, R. R. and Arnold, L. D. 1993. Don't look fossil gift horses in the mouth. *GAC/MAC Joint Annual Meeting, Edmonton. Program and Abstracts*, v. 18, A-14.

Crawford, M. H. 1998. *The Origins of Native Americans*. Cambridge: Cambridge University Press.

Dyke, A. S. and Prest, V. K. 1987a. Late Wisconsinian and Holocene history of the Laurentide ice sheet. *Geographie Physique et Quaternaire*, 41: 237–63.

Dyke, A. S. and Prest, V. K. 1987b. *Palaeogeography of Northern North America, 18,000–5,000 years ago*. Geological Survey of Canada, Map 1703a, scale 1:12,500,000.

Elias, S.,A., Short, S. K., Nelson, C. H. and Birks, H. H. 1996. Life and times of the Bering land bridge. *Nature*, 382: 60–3.

Faught, M. K., Anderson, D. G. and Gisiger, A. 1994. North American Paleoindian database: an update. *Current Research in the Pleistocene*, 11: 32–5.

Fisher, R. A. 1937. The wave of advance of advantageous genes. *Annals of Eugenics*, 7: 355–69.

Hansen, B. A. and Engstrom, D. R. 1996. Vegetation history of Pleasant Island, Southeastern Alaska, since 13,000 yr BP. *Quaternary Research*, 46: 161–75.

Hassan, F. A. 1981. *Demographic Archaeology*. London: Academic Press.

Hoffecker, J. F., Powers, W. R. and Goebel, T. 1993. The colonization of Beringia and the peopling of the New World. *Science*, 259: 46–53.

Kelly, R. L. 1995. *The Foraging Spectrum*. Washington: Smithsonian Institution Press.

Kot, M., Lewis, M. A. and van den Driessche, P. 1996. Dispersal data and the spread of invading organisms. *Ecology*, 77: 2027–42.

Lima, S. L. and Zollner, P. A. 1996. Towards a behavioral ecology of ecological landscapes. *Trends in Ecology and Evolution*, 11: 131–5.

Lozano-Garcia, M. S., Ortega-Guerrero, B., Caballero-Miranda, M. and Urrutia-Fucugauchi, J. 1993. Late Pleistocene and Holocene paleoenvironments of Chalco Lake, Central Mexico. *Quaternary Research*, 40: 332–42.

MacDonald, D. H. 1997. Hunter-gatherer mating distance and Early Paleoindian social mobility. *Current Research in the Pleistocene*, 14: 119–21.

Meltzer, D. J. 1993. *Search for the First Americans*. Washington, DC: Smithsonian Institution Press.

Meltzer, D. J. 1995. Clocking the first Americans. *Annual Review of Anthropology*, 24: 21–45.

Murray, J. D. 1990. *Theoretical Biology*. Berlin: Springer-Verlag.

Newman, W. I. 1980. Some exact solutions to a non-linear diffusion problem in population genetics and combustion. *Journal of Theoretical Biology*, 85: 325–34.

Overpeck, J., Webb, R. S. and Webb, T. 1992. Mapping eastern North American vegetation change of the past 18 ka: No-analogs and the future. *Geology*, 20: 1071–4.

Powell, J. F. and Steele, D. G. 1994. Diet and health of Paleoindians: an examination of early Holocene human dental remains. In *Paleonutrition: The Diet and Health of Prehistoric Americans* (ed. K. D. Sobolik). Carbondale: Southern Illinois University.

Press, W. H., Flannery, B. P., Teukolsky, S. A. and Veterling, W. T. 1986. *Numerical Recipes: The Art of Scientific Computing*. Cambridge: Cambridge University Press.

QEN Atlas Site: Review and Atlas of Palaeovegetation: Preliminary land ecosystem maps of the world since the Last Glacial Maximum. http://www.esd.ornl.gov/ern/qen/adams1.html

Shigesada, N. and Kawasaki, K. 1997. *Biological Invasions: Theory and Practice*. Oxford: Oxford University Press.

ShowTime 1995. NOAA Palaeoclimatology Program (downloadable shareware of North American pollen data since 15,000 BP). http://www.ngdc.noaa.gov/paleo/softlib.html

Skellam, J. G. 1951. Random dispersal in theoretical populations. *Biometrika*, 38: 196–218.

Steele, J., Gamble, C. S. and Sluckin, T. J. (in press) Estimating the velocity of Paleoindian expansion into South America. In *People as Agents of Environmental Change* (eds R. Nicholson and T. O'Connor). Oxford: Oxbow Books.

Steele, J., Sluckin, T. J., Denholm, D. R. and Gamble, C. S. 1995. Simulating the hunter-gatherer colonization of the Americas. *Analecta Praehistorica Leidensia*, 28: 223–7.

Tankersley, K. B. 1992. A geoarchaeological investigation of distribution and exchange in the raw material economies of Clovis groups in Eastern North America. In *Raw Material Economies among Prehistoric Hunter-Gatherers* (eds A. Montet-White and S. Holen). University of Kansas Publications in Anthropology 19, pp. 285–303.

Thompson, R. S., Whitlock, C., Bartlein, P. J., Harrison, S. P. and Spaulding, W. G. 1993. Climatic changes in the western United States since 18,000 yr. BP. In *Global Climates Since the Last Glacial Maximum* (eds H. E. Wright Jr., J. E. Kutzbach, T. Webb III, W. F. Ruddiman, F. A. Street-Perrott and P. J. Bartlein). Minneapolis: University of Minnesota Press, pp. 468–513.

Van den Bosch, F., Hengeveld, R. and Metz, J. A. J. 1992. Analyzing the velocity of animal range expansion. *Journal of Biogeography*, 19: 135–50.

Wells, G. L. 1992. The Aeolian landscape of North America from the Late Pleistocene. DPhil thesis, University of Oxford, UK.

Whitley, D. S. and Dorn, R. L. 1993. New perspectives on the Clovis vs. pre-Clovis controversy. *American Antiquity*, 58: 626–47.

Williamson, M. 1996. *Biological Invasions*. London: Chapman & Hall.

Young, D. A. and Bettinger, R. L. 1995. Simulating the global human expansion in the Late Pleistocene. *Journal of Archaeological Science*, 22: 89–92.

The population shuffle in the central Illinois valley: a diachronic model of Mississippian biocultural interactions

Dawnie Wolfe Steadman

Abstract

A new population genetics method is applied to discriminate between processes of extraregional gene flow and intraregional biological continuity within and among three temporally sequential prehistoric Native American cultures in the central Illinois valley. Within a population genetics framework, the impact of regional and interregional cultural changes on local population structure can be quantified and the magnitude of biocultural interaction can be inferred. The results suggest that population structure within the region was relatively unaffected by the cultural transition from Late Woodland to Mississippian or by significant interregional sociopolitical changes in neighboring regions later in the Mississippian period. Finally, a Bold Counselor Phase Oneota population was morphologically distinct from Mississippians, supporting the archaeological model that this Oneota group was an intrusive, frontier population from the upper Mississippi valley. A population genetic approach is highly recommended over traditional biodistance analyses to formally address how past demographic and biocultural processes affected local population structures.

Keywords

Population genetics; bioarchaeology; skeletal biology; central Illinois valley; Mississippian; Late Woodland; Oneota.

Introduction

Bioarchaeology can provide a unique and significant understanding of the complex relationships between cultural and demographic processes in ancient populations. By assuming that biological interactions provide an indirect measure of social interaction (Buikstra 1977; Conner 1987; Droessler 1981; Konigsberg 1988, 1990a, b), correlations between fluctuations in population structure and cultural processes can be detected from morphological traits of the skeleton. Within the past decade, the study of biocultural change in past populations has undergone significant theoretical and methodological advances as bioarchaeologists have begun to apply formal, model-bound population genetic models to elucidate specific parameters of ancient population structure (Konigs-berg 1987, 1990a; Langdon 1995; Steadman 1997). Though requiring more assumptions and complexity, model-bound analyses are superior to traditional model-free techniques because they are grounded in population genetic theory and are designed to identify the microevolutionary processes that produced and maintained variation within and among past populations (Relethford and Lees 1982). Most relevant for regional studies is the Relethford and Blangero (1990) model of within-group heterogeneity that detects differ-ential amounts of gene flow from an extraregional source. By applying this model to a regional skeletal analysis of three temporally sequential prehistoric Native American cultures, it is possible to determine if cultural transitions and large-scale sociopolitical changes involved interregional population movement.

Bioarchaeological setting

Diachronic interactions among three late prehistoric cultures from west-central Illinois, USA, are investigated in this study with emphasis on the fertile floodplain of the central Illinois valley (Fig. 1). Table 1 provides an overview of the cultures and their temporal relationships in west-central Illinois and the American Bottom. Late Woodland culture (*c.* AD 700–1050) in the central Illinois valley can be characterized by a hunting/gathering economy with evidence of some maize horticulture, a less complex social system than in the succeeding Mississippian period, and clay, grit or limestone tempered pottery with little decorative detail (Conrad 1991; Esarey 1997; Harn 1975). The subsequent Mississippian culture (AD 1050–1300) had a complex stratified social system as reflected in the settlement patterns and mortuary program, a maize-based subsistence economy, and a wide variety of elaborately decorated, shell tempered wares (Conrad 1991; Harn 1991a; Fowler and Hall 1972; Goldstein 1980; Griffin 1967; Pauketat 1994). Mississippians also had an extensive cultural distribution and trade network across the southeast United States (c.f. Smith 1990; Emerson and Lewis 1991). Finally, Bold Counselor phase Oneota groups appeared around AD 1300. They also practiced maize subsistence agriculture but had a less complex social organization than the Mississippians. Native American populations largely abandoned the central Illinois valley by AD 1450 (Conrad 1991; Harn 1991a).

Mississippian development in the central Illinois River valley

Studies of Mississippian development in the central Illinois valley are marked by controversy concerning the nature of the transition between Late Woodland and Missis-sippian cultures around AD 1050 (Blakely 1973; Conrad 1991; Harn 1991a; Wolf 1977). The central issue is whether Mississippian populations entered the region from the American Bottom or if Mississippian culture developed *in situ* from an indigenous Late Woodland base (Caldwell 1967; Conrad 1991; Harn 1991a; Griffin 1967). Based on discontinuities in ceramic styles, mortuary practices and housing structures, archaeological models contend that Mississippian populations entered the central Illinois valley during the Eveland phase and replaced or acculturated indigenous Late Woodland populations (Conrad 1991; Harn

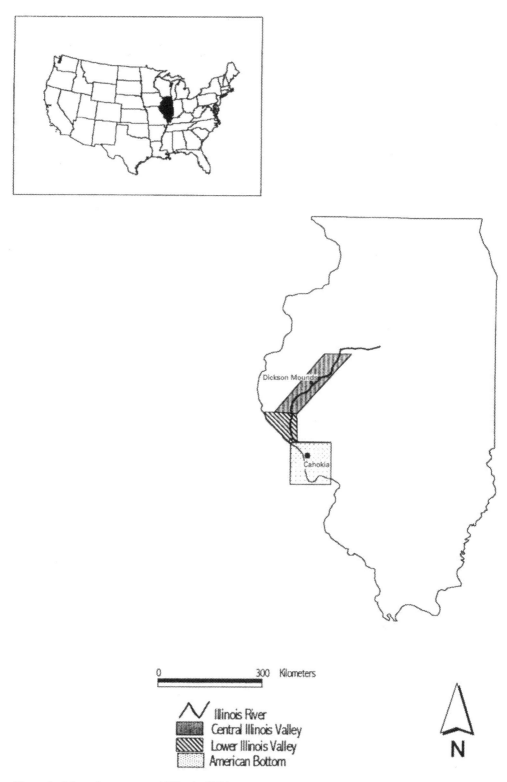

Figure 1   Map of west-central Illinois, USA.

Table 1 Late Woodland, Mississippian and Oneota chronologies for the central and lower Illinois River valleys and the American Bottom. Based on Harn (1991a), Conrad (1991), Kelly (1990) and Milner (1996).

A.D.	PERIOD	CULTURAL	UNITS	
		CENTRAL ILLINOIS VALLEY	LOWER ILLINOIS VALLEY	AMERICAN BOTTOM
1500	ONEOTA	Bold Counselor	Vulcan	Vulcan
1400				Sand Prairie
1300	MISSISSIPPIAN	Larson	Sand Prairie	Sand Prairie
1200		Orendorf	Moorehead	Moorehead
1100		Eveland	Stirling	Stirling
1000	EMERGENT MISSISSIPPIAN & LATE WOODLAND	Sepo Maples Mills Bauer Branch Myer/Dickson Late Woodland	Jersey Bluff Late Woodland	Lohmann
900				Emergent Mississippian
800				Patrick Late Woodland

1991a). However, there is little agreement concerning the magnitude of Mississippian movement into the region (Conrad 1991; Emerson 1991; Harn 1991a).

While the migration model has been supported by an intra-cemetery biological distance study of the Late Woodland and Mississippian skeletal samples at Dickson Mounds, Illinois (Blakely 1973), a different process of cultural transition occurred in the adjacent lower Illinois valley. Droessler (1981) examined seven Late Woodland and Mississippian skeletal samples from five cemeteries throughout the region and found that Mississippians were biologically more similar to Late Woodland samples within the same cemetery than to other Mississippian groups in the region. Thus, there was biological continuity within the region during a period of significant cultural change. If the same process was occurring in the central Illinois valley, a similar pattern of intra-cemetery and regional continuity is expected between Late Woodland and Mississippian populations.

The Mississippian period

Once established, Mississippian culture flourished for the next two centuries in the central Illinois valley (AD 1100–1300) (Harn 1991a; Conrad 1991). Much debate has centered on the economic, political and demographic relationships between Cahokia, located in the American Bottom, and surrounding regions. The traditional model contends that a Mississippian élite at Cahokia, the largest Mississippian regional center, had exclusive rights to production, trade and other cultural processes in distant regions (Dincauze and Hasenstab 1989; Goodman and Armelagos 1985; Goodman et al. 1984; Hall 1991; Kelly

1991b; Porter 1969). Peripheral regions, such as the central Illinois valley, are seen as Mississippian outposts that functioned only to extract raw materials and food from the local environment for export to the superordinate echelon at Cahokia (Kelly 1991a). In this view, Cahokia dominated and controlled all economic and politically based activities within its wide sphere of influence.

In contrast to a model of Cahokian dominance, a recent reinterpretation of Mississippian sociopolitical interaction suggests that the Cahokia polity was inherently unstable and its influence in the American Bottom and beyond periodically waned, allowing peripheral regions to control their own resources and production (Milner 1990). Even during the rise and pinnacle of Cahokia's power, there were other powerful, competing regional centers operating in the American Bottom (Milner 1990; Pauketat 1994). According to Milner (1990), settlements immediately surrounding Cahokia were directly under its control but distant communities developed quasi-autonomous political systems. During and succeeding Cahokia's decline and depopulation, other polities emerged in southern outlying areas, including Emerald Mounds and the Common Field site. Thus, while the impact of Cahokia's demise was certainly felt within the American Bottom, business continued as power cycled through other regional polities.

Milner (1990, 1996) argues that if the elite at Cahokia could not exert direct control over outlying communities within the American Bottom, it is unlikely that they could dominate production, trade and sociopolitical activities in distant regions. Harn (1991a) and Conrad (1991) support this view and contend that, while ceramic assemblages and mortuary practices were strongly influenced by Cahokia during the Eveland phase, central Illinois valley Mississippians quickly developed their own cultural subsystem. After AD 1100, central Illinois valley Mississippians had developed new, local ceramic complexes that were clearly distinct from contemporary assemblages in the American Bottom. Further, they fully participated in trade interactions within and outside of the Cahokia network (Conrad 1991).

While the material evidence may support a model of central Illinois valley autonomy, the impact of Cahokia's slow decline (AD 1200–50) on the population structure of central Illinois valley Mississippians could still have been dramatic. Prior to AD 1200, Mississippian occupation of the central Illinois valley region was limited to only a few habitation sites (Conrad 1991; Harn 1991a). Between AD 1100 and 1150, Mississippians abandoned the Eveland site and subsequently constructed as many as five sequential settlements at the Orendorf village over the course of the next century (Fig. 2) (Conrad 1991; Esarey and Conrad 1981). Orendorf was the first large town in the region and it does not appear that other large villages existed during this period (Conrad 1991; Harn 1991a). However, the succeeding Larson period (*c.* AD 1250–1300) was marked by the construction of six large temple towns (Larson, Hildemeyer, Walsh, Lawrenz Gun Club, Kingston Lake and Crable) and associated villages along a 160-mile stretch of the Illinois River (Harn 1994).

A key concern is whether the rise of these regional polities was concomitant with the influx of Mississippians from other regions or due to intraregional cultural and demographic expansion. Kelly (1991a) and Emerson (1991) have suggested that the Larson phase polities in the central Illinois valley competed with Cahokia and then flourished as Cahokia gradually crumbled. Therefore, it is conceivable that populations moved into the

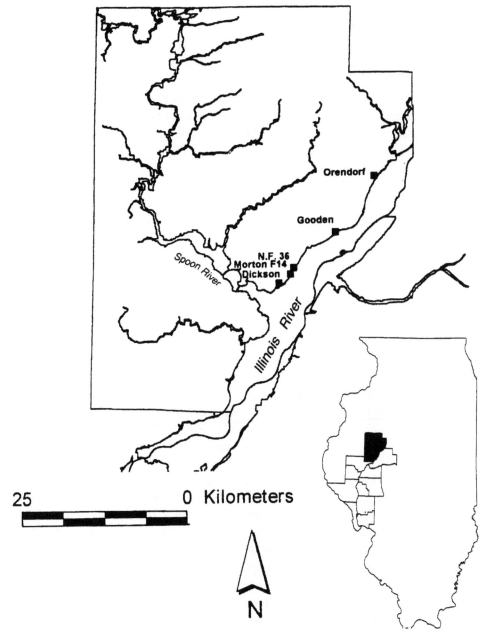

Figure 2 Map of study area: location of central Illinois River valley sites in Fulton County, Illinois.

region as political power shifted from the American Bottom to the central Illinois valley. In the southern reaches of the American Bottom, Milner (1990) found that populations abandoned Cahokia and surrounding floodplain sites and moved into the uplands where smaller, more stable polities were located. This pattern of regional center relocation and associated population redistribution is seen elsewhere in the southeast when Mississippian chiefdoms collapsed (e.g. Anderson 1994, 1996; Muller 1997). Settlement changes in the lower Illinois valley, the region lying between the central Illinois valley and the American Bottom, potentially parallel a shift of political power. Conner (1985) found a shift in Mississippian settlement location within the lower Illinois valley from the south, near the American Bottom, northwards toward the central Illinois valley by the end of the thirteenth century.

However, not all of the archaeological evidence points to migrations into the central Illinois valley. Ceramic studies in the central Illinois valley suggest that the few stylistic and technological changes between the Orendorf and Larson phases reflect *in situ* temporal variation rather than the introduction of new interregional styles (Conrad 1991; Harn 1991a). Further, since stable polities were present in the American Bottom to replace Cahokia during its decline, there may have been no real social, economic or political impetus for Mississippians to leave the region. Thus, Larson phase expansion in the central Illinois valley could be due to the propagation and dispersion of Orendorf phase Mississippians followed by small-scale movement of populations from one town to another, rather than significant interregional immigration.

Appearance of the Oneota

For reasons not yet understood, Mississippians abandoned their temple towns in the Spoon River Valley and moved to the southern part of the central Illinois valley around AD 1300 (Conrad 1991; Emerson 1991; Harn 1978, 1991a). There is evidence, however, that central Illinois valley Mississippians had not completely deserted the area when Bold Counselor Phase Oneota appeared in the region by AD 1300–25 (Conrad and Esarey n.d.). First believed to be an intrusive population from the upper Mississippi valley, archaeologists are struck by the similarities in ceramic styles between Oneota and Mississippian wares in the central Illinois valley (Conrad 1991; Conrad and Esarey n.d.; Gibbon 1982; Santure and Esarey 1990). It is unclear whether these similarities stem from acculturation upon their arrival in the region or previous exposure to Mississippian culture prior to leaving the upper Mississippi valley. However, in addition to the ceramic evidence, there are other indications of cultural interactions within the region. Most dramatically, 17 percent of the individuals in the Norris Farms #36 Oneota cemetery had warfare-related injuries, suggesting that the Oneota were neither alone nor particularly welcome in the region (Milner et al. 1991). Radiocarbon dates from terminal Mississippian sites in the region are later than AD 1300 (Esarey and Santure 1990), further suggesting that there could have been temporal overlap, and hence biological interaction, between the Oneota and Mississippians.

A population genetic approach

From this brief overview of late prehistoric cultural change in the central Illinois valley, two archaeological questions emerge. First, what is the mode of diachronic cultural transitions within this region? Second, what are the demographic implications of Cahokia's decline and associated sociopolitical changes on central Illinois valley Mississippian populations? With the development of new analytical models appropriate for morphological data, these questions can now be addressed by modeling them within a population genetics framework.

The Relethford and Blangero model

The Relethford and Blangero (1990) model of heterogeneity was used to detect differential access to external gene flow among central Illinois valley populations. According to population genetic theory, if all populations within a region exchange migrants from an outside source at an equal rate, the relationship between the average within-group variation and genetic distance to the centroid (the average heterozygosity of all subpopulations) for each population should be linear (the null hypothesis). However, when one population increases the rate of genetic exchange with external populations, their within-group heterogeneity will increase due to the influx of new genes and the linear relationship will be violated. Therefore, subpopulations that receive more extraregional gene flow will have greater within-group variation than expected by the null hypothesis. Conversely, if a population received less than average external gene flow their observed heterozygosities will be lower than expected.

The Harpending and Ward (1982) model of heterogeneity was based on allele frequencies but Relethford and Blangero (1990) modified it for use with continuous traits. The complete mathematical model is presented in Relethford and Blangero (1990), Relethford et al. (1997) and Steadman (1997), and is only summarized here. The average distance of each population to the regional centroid (r_{ii}), as well as the observed ($\bar{v}_i$) and expected $E(\bar{v}_i)$ heterozygosity values are calculated across all traits based on a relationship (R) matrix (Relethford and Blangero 1990). The unbiased R matrix is used in all computations to reduce sampling error (Relethford et al. 1997). The unbiased R matrix is scaled by weighting each sample by the estimated population size which accounts for differences in effective populations size, thereby statistically removing the potential effect of genetic drift in smaller populations (Relethford and Blangero 1990; Relethford et al. 1997). Therefore, differences in heterozygosity are assumed to reflect only migration and long-term population histories (Relethford 1996; Relethford et al. 1997). Table 2 includes the estimated census size for each sample in the central Illinois valley based on cemetery size or published estimates of associated village size. The estimates reflect a trend of increasing population density through time in the region as interpreted from the archaeological record (Conrad 1991; Harn 1991a, 1994; Santure 1981).

The difference between the expected and observed heterozygosity is the residual [$\bar{v}_i - E(\bar{v}_i)$]. The sign and magnitude of the residual indicates the relative extent of external gene flow into each population. Standard errors and significance levels of the residuals are estimated by jackknifing the residual variance over all variables (Miller 1974; Relethford and Harpending 1994; Williams-Blangero and Blangero 1990). The average distance to the centroid across all populations (average across all r_{ii}) is r_0, which is equivalent to the minimum F_{st}, a measure of minimum between-group differentiation that can be compared across populations (Relethford 1994; Relethford and Blangero 1990; Williams-Blangero and Blangero 1989).

Following Relethford and Harpending (1994) and Harpending and Jenkins (1973),

Table 2 Sample and census sizes and radiocarbon dates of central Illinois valley skeletal series.

Site	Cultural component	Sample size	Estimated census size	Radiocarbon date BP	Calendar date	Dendro-corrected date	Dating source	Reference
Dickson Mounds	Mississippian (Eveland phase)	19	350	Eveland site 865 ± 50 895 ± 55 820 ± 50	AD 1085 AD 1055 AD 1130	Average of AD 1177	charcoal, charred wood from Eveland village site	Bender et al. 1975 Harn 1994
Dickson Mounds	Mississippian (Larson phase)	40	1000	Larson site 765 ± 55 760 ± 55 835 ± 60 815 ± 55	AD 1185 AD 1190 AD 1115 AD 1135	Average of AD 1240	charcoal from features of the Larson site	Bender et al. 1975 Harn 1994
Gooden	Late Woodland	14	125	No RC dates	AD 700–900		ceramic chronology	Droessler 1976
Morton	Late Woodland	21	125	Village site 1350 ± 70	AD 600		charcoal from Feature 35	Santure et al. 1990
Morton	Mississippian	31	500	No RC dates. Ceramics suggest Larson phase	AD 1250–1300		ceramic chronology	Santure et al. 1990
Orendorf	Mississippian	29	500	Village 800 ± 55 865 ± 55 845 ± 65 810 ± 45 770 ± 55	AD 1150 AD 1085 AD 1105 AD 1140 AD 1180		charcoal, plant remains from the village site	Bender et al. 1975
Norris Farms #36	Oneota	85	500	1120 ± 70 690 ± 70 670 ± 70 390 ± 70	AD 830 AD 1260 AD 1280 AD 1560		ISGS-1349 ISGS-1348 ISGS-1377 ISGS-1415	Santure et al. 1990

genetic distances between populations are calculated by converting the elements of the R matrix into a distance matrix, $d_{ij}^2 = r_{ii} + r_{jj} - 2r_{ij}$. Multidimensional scaling (MDS) provides graphical representations of the biological distances (Kruskal 1964). The stress value of each MDS map represents the goodness-of-fit (Schiffman et al. 1981).

Samples

A total of 239 individuals from eight sites in the central Illinois valley are included in this analysis. Table 2 shows the cultural affiliations, sample sizes and available radiocarbon or relative dates for each site. Following Harn's (1980) cultural divisions based on ceramic typologies and burial practices, the Dickson Mounds Mississippian sample is separated into Eveland and Larson subphases. Although some cultural divisions within the cemetery have been debated (cf. Buikstra and Milner 1989), cultural material in Eveland phase burials is distinguishable from Larson phase wares placed in the later interments (Conrad 1991; Harn 1991a). Harn (1991b) suggests that the Mississippian burials in the Morton Mounds belong in the Larson phase, though absolute dates are not yet available. The specific cultural affiliation of the Morton Late Woodland sample is uncertain due to the small number of diagnostic grave goods in the cemetery.

Data

Cranial measurements were utilized as morphological indicators of the underlying genetic variation among populations. Cranial dimensions are polygenic traits and do not directly reflect allele frequencies since they have both genetic and environmental components. Extensive studies of polygenic inheritance and environmental variation have demonstrated that they can provide signals of microevolutionary events. For instance, Williams-Blangero and Blangero (1989) have shown that if there is no environmental variation between subpopulations, a fairly safe assumption in regional contexts within a relatively short time period, then the phenotypic distance between samples is less than or equal to the genetic distance. Cheverud (1988) found a very close correspondence between phenotypic and genotypic correlation matrices in a number of continuous traits, indicating that the assumption of zero environmental deviation is appropriate (Relethford and Blangero 1990; Relethford et al. 1997; Relethford and Harpending 1994; Williams-Blangero and Blangero 1989).

Following definitions found in Buikstra and Ubelaker (1994) and Droessler (1981), 48 measurements were recorded for each individual. The 32 measurements recommended by Buikstra and Ubelaker (1994) were derived from North American prehistoric Indian skeletal series, including a Dickson Mounds Mississippian sample. Variables are removed if they have significant intra-observer errors or are significantly correlated with age (arranged into young, middle and old adult categories). Most variables are affected by sexual dimorphism and some have age-related changes in craniofacial size. Such effects are statistically removed by standardizing the raw data within each age/sex category (Williams-Blangero and Blangero 1989, 1990). Z-score standardization is a common and accepted procedure to control age- and sex-related size variation (e.g. Konigsberg and Ousley 1995; Langdon 1995;

Relethford 1994; Relethford and Harpending 1994; Williams-Blangero and Blangero 1989, 1990). After extensive statistical screening the following eleven variables are used in this study: maximum cranial length, minimum frontal breadth, nasal height, frontal chord, occipital chord, minimum ramus breadth, biasterionic breadth, midfacial breadth, maximum malar length, occipital condyle breadth and maximum condyle length.

Results

The initial analysis is designed to understand the general relationships among all Late Woodland, Mississippian and Oneota samples within the region. The biological distance matrix in Table 3 shows that the Oneota–Mississippian distances are among the largest in the region while the Late Woodland group is close to both Morton and Eveland Mississippians. Eveland, the earliest Mississippian sample, has zero distances to the later Morton and Orendorf Mississippian samples, and a relatively small distance to the Larson Mississippian sample. The close relationship among Mississippian groups is demonstrated in the MDS map (Fig. 3). In two dimensions, the Late Woodland sample appears distant from the Morton Mississippians, but this is due to the large intergroup distances between Late Woodland and Orendorf groups.

The Relethford-Blangero results provide an interpretive framework for the biological distance patterns (Table 4). The Orendorf and Larson Mississippian populations have

Table 3   Minimum biological distances among central Illinois valley Late Woodland, Mississippian and Oneota groups based on the unbiased, scaled R matrix.

Group	Late Woodland	Morton	Eveland	Orendorf	Larson	Oneota
Late Woodland	0.000000	0.017211	0.024594	0.047721	0.028449	0.013270
Morton		0.000000	0.000000	0.010103	0.031740	0.027712
Eveland			0.000000	0.000000	0.006441	0.033333
Orendorf				0.000000	0.021517	0.074510
Larson					0.000000	0.038656
Oneota						0.000000

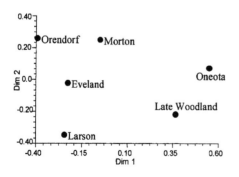

Stress = 0.000731

Figure 3 MDS map of the minimum biological distances among central Illinois valley Late Woodland, Mississippian and Oneota samples.

Table 4   Relethford and Blangero analysis of differential gene flow: Late Woodland, Mississippian and Oneota phenotypic distances to the centroid (r_{ii}), observed mean variance ($\bar{v}_i$), expected mean variances $E(\bar{v}_i)$ and residual variances $[\bar{v}_i - E(\bar{v}_i)]$.

Population	r_{ii}	$(\bar{v}_i)$	$E(\bar{v}_i)$	*Residual* $[\bar{v}_i - E(\bar{v}_i)]^*$
Late Woodland	0.029818	0.954	0.974	−0.020
Eveland	0.000000	0.942	1.003	−0.062
Morton	0.003387	0.935	1.000	−0.065
Orendorf	0.009889	1.050	0.994	0.056
Larson	0.000496	1.042	1.003	0.039
Oneota	0.024194	0.963	0.979	−0.016

Mean within-group phenotypic variance = 0.995
Unbiased minimum F_{st} = 0.008608
Standard error = 0.004209
*No residuals were significant at the 0.05 level

positive residual values, indicating they received greater than average external gene flow. However, neither sample is very far from the centroid, nor are the residuals significant, suggesting that the amount of external gene flow was not sufficient to substantially increase within-group heterogeneity and pull the populations away from the centroid. The other three samples, including the Late Woodland group, received slightly less than average external immigration. Overall, the small residuals indicate that there was little differential gene flow into the region over 500 years of occupation.

The Late Woodland–Mississippian transition

To examine the biological component of the Late Woodland–Mississippian cultural transition, the Oneota sample is excluded. The distance matrix (Table 5) and MDS map (Fig. 4) show that the Late Woodland sample is biologically similar to both the Morton and Eveland Mississippian groups. The former relationship is likely a reflection of intra-cemetery continuity between Morton Late Woodland and Mississippian groups, while Eveland is the earliest Mississippian group known in the region. These biodistance patterns are consistent with those in the lower Illinois valley (Droessler 1981), and suggest biological continuity between this Late Woodland group and Mississippians within the region. The Relethford and Blangero analysis (Table 6) supports this interpretation since the Late Woodland group was not receiving a greater number of extraregional immigrants than expected. Thus, both the biological distance and population genetic analyses indicate biological continuity between Late Woodland and early Mississippian populations within the central Illinois valley region.

Intraregional Mississippian relationships

Relationships among regional Mississippian samples can be investigated after excluding the Oneota and Late Woodland samples. While biological distances between populations

Table 5 Minimum biological distances among central Illinois valley Late Woodland and Mississippian groups based on the unbiased, scaled R matrix.

Group	Late Woodland	Morton	Eveland	Orendorf	Larson
Late Woodland	0.000000	0.018072	0.022891	0.044526	0.024810
Morton		0.000000	0.000452	0.011142	0.034314
Eveland			0.000000	0.000000	0.008969
Orendorf				0.000000	0.023811
Larson					0.000000

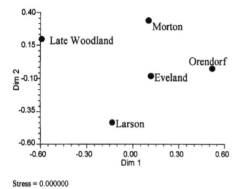

Stress = 0.000000

Figure 4 MDS map of the minimum biological distances among central Illinois valley Late Woodland and Mississippian samples.

Table 6 Relethford and Blangero analysis of differential gene flow: Late Woodland and Mississippian phenotypic distances to the centroid (r_{ii}), observed mean variance ($\bar{v}_i$), expected mean variances $E(\bar{v}_i)$ and residual variances $[\bar{v}_i - E(\bar{v}_i)]$.

Population	r_{ii}	$(\bar{v}_i)$	$E(\bar{v}_i)$	Residual $[\bar{v}_i - E(\bar{v}_i)]*$
Late Woodland	0.038502	0.951	0.955	−0.004
Eveland	0.000000	0.939	0.993	−0.054
Morton	0.005550	0.931	0.988	−0.057
Orendorf	0.002715	1.029	0.991	0.038
Larson	0.000000	1.023	0.993	0.030

Mean within-group phenotypic variance = 0.998
Unbiased minimum F_{st} = 0.005292
Standard error = 0.004661
*No residuals were significant at the 0.05 level

were small (Table 7), a multidiscriminant plot of only four samples is unrevealing and not included here. The Relethford and Blangero analysis (Table 8) shows that the Orendorf and Larson phase Mississippians were receiving more immigrants from an extraregional source, but the magnitude of external gene flow was small. Similarly, none of the Mississippian groups were receiving significantly less than expected external gene flow. This pattern is indicative of either external immigration of a consistent magnitude over time or a lack of significant interregional migration throughout the entire period.

Table 7   Minimum biological distances among central Illinois valley Mississippian groups based on the unbiased, scaled R matrix.

Group	Morton	Eveland	Orendorf	Larson
Morton	0.000000	0.001275	0.010660	0.030441
Eveland		0.000000	0.000000	0.007981
Orendorf			0.000000	0.020236
Larson				0.000000

Table 8   Relethford and Blangero analysis of differential gene flow: Mississippian phenotypic distances to the centroid (r_{ii}), observed mean variance ($\bar{v}_i$), expected mean variances $E(\bar{v}_i)$ and residual variances $[\bar{v}_i - E(\bar{v}_i)]$.

Population	r_{ii}	$(\bar{v}_i)$	$E(\bar{v}_i)$	Residual $[\bar{v}_i - E(\bar{v}_i)]$*
Eveland	0.000000	0.957	1.003	−0.046
Morton	0.007719	0.948	0.995	−0.047
Orendorf	0.000000	1.034	1.003	0.031
Larson	0.000000	1.026	1.003	0.023

Mean within-group phenotypic variance = 1.001
Unbiased minimum F_{st} = 0.001642
Standard error = 0.004799
*No residuals were significant at the 0.05 level

An interregional analysis of Late Woodland and Mississippian samples from the central and lower Illinois valleys provides support for the latter hypothesis. As shown by the MDS map in Figure 5, Late Woodland samples from both regions are closely related, suggesting significant amounts of interregional gene flow irrespective of geographic distance between sites. In contrast, Mississippian populations clustered exclusively by geographic region. Since geographic distances remained constant, it appears that cultural factors provided effective deterrents to gene flow. This pattern conforms to a classic isolation-by-distance model and indicates that there was little interregional migration throughout the Mississippian period.

It is important to note that overall genetic differentiation, as measured by the minimum

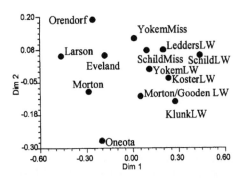

Stress = 0.069940

Figure 5 MDS map of the minimum biological distances among central and lower Illinois valley interregional samples.

F_{st}, decreased greatly when the Late Woodland and Oneota samples are removed. The F_{st} for all regional populations is 0.009 (Table 4), but the minimum genetic differentiation among the Mississippians is only 0.002. This low level of heterozygosity is typical of small tribal populations throughout the world (Jorde 1980). For instance, genetic variation within central Illinois valley Mississippian populations is smaller than differentiation among highly endogamous Jirel populations in Nepal (F_{st} = 0.01) (Relethford and Blangero 1990), as well as Iroquois (F_{st} = 0.053) (Langdon 1995) and Siberian samples (F_{st} = 0.109) (Ousley 1995). Comparisons of these F_{st} values are valid since they were all derived from continuous data.

Mississippian and Oneota relationships

To determine if there was continuity between Mississippians and the Oneota, the Late Woodland sample is removed from the analysis. According to the biodistance matrix (Table 9), distances between the Oneota and Mississippian groups are larger than any inter-group distance among Mississippians, except Morton and Larson (Fig. 6). The minimum genetic differentiation for the Mississippians and Oneota rises to 0.005, indicating that the Oneota sample contributed substantial variation to the regional gene pool (Table 10). Thus, within a regional context, there is little evidence of biological interaction between Bold Counselor Phase Oneota and Mississippians.

Table 9 Minimum biological distances among central Illinois valley Oneota and Mississippian groups based on the unbiased, scaled R matrix.

Group	Morton	Eveland	Orendorf	Larson	Oneota
Morton	0.000000	0.000000	0.009523	0.027943	0.025880
Eveland		0.000000	0.000000	0.005402	0.030992
Orendorf			0.000000	0.018413	0.067297
Larson				0.000000	0.032898
Oneota					0.000000

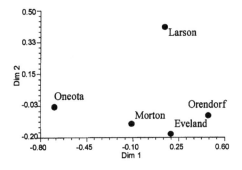

Stress = 0.000008

Figure 6 MDS map of the minimum biological distances among central Illinois valley Oneota and Mississippian samples.

Table 10 Relethford and Blangero analysis of differential gene flow: Oneota and Mississippian phenotypic distances to the centroid (r_{ii}), observed mean variance ($\bar{v}_i$), expected mean variances $E(\bar{v}_i)$ and residual variances $[\bar{v}_i - E(\bar{v}_i)]$.

Population	r_{ii}	$(\bar{v}_i)$	$E(\bar{v}_i)$	Residual $[\bar{v}_i - E(\bar{v}_i)]^*$
Eveland	0.000000	0.945	1.007	−0.062
Morton	0.004135	0.938	1.003	−0.065
Orendorf	0.006813	1.050	1.000	0.050
Larson	0.000000	1.042	1.007	0.035
Oneota	0.027796	0.966	0.979	−0.013

Mean within-group phenotypic variance = 0.988
Unbiased minimum F_{st} = 0.005292
Standard error = 0.004661
*No residuals were significant at the 0.05 level

A diachronic model of regional Mississippian interactions

The results of this study suggest that Mississippian development and expansion within the central Illinois valley was a local affair, such that *in situ* cultural transitions and intra-regional gene flow had a more significant impact on their population structure than inter-regional migration. The population genetic and biodistance results indicate that the Late Woodland and Eveland Mississippian samples were not as heterozygous as expected if the Mississippians were a genetically distinct population that entered the region around AD 1050. Though these interpretations are based on a pooled Late Woodland sample, the process of biocultural change in the central Illinois valley is entirely consistent with the pattern of cultural transition in the lower Illinois valley (Droessler 1981). Thus, at this time there is no evidence to suggest large-scale movement of Mississippians into either region between AD 1000 and 1100.

As predicted by ceramic analyses (Conrad 1991; Harn 1991a), the biodistance and population genetic results are indicative of a Mississippian lineage that is continuous through time and relatively unaffected by external gene flow (Konigsberg 1987; Relethford and Blangero 1990). Slight changes in the population structure of Orendorf and Larson phase samples are indicative only of small-scale immigration, not mass population movements associated with the decline of Cahokia or the simultaneous rise of multiple regional polities within the region. This interpretation is also appropriate if some of the populations were contemporaneous rather than sequential. Under this scenario, the results indicate that intraregional gene flow among contemporary populations was extensive and immigration from outside of the region was nominal, even during periods of great cultural upheaval and change. Thus, despite unclear microchronologies, the inference remains that sociopolitical and demographic processes in the American Bottom had little impact on Mississippian population structure in the central Illinois valley.

The pattern of intraregional biological continuity appears to be broken upon the arrival of the Oneota. The Oneota were distinct from all Mississippian populations, particularly Orendorf and Larson, the later Mississippian samples. Although the conclusions should be viewed tentatively since only one Oneota skeletal sample is available for study, they do support a model of Oneota expansion into the region as Mississippians retreated.

Conclusions

The Relethford and Blangero (1990) population genetics model is an ideal method to apply to archaeological problems in the central Illinois valley for it discriminates between the processes of extraregional immigration and intraregional biological continuity. This study has shown that, although small-scale interregional immigration may have been associated with the decline of Cahokia, intraregional growth and population shuffling were the dominant demographic processes that shaped the population structure of central Illinois valley Mississippians. Further, the biological evidence supports the most recent archaeological model that the central Illinois valley Mississippian populations were a relatively autonomous entity in the Mississippian world.

Acknowledgements

I would like to give special thanks to John Relethford whose professionalism, patience and boundless knowledge lies at the root of this work. Thanks also go to Jane Buikstra, Lyle Konigsberg, George Milner and John Blangero for their direct contributions to this project. I would like to acknowledge Alan Harn, Duane Esarey, Della Cook and Larry Conrad for facilitating data collection and sharing their vast archaeological knowledge and insight. This work was supported by a grant from the Wenner-Gren Foundation for Anthropological Research (Gr. 5898).

Department of Anthropology
Iowa State University
Ames, Iowa 50011-1050, USA

References

Anderson, D. G. 1994. *The Savannah River Chiefdoms: Political Change in the Late Prehistoric Southeast*. Tuscaloosa: University of Alabama Press.

Anderson, D. G. 1996. Chiefly cycling and large-scale abandonments as viewed from the Savannah River Basin. In *Political Structure and Change in the Prehistoric Southeastern United States* (ed. John F. Scarry). Gainesville: University Press of Florida, pp. 150–91.

Bender, M., Bryson, R. A. and Baerreis, D. A. 1975. University of Wisconsin radiocarbon dates XII. *Radiocarbon*, 17: 121–34.

Blakely, M. 1973. Biological variation among and between two prehistoric Indian populations at Dickson Mound. Unpublished PhD dissertation. Indiana University, Bloomington.

Buikstra, J. E. 1977. Biocultural dimensions of archeological study: a regional perspective. In *Biocultural Adaptation in Prehistoric America* (ed. R. L. Blakely). Athens: University of Georgia Press, pp. 67–84.

Buikstra, J. E. and Milner, G. R. 1989. *The Dickson Mounds Site: An Annotated Bibliography.* Springfield: Illinois State Museum. Reports of Investigations, No. 44.

Buikstra, J. E. and Ubelaker, D. H. (eds) 1994. *Standards for Data Collection from Human Skeletal Remains.* Fayetteville: Arkansas Archeological Survey Research Series No. 44.

Caldwell, J. R. 1967. New discoveries at Dickson Mounds. *The Living Museum*, 29: 139–42.

Cheverud, J. M. 1988. A comparison of genetic and phenotypic correlations. *Evolution*, 42: 958–68.

Cole, F. and Deuel, T. 1937. *Rediscovering Illinois: Archaeological Explorations in and around Fulton County.* Chicago: University of Chicago Press.

Conner, M. D. 1984. Population structure and biological variation in the Late Woodland of west-central Illinois. PhD dissertation. Department of Anthropology, University of Chicago.

Conner, M. D. (ed.) 1985. *The Hill Creek Homestead and Late Mississippian Settlement in the Lower Illinois Valley.* Kampsville, Illinois: Center for American Archeology, Kampsville Archeological Center, Research Series, Vol. 1.

Conrad, L. A. 1991. The Middle Mississippian cultures of the Central Illinois Valley. In *Cahokia and the Hinterlands: Middle Mississippian Cultures of the Midwest* (eds T. E. Emerson and R. B. Lewis). Urbana: University of Illinois Press, pp. 119–56.

Conrad, L. A. and Esarey, D. n.d. The Bold Counselor phase Oneota occupation of the Central Illinois River Valley. Unpublished manuscript on file at Dickson Mounds Museum, Lewistown, Illinois.

Dincauze, D. F. and Hasenstab, R. J. 1989. Explaining the Iroquois: tribalization on a prehistoric periphery. In *Centre and Periphery: Comparative Studies in Archaeology* (ed. Timothy C. Champion). London: Unwin Hyman, pp. 67–87.

Droessler, J. 1976. Late Woodland Maples Mills focus populations in the Illinois valley: cultural affinities and biological distance. *Indiana Academy of Science*, Proceedings No. 85, pp. 66–73.

Droessler, J. 1981. *Craniometry and Biological Distance: Biocultural Continuity and Change at the Late Woodland–Mississippian Interface.* Evanston, IL: Center for American Archaeology at Northwestern University.

Emerson, T. E. 1991. Some perspectives on Cahokia and the northern Mississippian expansion. In *Cahokia and the Hinterlands: Middle Mississippian Cultures of the Midwest* (eds E. Emerson and R. B. Lewis). Urbana: University of Illinois Press, pp. 221–36.

Emerson, T. E. and Lewis, R. B. (eds) 1991. *Cahokia and the Hinterlands: Middle Mississippian Cultures of the Midwest.* Urbana: University of Illinois Press.

Esarey, D. 1997. The Late Woodland Maple Mills and Mossville Phase sequence in the central Illinois River valley. Paper presented at the Urbana Late Woodland Conference, Urbana, Illinois.

Esarey, D. and Conrad, L. A. 1981. The Orendorf site preliminary working papers. Archaeological Research Laboratory, Western Illinois University, Macomb.

Esarey, D. and Santure, S. K. 1990. The Morton site component and the Bold Counselor phase. In *Archaeological Investigations at the Morton Village and Norris Farms 36 Cemetery* (eds S. K. Santure, A. D. Harn and D. Esarey). Springfield: Illinois State Museum Reports of Investigations, No. 45, pp. 162–6.

Fowler, M. L. and Hall, R. L. 1972. Archaeological phases at Cahokia. *Papers in Anthropology* 1. Springfield: Illinois State Museum.

Gibbon, G. 1982. Oneota origins revisited. In *Oneota Studies* (ed. Guy E. Gibbon). Minneapolis: University of Minnesota, Publications in Anthropology No. 1, pp. 85–90.

Goldstein, L. G. 1980. *Mississippian Mortuary Practices: A Case Study of Two Cemeteries in the Lower Illinois Valley.* Evanston: Northwestern University Archeological Program, Scientific Papers No. 4.

Goodman, A. H. and Armelagos, G. J. 1985. Disease and death at Dr Dickson's Mounds. *Natural History*, 94(9): 12–18.

Goodman, A. H., Lallo, J. W., Armelagos, G. J. and Rose, J. C. 1984. Health changes at Dickson Mounds, Illinois (AD 950–1300). In *Paleopathology at the Origins of Agriculture* (eds M. N. Cohen and G. G. Armelagos). Orlando: Academic Press, pp. 271–305.

Griffin, J. B. 1967. Eastern North American archaeology: a summary. *Science*, 156: 175–91.

Hall, R. L. 1991. Cahokia identity and interaction models of Cahokia Mississippian. In *Cahokia and the Hinterlands: Middle Mississippian Cultures of the Midwest* (eds E. Emerson and R. B. Lewis). Urbana: University of Illinois Press, pp. 3–34.

Hally, D. J. 1996. Platform mound construction and the instability of Mississippian chiefdoms. In *Political Structure and Change in the Prehistoric Southeastern United States* (ed. J. F. Scarry). Gainesville: University Press of Florida, pp. 92–127.

Harn, A. D. 1975. Cahokia and the Mississippian emergence in the Spoon River area of Illinois. *Transactions, Illinois State Academy of Science*, 68: 414–34.

Harn, A. D. 1978. Mississippian settlement patterns in the Central Illinois River Valley. In *Mississippian Settlement Patterns* (ed. B. D. Smith). New York: Academic Press, pp. 233–68.

Harn, A. D. 1980. *The Prehistory of Dickson Mounds: The Dickson Excavations*. Springfield: Illinois State Museum Reports of Investigations, No. 35.

Harn, A. D. 1991a. The Eveland site: inroad to Spoon River Mississippian society. In *New Perspectives on Cahokia: Views from the Periphery* (ed. J. B. Stoltman). Madison: Prehistory Press, Monographs in World Archaeology, No. 2, pp. 129–53.

Harn, A. D. 1991b. Comments on subsistence, seasonality, and site function at upland subsidaries in the Spoon River area: Mississippianization at work on the northern frontier. In *Cahokia and the Hinterlands: Middle Mississippian Cultures of the Midwest* (eds T. E. Emerson and R. B. Lewis). Urbana: University of Illinois Press, pp. 157–63.

Harn, A. D. 1994. *Variation in Mississippian Settlement Patterns: The Larson Settlement System in the Central Illinois River Valley*. Springfield: Illinois State Museum Reports of Investigations, No. 50.

Harpending, H. and Jenkins, T. 1973. Genetic distance among southern African populations. In *Methods and Theories of Anthropological Genetics* (eds M. H. Crawford and P. L. Workman). Albuquerque: New Mexico Press, pp. 177–99.

Harpending, H. and Ward, R. H. 1982. Chemical systematics and human populations. In *Biochemical Aspects of Evolutionary Biology* (ed. M. H. Nitecki). Chicago: University of Chicago Press, pp. 213–56.

Jorde, L. B. 1980. The genetic structure of subdivided human populations. In *Current Developments in Anthropological Genetics* (eds James H. Mielke and Michael M. Crawford). New York: Plenum Press, pp. 135–208.

Kelly, J. C. 1990. The emergence of Mississippian culture in the American Bottom region. In *The Mississippian Emergence* (ed. B. D. Smith). Washington, DC: Smithsonian Press, pp. 113–52.

Kelly, J. E. 1991a. Cahokia and its role as a gateway center in interregional exchange. In *Cahokia and the Hinterlands: Middle Mississippian Cultures of the Midwest* (eds T. E. Emerson and R. B. Lewis). Urbana: University of Illinois Press, pp. 61–80.

Kelly, J. E. 1991b. The evidence for prehistoric exchange and its implications for the development of Cahokia. In *New Perspectives on Cahokia: Views from the Periphery* (ed. J. B. Stoltman). Madison: Prehistory Press, Monographs in World Archaeology, No. 2, pp. 65–89.

Konigsberg, L. W. 1987. Population genetic models for interpreting prehistoric intra-cemetery biological variation. PhD dissertation. Department of Anthropology, Northwestern University, Chicago.

Konigsberg, L. W. 1988. Migration models of prehistoric postmarital residence. *American Journal of Physical Anthropology*, 77: 471–82.

Konigsberg, L. W. 1990a. Analysis of prehistoric biological variation under a model of isolation by geographic and temporal distance. *Human Biology*, 62(1): 49–70.

Konigsberg, L. W. 1990b. Temporal aspects of biological distance: serial correlation and trend in a prehistoric skeletal lineage. *American Journal of Physical Anthropology*, 82: 45–52.

Konigsberg, L. W. and Ousley, S. D. 1995. Multivariate quantitative genetics of anthropometric traits from the Boas data. *Human Biology*, 67: 481–98.

Kruskal, J. B. 1964. Nonmetric multidimensional scaling: A numerical method. *Psychometrika*, 29: 1–27, 115–29.

Langdon, S. P. 1995. Biological relationships among the Iroquois. *Human Biology*, 67: 355–74.

Miller, R. G. 1974. The jackknife – a review. *Biometrika*, 61(1): 1–15.

Milner, G. R. 1990. The late prehistoric Cahokia cultural system of the Mississippi River Valley: Foundations, florescence, and fragmentation. *Journal of World Prehistory*, 4(1): 1–43.

Milner, G. R. 1991. American Bottom Mississippian culture: internal developments and external relations. In *New Perspectives on Cahokia: Views from the Periphery* (ed. J. B. Stoltman). Madison: Prehistory Press, Monographs in World Archaeology, No. 2, pp. 29-48.

Milner, G. R. 1996. Development and dissolution of a Mississippian society in the American Bottom, Illinois. In *Political Structure and Change in the Prehistoric Southeastern United States* (ed. J. F. Scarry). Gainesville: University Press of Florida, pp. 27–52.

Milner, G. R., Smith, V. G. and Anderson, E. 1991. Conflict, mortality, and community health in an Illinois Oneota population. In *Between Bands and States* (ed. S. A. Gregg). Carbondale: Southern Illinois University, Center for Archaeological Investigations, Occasional Paper No. 9, pp. 245–64.

Muller, J. 1997. *Mississippian Political Economy*. New York: Plenum Press.

Ousley, S. D. 1995. Relationships between Eskimos, Amerindians, and Aleuts: old data, new perspectives. *Human Biology*, 67: 427–58.

Pauketat, T. R. 1994. *The Ascent of Chiefs: Cahokia and Mississippian Politics in Native North America*. Tuscaloosa: University of Alabama Press.

Porter, J. W. 1969. The Mitchell site and prehistoric exchange systems at Cahokia: AD 1000 ± 300. In *Explorations into Cahokia Archaeology* (ed. M. L. Fowler). Urbana: Illinois Archaeological Survey Bulletin No. 7, pp. 137–64.

Relethford, J. H. 1994. Craniometric variation among modern human populations *American Journal of Physical Anthropology*, 95: 53–62.

Relethford, J. H. 1996. Genetic drift can obscure population history: problem and solution. *Human Biology*, 68: 29–44.

Relethford, J. H. and Blangero, J. 1990. Detection of differential gene flow from patterns of quantitative variation. *Human Biology*, 62: 5–25.

Relethford, J. H. and Harpending, H. 1994. Craniometric variation, genetic theory, and modern human origins. *American Journal of Physical Anthropology*, 95: 249–70.

Relethford, J. H. and Lees, F. C. 1982. The use of quantitative traits in the study of human population structure. *Yearbook of Physical Anthropology*, 25: 113–32.

Relethford, J. H., Crawford, M. N. and Blangero, J. 1997. Genetic drift and gene flow in post-famine Ireland. *Human Biology*, 69: 443–65.

Santure, S. K. 1981. The changing community plan of settlement C. In *The Orendorf Site Preliminary Working Papers* (eds D. Esarey and L. A. Conrad). Macomb: Western Illinois University, Archaeological Research Laboratory, pp. 5–80.

Santure, S. K. and Esarey, D. 1990. Analysis of artifacts from the Oneota mortuary component. In *Archaeological Investigations at the Morton Village and Norris Farms 36 Cemetery* (eds S. K. Santure, A. D. Harn and D. Esarey). Springfield: Illinois State Museum Reports of Investigations, No. 45, pp. 75–110.

Schiffman, S., Reynolds, M. L. and Young, F. W. 1981. *Introduction to Multidimensional Scaling: Theory, Methods and Applications*. New York: Academic Press.

Smith, Bruce D. (ed.) 1990. *The Mississippian Emergence*. Washington DC: Smithsonian Institution Press.

Steadman, D. W. 1997. Population genetic analysis of regional and interregional prehistoric gene flow in west-central Illinois. PhD dissertation. Department of Anthropology, University of Chicago.

Williams-Blangero, S. and Blangero, J. 1989. Anthropometric variation and the genetic structure of the Jirels of Nepal. *Human Biology*, 62: 131–46.

Williams-Blangero, S. and Blangero, J. 1990. Effects of population structure on within-group variation in the Jirels of Nepal. *Human Biology*, 61: 1–12.

Wolf, D. J. 1977. Middle Mississippian: a prehistoric cultural system viewed from a biological perspective. In *Biocultural Adaptation in Prehistoric America* (ed. R. L. Blakely). Athens: University of Georgia Press, pp. 27–44.

Using stable nitrogen-isotopes to study weaning behavior in past populations

Mark R. Schurr

Abstract

Several different methods have been used to explore weaning behavior in past populations, including demographic profiles, non-specific osteological indicators of stress, and bone chemistry studies. Stable nitrogen-isotope ratios of prehistoric bone proteins provide an especially useful method for reconstructing the weaning patterns of archaeological populations. A demographic measure of fertility (the D30+/D5+ ratio) is compared with age-related changes in stable nitrogen-isotope ratios for human burials from one historic cemetery and two prehistoric ones. The stable nitrogen-isotope ratios show that each population had a characteristic and distinctive combination of weaning time and rate, and that neither the timing nor tempo of weaning was clearly correlated with the demographic measure of fertility. These results demonstrate the feasibility of using stable nitrogen-isotope ratios to compare weaning patterns and fertility in past populations. This example also shows that the relationship between fertility and weaning behavior is complex.

Keywords

Paleodemography; weaning; stable nitrogen-isotopes; eastern North America; childhood diet.

Introduction

The apparent age-specific mortality in a skeletal series is not determinant in the sense that age distributions are not determined by a single variable. This is a major disadvantage of using age profiles of skeletal series as the sole measure of demographic characteristics of a past population. In its most extreme interpretation, this observation leads to a complete rejection of paleodemography (Boquet-Appel and Masset 1982). A less extreme position implies that paleodemographic mortality profiles may have so many potential underlying causes that they cannot be reliably interpreted with current knowledge (Wood et al. 1992). For example, a high proportion of infant burials can be interpreted as evidence for high infant mortality due to weaning, or for high fertility. Paleodemographic data from skeletal

World Archaeology Vol. 30(2): 327–342 *Population and Demography*
© Routledge 1998 0043–8243

series must be interpreted within the context of many different sources of data about fertility and mortality. It may be impossible to determine the relative contributions of fertility and mortality or the role of weaning in mortality unless independent evidence about these aspects of past human behavior is available. Thus, the development of new methods for examining aspects of past human biology is extremely important for understanding the demography of past populations. Stable nitrogen-isotope ratios of protein extracted from human skeletons have recently been used to identify infant feeding practices in past populations (Fogel et al. 1989; Katzenberg et al. 1993; Schurr 1997). This is one example of a new technique than can be used to measure one or more variables that could not be measured before. In this example, a demographic measure of fertility (the D30+/D5+ ratio) is compared with weaning times and rates determined with stable nitrogen-isotope ratios to compare fertility and weaning behavior in three archaeological populations.

Estimating weaning and fertility in past populations

Estimating weaning time

For some historic populations, weaning practices and female fertility can be estimated from historic records. In many cases though, the necessary information is not available, and written documents are of course completely unavailable for prehistoric populations. Several different methods have been used to estimate weaning times in past populations. These include demographic methods (Clarke 1977; Cook 1976; Lallo 1973), non-specific measures of stress (Clarke 1980; Corruccini et al. 1985; Goodman and Rose 1990; Larsen 1995; Martin et al. 1985), and bone chemistry studies (Fogel et al. 1989; Katzenberg et al. 1996; Katzenberg et al. 1993; Schurr 1997; Sillen and Smith 1984; White and Schwarcz 1994). Katzenberg et al. (1996) provide an excellent review of the archaeological uses of the term 'weaning' and clearly explain why weaning is best viewed as a process rather than an event.

Demographic measures

Demographic measures were the earliest measures used to infer weaning behavior in past populations. The age at death of juveniles can be determined with precisions ranging from a few months to a few years using osteological indicators of age such as the degree of dental development, dental wear, limb bone growth rates, and timing of epiphysial closures (Bass 1971; Schwartz 1995; Ubelaker 1978). The numbers of individuals in the sample that died at each age or age interval are used to construct a life table and to calculate various demographic measures such as probability of dying or mortality for each age group. If the skeletal series provides an accurate representation of the demographic structure of the population, then weaning time might be revealed by a peak in early childhood mortality caused by poor nutrition, greater exposure to environmental pathogens, or the like.

The uncritical use of life tables from skeletal samples has been widely and justifiably criticized (most recently by Wood et al. 1992). Problems of under-enumeration of infants, whose fragile remains are less likely to be preserved than the more robust remains of adults, or who may not even have been buried by some cultures, are well recognized. It has also been shown that juvenile mortality profiles from skeletal series are more strongly associated with fertility than they are with mortality (Buikstra et al. 1986; Sattenspiel and

Harpending 1983). As noted above, it cannot be determined whether high numbers of infants reflect high infant mortality or high fertility solely on the basis of a life table.

Non-specific measures of biological stress

Anthropologists have used non-specific measures of biological stress (such as Harris lines or linear enamel hypoplasias) to avoid the limitations of demographic profiles. As their name suggests, these non-specific measures of biological stress can have many causes (Katzenberg et al. 1996). Thus, for example, there is no certainty that a peak in the intensity of enamel hypoplasias at a given age was produced by weaning at that age, and it is not possible to distinguish the effects of diet from other possible stresses using these methods. If a population experienced more opportunities for exposure to infectious disease, the frequency of developmental defects such as linear enamel hypoplasias among infants could increase without a change in weaning behavior or nutritional status.

Chemical methods

Chemical methods for the reconstruction of prehistoric diet offer the best potential for examining weaning behavior in prehistoric populations because they provide the most specific information about the actual content of the diet itself. Based on the principle that 'you are what you eat', chemical methods are used to determine the chemical composition of bone which can then be related to the consumption of foods with differing chemical compositions. Two primary chemical phases are preserved in ancient human bone. The organic phase largely consists of the protein collagen, a very high molecular weight protein that is very resistant to degradation compared to most other proteins. Under favorable conditions, collagen can be preserved for up to 70,000 years (Bocherens et al. 1994). The collagen portion of bone provides an organic support for the inorganic phase, the bone mineral calcium hydroxyapatite, which is largely composed of calcium and phosphate ions mixed with small amounts of associated trace elements. Appropriate chemical techniques have been developed for the analysis of both chemical phases (Katzenberg 1992; Schwarcz and Schoeninger 1991). These techniques include procedures to purify collagen that is contaminated or degraded, and methods to identify specimens that have been so badly degraded that they are unlikely to reliably reflect the original diet. The criteria most commonly used to verify the integrity of collagen samples include extraction yield (Ambrose 1990) and the carbon to nitrogen (C/N) ratio of the collagen (DeNiro 1985).

The ratio of strontium to calcium (Sr/Ca) in bone mineral has been used to determine weaning time in a prehistoric population from arid Sudanese Nubia (Sillen and Smith 1984). However, as the mineral phase of bone is relatively susceptible to contamination or alteration when exposed to moisture, the analysis of Sr/Ca ratios may not be easily applied to samples from areas or sites where the soil moisture is high. The general utility of Sr/Ca ratios has not been determined.

Stable nitrogen-isotope ratios are the most broadly applicable of the two chemical methods because the organic portion of the bone is more resistant to contamination after burial than the inorganic fraction is, and the presence of contaminants or degraded proteins that might provide misleading results can be identified during analysis. Stable isotope analysis can also be used to analyze other proteins such as those in hair or nails, and can therefore be applied to living populations for comparative purposes (Fogel et al. 1989; Schoeller et al. 1986).

The ratio of the stable nitrogen-isotopes nitrogen-15 to nitrogen-14 (the ratio ^{15}N/^{14}N) is expressed as δ^{15}N in 'per mil' [‰] using the standard 'delta' notation. Changing δ^{15}N values of bone collagen with age provide evidence of prehistoric weaning behavior (Fogel et al. 1989; Katzenberg et al. 1993; Schurr 1997). Because collagen is a protein, it contains relatively large amounts of nitrogen. The isotopic composition of the nitrogen in collagen reflects that of dietary proteins. A new-born infant has an isotopic composition that appears identical to that of its mother (Katzenberg et al. 1996). For a breast-feeding child, the only source of dietary nitrogen is via the mother's milk, and the isotopic composition of the child's collagen will therefore be directly related to that of breast-milk. Breast-milk is enriched in ^{15}N by 2 to 3 per mil compared to the mother's diet (Fogel et al. 1989; Steele and Daniel 1978). This difference is an example of a fractionation effect, produced when the metabolic processes that synthesize a tissue preferentially incorporate one isotope into the end product over another. As a breast-feeding infant synthesizes new bone collagen over time, the ^{15}N content of the new collagen will increase, because the diet contains more ^{15}N than that of the mother. If breast-milk was the only food consumed, and nursing continued indefinitely, the δ^{15}N value of the bone collagen would eventually approach a maximum value that would be 2 to 3 per mil higher than the mother's diet. Most foods contain less ^{15}N than breast-milk, especially typical weaning foods such as cereal (Katzenberg et al. 1993). Unless a child consumed a very unusual diet, the onset of weaning will be marked by a gradual decline in the δ^{15}N value of collagen as new foods that contain less ^{15}N than breast-milk enter the diet, and as new collagen reflecting the lower ^{15}N content of the new diet is synthesized. The age profile of nitrogen stable-isotope ratios will therefore follow the pattern shown in Figure 1, with an increase in δ^{15}N values during the first months of life when nursing occurs. A maximum value will be reached at the onset of weaning, followed by a gradual decline as weaning continues. The onset of the decline in δ^{15}N values after the peak value is reached indicates that weaning has begun. The rate of the decline after the onset of weaning reflects the isotopic content of the juvenile diet, how rapidly new foods replace breast-milk, the rate at which new collagen is synthesized, and any fractionation effects that operated when the collagen was synthesized.

Stable nitrogen-isotope ratios have not been widely used to study prehistoric weaning

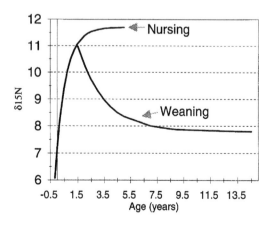

Figure 1 Expected changes in stable nitrogen-isotope ratios with age during nursing and weaning.

for several reasons. First, the technique is relatively new and is not widely known. Second, it has been technically difficult and time-consuming to prepare samples for nitrogen isotope analysis because nitrogen gas is relatively difficult to purify and samples can easily be contaminated by atmospheric nitrogen. New continuous flow instrument configurations, which convert samples into gas with an elemental analyzer, purify the gases chromatographically, and then immediately measure the isotope ratios of the gases, have eliminated these technical barriers (Newman 1996). Finally, a relatively large sample of subadult skeletons (from 15 to 20) that are accurately aged must be available. This means that only relatively large skeletal series are suitable for this type of study. And although many such series from throughout the world are available, the juvenile portions of such series have often been neglected in paleobiological studies.

Estimating fertility

The earliest method used to estimate prehistoric fertility was by the use of so-called 'parity pits' (Angel 1969). This method is no longer considered to be reliable (Buikstra et al. 1986). The best available estimate of prehistoric fertility is based on a demographic measure (similar to the concept of the use of demographic measures for weaning). Computer simulations have shown that the ratio D30+/D5+, the ratio of individuals aged over age 30 (D30+) to individuals over age 5 (D5+) is strongly correlated with fertility (Buikstra et al. 1986; Sattenspiel and Harpending 1983). When ages are available for each individual in the series, this ratio can easily be calculated from burial data.

An example application

Suitable samples are available to show how stable nitrogen-isotope ratios and demographic estimates of fertility can be used to compare weaning and reproductive behaviors across past populations. Three sites in North America (Fig. 2) have produced data that are suitable for demonstrating how stable nitrogen-isotope ratios can be used to examine relations between fertility and weaning. The stable nitrogen-isotope ratios for juvenile burials from these sites, the methods used to evaluate the reliability of the isotope ratios, and detailed discussions of the methods used to age the skeletons were originally reported elsewhere (Katzenberg and Pfeiffer 1995; Katzenberg et al. 1993; Schurr 1997). This article uses the reliable isotope ratios (based on extraction yields and C/N ratios) and the age determinations from the original reports to examine issues of weaning and demography that were not examined in the original publications. The three sites are scattered in space and time but illustrate the potential uses of stable nitrogen-isotopes for the study of childhood diets in ancient populations. The sites are also used to explore the relationships between fertility and weaning amongst agriculturalists.

The Angel site

The Angel site was a late prehistoric Middle Mississippian civic and ceremonial center along the Ohio River in southern Indiana (Black 1967). It was inhabited between about

Figure 2   Locations of Angel, MacPherson, and Prospect Hill.

AD 1200 to 1450 (Hilgeman 1996). Excavations conducted over a span of 50 years recovered human remains from more than 300 individuals, most of which date to around AD 1350 (Schurr 1992). The site was the central settlement of a chiefdom whose members supported themselves through maize agriculture and the hunting and gathering of wild resources. The dog was the only domesticated animal. It is not known if dogs were eaten at Angel, as was the often the case at later Historic Period Native American sites (Heidenreich 1971; Wrong 1939).

Stable carbon-isotope ratios of human burials from Angel show that the Angel chiefdom relied on intensive maize cultivation to support its population (Schurr and Schoeninger 1995). The stable carbon-isotope ratio is the ratio of carbon-13 (^{13}C) to carbon-12 (^{12}C). It is expressed using the standard 'delta' notation ($\delta^{13}C$) in per mil (‰) relative to the PeeDeeBelemnite (PDB) standard. Because most organic materials have a lower ^{13}C content than the PDB standard, most biological materials have $\delta^{13}C$ values that are less than 0.0 (and hence represented with negative numbers). In areas of eastern North America where marine foods were not consumed, more positive (less negative)

δ^{13}C values indicate higher maize consumption. The average adult δ^{13}C for Angel was –9.0 per mil (± 1.07, n = 47) (Schurr 1992), a value indicating relatively high maize consumption compared to most other sites in eastern North America (Buikstra et al. 1988).

The MacPherson site

The MacPherson site was a Proto-Historic village located in what is now Ontario, Canada (Katzenberg et al. 1993). The site was inhabited by the Neutrals, an Iroquoian tribe, during the sixteenth century when extensive contact between Native Americans and Europeans was just beginning in this area. The site expanded in size over several decades to ultimately house a maximum population of approximately 725 persons. The expansion appears to have been partially due to successive waves of immigration. The mortuary sample from the site is relatively small, with only 31 burials recovered by excavation.

The subsistence activities at MacPherson were similar to those at Angel, but stable carbon- and nitrogen-isotope ratios show that the MacPherson population was less agricultural than the Angel population in the sense that they consumed less maize. The average δ^{13}C value of –10.6 per mil (± 0.94, n = 15) for adults from MacPherson (calculated from Katzenberg et al. (1993); Table 1) is slightly but significantly lower than the average adult δ^{13}C value for Angel adults. Stable nitrogen-isotope ratios from MacPherson show that fish from the Great Lakes were an important part of the diet (Katzenberg 1989).

The MacPherson site was inhabited during a period of rapid demographic change. The site was established shortly after an epidemic of European diseases had sharply reduced the indigenous population. There is abundant archaeological and historical evidence for immigration and regional conflict as well (Mason 1981). These would also have influenced the demographic structure of the population.

Prospect Hill

The Prospect Hill site, also in Canada, was a Methodist cemetery in New Market, Ontario, used between about AD 1824 and 1879 (Katzenberg and Pfeiffer 1995; Pfeiffer et al. 1989). New Market was a relatively small town by modern standards with a population of around 1,400. This is similar in magnitude to population estimates for Angel (Black 1967; Green and Munson 1978) and about twice the size of the maximum estimate for MacPherson. Most of the people buried in the cemetery probably lived in town, supporting themselves by trade or crafts, and were not directly involved in agriculture. In that sense, it was the most agriculturally dependent site.

The mean δ^{13}C value for adults from MacPherson was –19.6 per mil (± 0.66, n = 27) (calculated from Katzenberg and Pfeiffer (1995); Table 1), indicating very little use of C4 plants. Maize or cane sugar (not available to the inhabitants of the Native American sites) were probably consumed in small amounts (Katzenberg and Pfeiffer 1995).

Fertility

At all three sites, bone preservation was excellent so that all age ranges were represented. In addition, all three sites have produced plausible age distributions suggesting that all members of the population were buried on site. Fertility at each site was estimated by calculating the ratio D30+/D5+ for each site from the previously published data on the ages of burials at the site (Table 1). Fertility is inversely related to the D30+/D5+ ratio, with lower values of D30+/D5+ correlating with higher fertility. The MacPherson population appears to have had the highest fertility, followed closely by the Angel population, with Prospect Hill having a higher D30+/D5+ than the two Native American sites (and thus a lower apparent fertility). The ratios of D30+/D5+ for the two prehistoric sites are very similar to values reported for late prehistoric agriculturalists of the Illinois Valley region (Buikstra et al. 1986). Relatively high levels of fertility seem to be characteristic of many populations in eastern North America during the Late Prehistoric period.

Buikstra et al. (1986) use a complicated graphical method to estimate 95 per cent confidence intervals for the D30+/D5+ ratios. Their method is not reproduced here, but it should be noted that their average confidence interval is approximately ± 0.1000. The difference between the D30+/D5+ ratios for Angel and MacPherson are much smaller than this, and the ratios may not be significantly different, especially given the small size of the MacPherson sample. The D30+/D5+ ratio for Prospect Hill appears to be very different from those of the two Native American sites.

Prospect Hill seems to have a much lower fertility, but this might also indicate lower mortality as well. The site was occupied after scientific medical ideas began to improve health and sanitation. The town had several doctors and one dentist, so professional medical care was available (Katzenberg and Pfeiffer 1995). As comparisons are more likely to be meaningful between populations with similar medical practices, caution must be used when comparing the demographic profiles of these sites. None of these sites appears to fit the stable population model. The MacPherson site was inhabited just after a demographic catastrophe. The inhabitants of Prospect Hill were participants in the great demographic transition to lower mortality and fertility of the nineteenth and twentieth centuries. The demographic circumstances of the Angel site are less clear because the site was abandoned around AD 1450 and no historic documents are available from the region. The abandonment of the Angel site and the accompanying depopulation of the surrounding region (Williams 1990) suggests some sort of demographic collapse or extensive out-migration occurred.

Weaning

Adult stable nitrogen-isotope ratios vary considerably between the sites, with the Canadian sites having much higher values than Angel. Values for adults from each of the sites show that adult diets at the Canadian sites contained much higher levels of ^{15}N than was the case for Angel (Table 2). This reflects differing diets at each of the sites. At Angel,

Table 1 Calculation of the D30+D5+ ratios.

Site	N	D30+	D5+	D30/D5+
Angel	281	87	179	0.4860
MacPherson	29	7	17	0.4118
Prospect Hill	77	34	52	0.6538

Table 2 Estimates of weaning parameters from isotopic data.

Site	Time period	Mean adult $\delta^{15}N$	Mean child $\delta^{15}N$ (weaned)	Age of weaning onset (years)
Angel	Prehistoric	8.1	7.8	~1.75
MacPherson	Proto-Historic	11.4	12.0	~0.75
Prospect Hill	Historic	12.2	12.0	~1.25

the primary sources of dietary nitrogen were maize, wild plants, and wild animals that inhabited a midcontinental riverine ecosystem. At MacPherson, higher $\delta^{15}N$ values reflect the consumption of animals and fish from the Great Lakes ecosystem with higher average ^{15}N contents than ones from terrestrial ecosystems (Katzenberg 1989). As discussed above, maize was slightly less important in the MacPherson diet than it was at Angel, and more consumption of meat and fish at MacPherson may also have increased $\delta^{15}N$ values (Minagawa and Wada 1984; Schoeninger 1985; Schoeninger et al. 1983). The stable nitrogen-isotope ratios for the Prospect Hill burials are very similar to those from Mac-Pherson, suggesting that the types and amounts of protein in both Canadian diets were relatively similar, despite their different forms (with domesticated animals probably being a major source of dietary protein at Prospect Hill).

Because of the differences in the adult diets at each of the sites, it was necessary to normalize the juvenile data so that comparisons could be made between the sites. The childhood data were normalized using the equation:

$$\delta^{15}N_{norm} = (\delta^{15}N - \delta^{15}N_{child})/3.6$$

where:

$\delta^{15}N_{norm}$ = the normalized value for each individual

$\delta^{15}N$ = the stable nitrogen-isotope ratio for each individual as originally reported

$\delta^{15}N_{child}$ = the average $\delta^{15}N$ value for all the children from the site aged 5 to 10 years as a baseline estimate of the isotopic composition produced by the post-weaning diet

3.6 = an estimate of the typical enrichment between the mother's diet and the isotopic composition of her milk. This value has not been well-established, and has been estimated to range from 2.4 per mil (Katzenberg et al. 1996) to 3.6 per mil (Steele and Daniel 1978). The value of 3.6 probably represents a maximum estimate for this fractionation effect and is consistent with the results from the Angel site (see below).

The normalized data were then grouped into six month intervals and the average normalized value for each interval was plotted against age using the midpoint of the age interval as the X coordinate (Fig. 3).

Each site reaches its maximum value at a different age (Table 2). MacPherson reaches its maximum at 0.75 years, Prospect Hill reaches its maximum at 1.25 years, and Angel reaches its maximum at 1.75 years. As discussed above, weaning can be detected when the $\delta^{15}N$ values begin to decline after reaching their maximum value. This suggests that

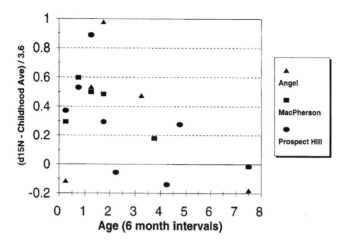

Figure 3 Normalized stable nitrogen-isotope ratios for six month age intervals at Angel, MacPherson, and Prospect Hill.

weaning was initiated earliest at MacPherson and latest at Angel. The normalized maximum values obtained at each site are consistent with the conclusion that the peak times correspond to the onset of weaning. Only at Angel, where breast-milk seems to provide most of the dietary protein up to almost age 2, does the isotopic composition approach the theoretical maximum limit of the childhood average plus 3.6 per mil (normalized to 1.0). As shown in Figure 1, the theoretical maximum $\delta^{15}N$ value is reached only after prolonged and exclusive breast-feeding. When weaning begins before the theoretical maximum is attained, the actual maximum value will be less than the theoretically maximum possible value. At MacPherson and Prospect Hill, weaning begins before the maximum value is attained, with Prospect Hill reaching 90 per cent of the theoretical maximum and MacPherson reaching only 60 per cent of the maximum (suggesting very early weaning or supplementation at this Native American site). The locations and amplitudes of the peaks for the $\delta^{15}N$ age profile curves are consistent with expectations about the relationship between collagen $\delta^{15}N$ values and weaning behavior.

The dietary patterns after the onset of weaning are not directly tied to the weaning time. Prospect Hill shows the most rapid decline in $\delta^{15}N$ values after the peak, suggesting that weaning in this society was characterized by rapid substitution of foods other than breast-milk. Both Angel and MacPherson show more gradual declines in $\delta^{15}N$ values, suggesting that weaning was a much more gradual process at these sites. Given the similar rates of decline in the normalized isotope ratios from Angel and MacPherson, infant feeding practices after the onset of weaning must have been very similar in these two populations in spite of the differing times when weaning was initiated.

Uncertainties in the dietary reconstruction

These interpretations of the stable nitrogen-isotope ratios assume that the $\delta^{15}N$ value of collagen is directly related to the ^{15}N content of the diet in ways that are consistent at all three sites. Feeding studies have shown different bones from animals that consumed monotonous diets have identical isotopic compositions (Schoeninger and DeNiro 1984). However, the isotopic compositions of bones from an animal that consumed a diet with a changing isotopic composition over time may depend on when the protein in the bone was synthesized. For example, collagen extracted from the dentine of adult cave bear teeth reflects the nursing diet of the bears when the teeth were formed (Bocherens et al. 1994). Other bones that are continuously remodeled throughout life are more likely to reflect the average diet over many years because of the slow metabolic turnover rate of collagen in adults (Stenhouse and Baxter 1979). At the sites of MacPherson and Prospect Hill, collagen samples were obtained from ribs (Katzenberg et al. 1993; Katzenberg and Pfeiffer 1995). For the Angel sample, collagen was extracted from long bone diaphyses (where growth occurs) to measure the isotopic composition of the diet as closely as poss-ible to the time of death. The stable nitrogen-isotope ratios of juvenile ribs vary with age (Katzenberg et al. 1993; Katzenberg and Pfeiffer 1995) in a pattern that closely resembles the variation in long bone diaphyses (Schurr 1997). Thus, the isotopic contents of both regions of the skeleton appear to closely track the isotopic composition of the diet in young juveniles, and differences in the isotopic content of juvenile ribs and long bone diaphyses appear to be insignificant based on data presently available. The stable nitrogen-isotope ratios of collagen from bones that are constantly remodeled appears to reflect the average diet over the child's life span.

At both Angel and Prospect Hill (Table 2), the average $\delta^{15}N$ value for weaned children (children aged 5 to 10 years) was slightly lower than the average for adults (by 0.2 to 0.3 per mil). The mean value for children aged 5 to 10 at MacPherson was higher than the adult average (by 0.6 per mil). The reasons for these variations are unknown. Animal studies show that collagen ^{15}N content is a function of the ^{15}N content of the diet, water availability (Ambrose and DeNiro 1986), and perhaps diet quality (Cormie and Schwarcz 1996; Hobson and Clark 1992). Growth rates may also be important, as growing animals that are rapidly synthesizing proteins would have a high need for nitrogen, reducing the fractionation between diet and collagen (Schurr 1997). Each of these (except perhaps water availability at the three sites discussed here), may play a role in determining varia-tions in childhood $\delta^{15}N$ values. Estimates of fractionation effects in collagen synthesis (also known as 'the trophic level effect') are derived from the isotope ratios of adult wild animals that ate uncontrolled diets (Ambrose and DeNiro 1986; Cormie and Schwarcz 1996; Minagawa and Wada 1984), on laboratory animals fed monotonous diets (DeNiro and Schoeninger 1983), or whose metabolism may differ from that of humans (Hobson and Clark 1992; Steele and Daniel 1978). Relatively little is known about nitrogen metabolism and its isotopic expression in the bone collagen of human juveniles. Cleverly-designed studies of stable nitrogen-isotope metabolism in living human populations under well-controlled or well-monitored conditions are needed to clarify these issues.

Comparisons between weaning behavior and fertility

Taken as a group, the three sites clearly indicate that there is no simple correlation between the timing or rate of weaning and the ratio D30+/D5+ as a measure of fertility. There is also no direct correlation between weaning time and agricultural dependency. These results are not surprising given the diverse nature of the three sites.

The results for the two Native American sites are especially interesting. The inhabitants of the Proto-Historic period MacPherson site lived during a time of great social upheaval and demographic stress caused in large part by contact with Europeans. Based on the data from MacPherson, the Iroquoian population of this site apparently responded to this stress in part by maintaining high fertility. Rapid initiation of weaning was apparently one mechanism that the MacPherson site residents used to maintain a relatively high level of fertility, a conclusion that is supported by Katzenberg et al.'s (1993) interpretation of high infant stable carbon-isotope ratios at the site as evidence for use of maize gruel as a weaning food. While the prehistoric Angel site also had relatively high fertility, the inhabitants did not attempt to increase their fertility further by shortening the nursing period.

The very early weaning time at Prospect Hill is not correlated with high fertility according to the D30+/D5+ ratio. Based on the D30+/D5+, this site would have the lowest fertility of the three, as the D30+/D5+ ratio is inversely correlated with fertility.

Conclusions

Stable nitrogen isotopes can be used to determine both the timing and rates of weaning in past populations. Both timing and rates are important parameters that may vary independently. For this sample, there is no simple correlation between the D30+/D5+ ratio, a demographic measure of fertility calculated from skeletal series, and weaning time or rate measured by stable nitrogen-isotope ratios.

This method can be used to solve one of the key problems associated with the origins of food production: whether world population growth was a result of reduced birth intervals associated with increased sedentism, or of some other factor. If sedentism increased fertility, then some ancient hunter-gatherers, such as those of the American Midcontinental Archaic, the Danish Mesolithic, or the Natufian of the Near East might show high levels of fertility and early weaning long before the appearance of food production. If increased fertility was not the major determinant of population growth, then other things, such as improved access to weaning foods (Buikstra et al. 1986), deliberate attempts to increase populations to provide more labor in agricultural societies (Boserup 1965), or reductions in childhood mortality from improved nutrition (Pennington 1996), may be more important.

One practical drawback to using stable nitrogen-isotopes to determine prehistoric weaning behavior is the need for relatively large samples of juveniles (preferably 20 or more) spanning all or most of the ages prior to adulthood. This clearly limits its application to the obvious problem of determining whether changes in weaning time accompanied the development of food production, because, in many areas of the world, the populations that preceded food production either left few burials behind, or juveniles have not been recovered by archaeologists. Examples of these situations include the Early Archaic of eastern North America (Smith 1986) and the Mesolithic of northern continental Europe (Price et al. 1995). In other areas or at other times, pure hunter-gatherers or hunter-gatherers experimenting with food production became semi-sedentary and produced large cemeteries with abundant juvenile remains. Examples of this situation include the Late Archaic of eastern North America (Charles and Buikstra 1983) and the Danish Mesolithic (Price et al. 1995). In these cases, stable nitrogen-isotope ratios of the first semi-sedentary populations could be compared with those of succeeding fully sedentary populations to evaluate the effects of increased sedentism and agricultural intensification on infant feeding behavior, but the results may not be directly applicable to dietary changes associated with the first appearance of food production.

Discussions of prehistoric population growth usually give priority to increased fertility as a mechanism, with reduced birth intervals as the primary cause of high fertility (Buikstra et al. 1986; Sattenspiel and Harpending 1983). Reduced birth intervals are just one possible cause of increased fertility, because fertility can also be increased by increasing the portion of the female fertile period that is used for reproduction and by increasing the number of females that reproduce (through earlier reproduction, high proportions of reproducing females, more frequent or rapid return to reproductive status after widowhood or divorce, etc.; Livi-Bacci 1997). Population growth can also occur under conditions of stable fertility and an increase in over-all mortality when there are small reductions in early childhood mortality (Pennington 1996). These variables may be accessible for historic populations with good demographic records, but for most historic populations, and for all prehistoric ones, they must be inferred from other data. For example, earlier female reproduction might be revealed by an earlier rise in the female mortality curve after puberty. In a similar fashion, rapid remarriage after widowhood might be distinguished by higher female mortality in the late reproductive years coupled with high male mortality in early and middle adulthood. Stable isotope analysis of burials from historic cemeteries, where factors controlling fertility can be approximated with non-paleodemographic methods, or the isotopic analysis of hair or fingernails from living populations where demographic parameters can be observed directly, would clearly be very useful for evaluating the effect of weaning behavior on fertility and childhood mortality.

Fertility and weaning behavior depend on many things, including the types of foods available, cooking practices, the quality of medical care available to children, and the society's perceived need for labor. The relations between fertility and weaning are diverse in the very small sample used here, and can be expected to appear even more diverse as more skeletal samples are analyzed. Stable nitrogen-isotope analysis provides an especially promising method for the investigation of the connections between fertility, mortality, and weaning behavior in past and present populations.

Acknowledgments

An earlier version of this manuscript was presented at the symposium 'Biocultural Perspectives on Childhood Health and Adaptation'. The symposium was sponsored by the Paul M. and Barbara Jean Henkels Visiting Scholars Series, and the Departments of Anthropology, Psychology, and Biology at the University of Notre Dame. I received many useful comments from participants in the symposium, and especially from Barry Bogin, Katherine Dettwyler, James McKenna, and Susan Guise Sheridan. Editorial changes suggested by M. Anne Katzenberg, Stephen Shennan, and one or more anonymous reviewers were very helpful. Any errors or omissions remain my own.

Department of Anthropology
University of Notre Dame
Notre Dame, IN 46556, USA

References

Ambrose, S. H. 1990. Preparation and characterization of bone and tooth collagen for isotopic analysis. *Journal of Archaeological Science*, 17: 431–51.

Ambrose, S. H. and DeNiro, M. J. 1986. The isotopic ecology of East African mammals. *Oecologica*, 69: 395–409.

Angel, J. L. 1969. The basis of paleodemography. *American Journal of Physical Anthropology*, 30: 427–37.

Bass, W. M. 1971. *Human Osteology: A Laboratory and Field Manual of the Human Skeleton*. Columbia: Missouri Archaeological Society.

Black, G. A. 1967. *Angel Site: An Archaeological, Historical, and Ethnological Study*. Indianapolis: Indiana Historical Society.

Bocherens, H., Fizet, M. and Mariotti, A. 1994. Diet, physiology, and ecology of fossil mammals as inferred from stable carbon and nitrogen isotope biogeochemistry: implications for Pleistocene bears. *Palaeogeography, Palaeoclimatology, Palaeoecology*, 107: 213–25.

Boquet-Appel, J. P. and Masset, C. 1982. Farewell to paleodemography. *Journal of Human Evolution*, 11: 321–33.

Boserup, E. 1965. *The Conditions of Agricultural Growth: The Economics of Agrarian Change Under Population Pressure*. Chicago: Aldine Publishing Company.

Buikstra, J. E., Autry, W., Breitburg, E., Eisenberg, L. and van der Merwe, N. 1988. Diet and health in the Nashville Basin: human adaptation and maize agriculture in middle Tennessee. In *Diet and Subsistence: Current Archaeological Perspectives* (eds B. V. Kennedy and G. M. LeMoine). Ontario: Archaeological Association of the University of Calgary, pp. 243–59.

Buikstra, J. E., Konigsberg, L. W. and Bullington, J. 1986. Fertility and the development of agriculture in the prehistoric Midwest. *American Antiquity*, 51: 528–46.

Charles, D. K. and Buikstra, J. E. 1983. Archaic mortuary sites in the central Mississippi drainage: distribution, structure, and behavioral implications. In *Archaic Hunters and Gatherers in the American Midwest* (eds J. L. Phillips and J. A. Brown). New York: Academic Press, pp. 117–46.

Clarke, S. K. 1977. Mortality trends in prehistoric populations. *Human Biology*, 49: 181–6.

Clarke, S. K. 1980. Early childhood morbidity trends in prehistoric populations. *Human Biology*, 52: 79–85.

Cook, D. C. 1976. Pathologic states and disease process in Illinois Woodland populations: an epidemiologic approach. Unpublished PhD dissertation, Department of Anthropology, University of Chicago.

Cormie, A. B. and Schwarcz, H. P. 1996. Effects of climate on deer bone $\delta^{15}N$ and $\delta^{13}C$: Lack of precipitation effects on $\delta^{15}N$ for animals consuming low amounts of C_4 plants. *Geochimica et Cosmochica Acta*, 60: 4161–6.

Corruccini, R. S., Handler, J. S. and Jacobi, K. P. 1985. Chronological distribution of enamel hypoplasias and weaning in a Carribean slave population. *Human Biology*, 57: 699–711.

DeNiro, M. J. 1985. Postmortem preservation and alteration of in vivo bone collagen isotope ratios in relation to paleodietary reconstruction. *Nature*, 31: 806–9.

DeNiro, M. J. and Schoeninger, M. J. 1983. Stable carbon and nitrogen isotopes of bone collagen: variations within individuals, between sexes, and within populations raised on monotonous diets. *Journal of Archaeological Science*, 10: 199–203.

Fogel, M. L., Tuross, N. and Owsley, D. W. 1989. Nitrogen isotope tracers. *Carnegie Institution Year Book*, 88: 133–4.

Goodman, A. H. and Rose, J. C. 1990. Assessment of systematic physiological perturbations from dental enamel hypoplasias and associated histological structures. *Yearbook of Physical Anthropology*, 33: 59–110.

Green, T. J. and Munson, C. A. 1978. Mississippian settlement patterns in southwestern Indiana. In *Mississippian Settlement Patterns* (ed. B. D. Smith). New York: Academic Press, pp. 293–330.

Heidenreich, C. E. 1971. *Huronia: A History and Geography of the Huron Indians 1600–1650.* Toronto: McClellen & Stewart.

Hilgeman, S. L. 1996. Pottery and chronology at the Angel site, a Middle Mississippian center in the lower Ohio Valley. Unpublished PhD thesis, Indiana University, Bloomington.

Hobson, K. A. and Clark, R. G. 1992. Assessing avian diets using stable isotopes II: factors influencing diet-tissue fractionation. *The Condor*, 94: 189–97.

Katzenberg, M. A. 1989. Stable isotope analysis of archaeological faunal remains from southern Ontario. *Journal of Archaeological Science*, 16: 319–29.

Katzenberg, M. A. 1992. Advances in stable isotope analysis of prehistoric bones. In *Skeletal Biology of Past Peoples: Research Methods* (eds S. R. Saunders and M. A. Katzenberg). New York: Wiley-Liss, pp. 105–20.

Katzenberg, M. A. and Pfeiffer, S. 1995. Nitrogen isotope evidence for weaning age in a nineteenth century Canadian skeletal sample. In *Bodies of Evidence* (ed. A. L. Grauer). New York: John Wiley & Sons, pp. 221–35.

Katzenberg, M. A., Herring, D. A. and Saunders, S. R. 1996. Weaning and infant mortality: evaluating the skeletal evidence. *Yearbook of Physical Anthropology*, 39: 177–99.

Katzenberg, M. A., Saunders, S. R. and Fitzgerald, W. R. 1993. Age differences in stable carbon and nitrogen isotope ratios in a population of prehistoric maize horticulturalists. *American Journal of Physical Anthropology*, 90: 267–81.

Lallo, J. 1973. The skeletal biology of three prehistoric American Indian societies from Dickson Mounds. Unpublished PhD dissertation, Department of Anthropology, University of Massachusetts, Amherst.

Larsen, C. S. 1995. Biological changes in human populations with agriculture. *Annual Review of Anthropology*, 24: 185–213.

Livi-Bacci, M. 1997. *A Concise History of World Population* (trans C. Ipsen). Oxford, UK: Blackwell.

Martin, D. L., Goodman, A. H. and Armelagos, G. J. 1985. Skeletal pathologies as indicators of quality and quantity of diet. In *The Analysis of Prehistoric Diets* (eds R. I. Gilbert Jr. and J. H. Mielke). Orlando, Florida: Academic Press, pp. 227–79.

Mason, R. J. 1981. *Great Lakes Archaeology*. New York: Academic Press.

Minagawa, M. and Wada, E. 1984. Stepwise enrichment of ^{15}N along food chains: further evidence and the relation between $\delta^{15}N$ and animal age. *Geochimica et Cosmochimica Acta*, 48: 1135–40.

Newman, A. 1996. The precise world of isotope ratio mass spectrometry. *Analytical Chemistry*, 68: 373A–77A.

Pennington, R. L. 1996. Causes of early human population growth. *American Journal of Physical Anthropology*, 99: 259–74.

Pfeiffer, S., Dudar, J. C. and Austin, S. 1989. Prospect Hill: skeletal remains from a 19th-century Methodist cemetery, New Market, Ontario. *Northeast Historical Archaeology*, 18: 29–48.

Price, T. D., Gebauer, A. B. and Keely, L. H. 1995. The spread of farming into Europe north of the Alps. In *Last Hunters, First Farmers: New Perspectives on the Prehistoric Transition to Agriculture* (eds T. D. Price and A. B. Gebauer). Santa Fe, New Mexico: School of American Research Press, pp. 95–126.

Sattenspiel, L. and Harpending, H. 1983. Stable populations and skeletal age. *American Antiquity*, 48: 489–98.

Schoeller, D. A., Minagawa, M., Slater, R. and Kaplan, I. R. 1986. Stable isotopes of carbon, nitrogen, and hydrogen in the contemporary North American food web. *Ecology of Food and Nutrition*, 18: 159–70.

Schoeninger, M. J. 1985. Trophic effects on 15N/14N and 13C/12C ratios in human bone collagen and strontium levels in bone mineral. *Journal of Human Evolution*, 14: 515–25.

Schoeninger, M. J. and DeNiro, M. J. 1984. Nitrogen and carbon isotopic composition of bone collagen from marine and terrestrial mammals. *Geochimica et Cosmochimica Acta*, 48: 625–39.

Schoeninger, M. J., DeNiro, M. J. and Tauber, H. 1983. Stable nitrogen isotope ratios of bone collagen reflect marine and terrestrial components of human diet. *Science*, 20: 1381–3.

Schurr, M. R. 1992. Mortuary and isotopic variation in a Middle Mississippian population. *American Antiquity*, 54: 300–20.

Schurr, M. R. 1997. Stable isotopes as evidence for weaning at the Angel site: a comparison of isotopic and demographic measures of weaning age. *Journal of Archaeological Science*, 24: 919–27.

Schurr, M. R. and Schoeninger, M. J. 1995. Associations between agricultural intensification and social complexity: an example from the prehistoric Ohio Valley. *Journal of Anthropological Archaeology*, 14: 315–39.

Schwarcz, H. P. and Schoeninger, M. J. 1991. Stable isotope analysis in human nutritional ecology. *Yearbook of Physical Anthropology*, 34: 283–321.

Schwartz, J. H. 1995. *Skeleton Keys: An Introduction to Human Skeletal Morphology, Development, and Analysis*. Oxford: Oxford University Press.

Sillen, A. and Smith, P. 1984. Sr/Ca ratios in juvenile skeletons portray weaning in a Medieval Arab population. *Journal of Archaeological Science*, 11: 237–45.

Smith, B. D. 1986. The archaeology of the Southeastern United States: from Dalton to De Soto, 10,500-500 B.P. In *Advances in World Archaeology* (eds F. Wendorf and A. E. Close). New York: Academic Press, pp. 1–92.

Steele, K. W. and Daniel, R. M. 1978. Fractionation of nitrogen isotopes by animals: a further complication to the use of variations in the natural abundance of 15N for tracer studies. *Journal of Agricultural Science*, 90: 7–9.

Stenhouse, M. J. and Baxter, M. S. 1979. The uptake of bomb ^{13}C in humans. In *Radiocarbon Dating: Proceedings of the Ninth International Conference, Los Angeles and La Jolla, 1976* (eds R. Berger and E. Suess). Berkeley: University of California Press, pp. 324–41.

Ubelaker, D. H. 1978. *Human Skeletal Remains: Excavation, Analysis, Interpretation*. Chicago: Aldine.

White, C. D. and Schwarcz, H. P. 1994. Temporal trends in stable isotopes for Nubian mummy tissues. *American Journal of Physical Anthropology*, 93: 165–87.

Williams, S. 1990. The Vacant Quarter and other late events in the lower Valley. In *Towns and Temples Along the Mississippi* (eds D. H. Dye and C. A. Cox). Tuscaloosa: University of Alabama Press, pp. 170–80.

Wood, J. W., Milner, G. R., Harpending, H. C. and Weiss, K. M. 1992. The osteological paradox. *Current Anthropology*, 33: 343–70.

Wrong, G. M. (eds) 1939. *Father Gabriel Sagard: The Long Journey to the Country of the Hurons*. Toronto: The Champlain Society.

Contributors

Jonathan Adams is Wigner Fellow in the Environmental Sciences Division, Oak Ridge National Laboratory, where he works on the carbon cycle. His focus is on variation in total land carbon storage during the last glacial and the present interglacial, and he is also working on the relationship between global ecological change and modern human dispersals. He is Secretary of INQUA's Commission on Terrestrial Carbon. From October 1998 he will be a Lecturer in Physical Geography at the University of Adelaide.

Rose-Marie Arbogast is a researcher at the Centre National de la Recherche Scientifique, zooarchaeologist at the Laboratoire de ChronoEcologie at Besançon (France) and focuses her research on the Neolithic fauna and on the techniques of husbandry and hunting north-west of the Alps.

Deborah Blom holds an MA in Anthropology from the University of Chicago, where she is currently completing her PhD. During the 1998 academic year, she will begin a position as Assistant Professor of Anthropology at the University of Vermont. Her research interests include bioarchaeology and prehistoric complex societies. Her present research is focused in Andean South America.

Christine Bourquin-Mignot is ingénieur d'étude at the Centre National de la Recherche Scientifique and a specialist in wood identification at the Laboratoire de Chrono-Ecologie at Besançon (France). She works on archaeological wood in order to reconstruct the environment and human impact on the environment, from the Neolithic to the Middle Ages.

Jane E. Buikstra is a Distinguished Professor in Anthropology at the University of New Mexico, the Director of the Center for American Archaeology, and a member of the National Academy of Sciences. She holds an MA and PhD from the University of Chicago. Her research interests combine biological anthropology and archaeology, and she has conducted research through the Americas and Europe.

Alexander Christensen teaches in the Department of History and Anthropology at Augusta State University and is continuing his research into the biological structure of Mesoamerican populations.

Bruno David is based in the Department of Geography and Environmental Science at Monash University (Australia).

L. Ellis received a PhD and MA in Anthropology from Harvard University, and a BA in Anthropology from UCLA. Her areas of specialization are the archaeology of Eastern Europe from the Neolithic to the Roman period, the analysis of ancient pyrotechnologies, and the applications of the physical sciences in archaeology. She has conducted archaeological research in Romania since 1979. Currently, L. Ellis is full professor in the Department of Classics and Classical Archaeology and the Director of the MA program in Museum Studies at San Francisco State University.

Benedikt Hallgrímsson received his PhD in Biological Anthropology from the University of Chicago in 1995, and is currently Assistant Professor of Anatomy in the University of Puerto Rico School of Medicine. His research deals with developmental and morphometric approaches to variation and evolution.

Linda Keng is an Instructor of Anthropology at the University of Houston, where she received her MA degree in 1997. Her research interests include human oesteology, paleopathology, and demography of complex New World societies. She has spent the last three years conducting research in Honduras and coastal Peru.

Catherine Lavier is assistante-ingénieur détachée, at the Centre National de la Recherche Scientifique and a dendrochronologist at the Laboratoire de Chrono-Ecologie at Besançon (France). She has established the chronological framework of the agricultural communities of Chalain and Clairvaux during the fourth and third millennium BC as well as carrying out various other studies.

Harry Lourandos is based in the Department of Anthropology and Sociology at the University of Queensland (Australia).

María C. Lozada recently graduated with a PhD from the Department of Anthropology of the University of Chicago. She is currently a lecturer of Anthropology and Romance Languages at the University of Chicago. Her research interests focus on bioarchaeology of Andean South America.

Pierre Pétrequin is research-director at the Centre National de la Recherche Scientifique and head of the Laboratoire de Chrono-Ecologie at Besançon (France). He has proposed three archaeological approaches, complementary and interlinked: the modelling of ethnological studies in New-Guinea; the application of such models, as working hypotheses, to the Neolithic situations of the north-western Alps; and life-size experimental reconstructions.

Mark Schurr is an Assistant Professor in the Department of Anthropology at the University of Notre Dame. His research interests include the origins of social complexity and the archaeology of eastern North America (especially the Southeast and the Lower Great Lakes region). He also explores the applications of archaeological chemistry to the reconstruction of prehistoric diet and fluoride dating.

Tim Sluckin is Professor of Mathematics in the University of Southampton. In addition to working in industrial applied mathematics, he is a convenor of the Southampton Mathematical Biology Seminar and teaches Theoretical Genetics. He is currently working on modelling human dispersals, and on the evolution of co-operation in large social groups.

James Steele is Lecturer in the Department of Archaeology, University of Southampton. His research focuses on behavioural ecological approaches to hominid social and ranging behaviour, and on modelling the spread of modern humans (with particular reference to Paleoindian dispersals into the Americas). He also works on cognitive evolution and handedness.

Amandine Viellet, a doctoral candidate at the Laboratoire de Chrono-Ecologie at Besançon (France), is writing a dissertation on dendrochronology, to investigate the chronology and the management of woodland in the Neolithic villages of Chalain and Clairvaux.

Dawnie Wolfe Steadman is an assistant professor of physical anthropology at Iowa State University. She received her PhD from the University of Chicago, Department of Anthropology in 1997.

Notes to contributors

Manuscripts should not normally exceed 5,000 words. They should be typed on good quality A4 paper (i.e. approx. 300mm x 210mm), using double spacing throughout, including the References. Two copies of the manuscript should be submitted, the authors retaining another. Unsolicited contributions and related correspondence should be addressed to the Executive Editor (see front of current issue for address).

Referencing should follow the modern scientific convention. Footnotes should be avoided. Bibliographic references within the text should list the author's last name, date of publication and number of page, e.g. (Clarke 1952: 211). Where an author's name has just been cited in the text, references need be made only to the date of publication and page, e.g. (1952: 211). Extended references should be listed alphabetically at the end of the paper, e.g.

Brumfiel, E. M. and Earle, T. K. 1987. Specialization, exchange and complex societies: an introduction. In *Specialization, Exchange, and Complex Societies* (eds E. M. Brumfiel and T. K. Earle). Cambridge: Cambridge University Press, pp. 1–9.

Casey, J. 1986. *Understanding Ancient Coins*. London: Batsford.

Mezzena, F. and Palma di Cesnola, A. 1973. Oggetti d'arte mobilare di età gravettiana ed epigravettiana nella Grotta Paglicci (Foggia). *Rivista di Scienze Preistoriche*, 27: 211–24.

Schick, K. A. 1984. Processes of Paleolithic site formation: an experimental study. Doctoral dissertation. Department of Anthropology, University of California, Berkeley.

Text figures, site plans, maps, etc., should be drawn on strong paper, white card, or good quality tracing film, and be suitably lettered for printing. They should measure approximately twice the intended final size which should be indicated where possible. A published full-page illustration may not exceed 205mm x 155mm. Plates should be printed on glossy paper and mounted on thin card. Figures, maps and plates should be titled and numbered; originals should be numbered in pencil only. A list of captions to figures and plates must be provided on separate sheets. Authors must obtain approval, before submission, for reproduction of illustrations or other material if not their own.

It is important that authors submit accurate, well-prepared copy for the printer. Re-drawing or lettering of maps or figures cannot be undertaken by the editors, who may return sub-standard work to contributors for re-presentation in an improved form.

Each contribution should be accompanied by an abstract of 100–150 words. In addition up to 6 keywords, suitable for abstracting and indexing services, should be listed.

A short note on individual contributors should also be supplied.

Page proofs only will be sent to authors, who are reminded that these are intended for checking, not re-writing. Failure to return proofs by the required date may lead to substitution of the editor's corrected proofs.

One copy of the journal and twenty-five offprints will be supplied free to authors on publication of a paper; these must be shared in case of joint authorship. A memorandum of agreement between author and publisher will be sent at a preliminary stage.

Please Note
It is not current editorial policy to publish book reviews as a regular feature of the journal, although review articles may be submitted covering recent publications in particular fields.

Notes on style

It would be helpful if contributors were to bear in mind the following points of style when preparing their papers for *World Archaeology*:

1. *Initial capital letters*: Use as seldom as possible.
   North, south, etc. are only capitalized if used as part of a recognized place name e.g. Western Australia, South Africa; use lower case for general terms e.g. eastern France, south of Scotland.
   'vol.' and 'p.' to be lower roman if used, but delete if possible.
2. *Italics*: Use mainly for book titles and foreign words and phrases.
   'et al.' 'ibid.' and 'op. cit.' to be roman, *not* italicized, ('ibid.' always lower case).
3. *Full points*: No full points in HMSO, USA, NATO, plc, etc. Omit full points after contractions which end in the last letter of the word, e.g. Dr, Mr, St, edn, eds, Ltd, and after metric units, e.g. cm, m, km, kg, etc.
   Abbreviations, where the end of the word is cut, do have full points e.g. p.m., ed., e.g., i.e., vol., etc., etc.
4. *Quotations*: Use single quotation marks, but double within quotations. Do not use leader dots at the beginning or end of a quotation unless the sense absolutely demands. For ellipsis within a quotation use three leader dots for a mid-sentence break, four if the break is followed by a new sentence.
   Quotations of over 40 words should be extracted and indented.
5. *Numerals*: Use minimum numbers for pages and dates e.g. 25–8, 136–42, 150–1, but 12–16; 1980–1, 1487–92, 1914–18.
   Use words for under a hundred, unless paired or grouped.
   Insert comma for both thousands, and tens of thousands, e.g. 1,000 and 10,000.
   Always have numerals on both sides of the decimal point, e.g. 0.5.
   The percentage sign (%) should not be used in the text, only in tables and figures. The number always appears in numerals, e.g. 87 per cent.
   Use numerals, not words, for measurement, e.g. 12km, 5m, and ages, e.g. 10 years old.
6. *Dates*: Usual order, 8 July 1980 (no comma); on 14 September, or on the 14th.
   1980s, not spelt out, no apostrophes.
   Nineteenth century, not 19th century, (adjective nineteenth-century).
   AD usually precedes the year number (AD 30), but fifth century AD.
   BC and BP follow the date (1232 BC).
   There are usually no commas in dates, but BP dates do have a comma or space when they consist of five or more digits, e.g. 13,500 BP.

Dating conventions

1. In accordance with international convention, radiocarbon dates should be expressed as mean and standard deviation, together with the number of the issuing laboratory.
   e.g. a date of 3600 ± 600 BP (AA-50)
   or: the date was: K-3921 5540 ± 65 BP.
2. Calibrated dates should be indicated as follows: cal. AD 200; 250 cal. BC; a date in the range cal. AD 90–440.
   It may be useful to insert the phrase (calibrated date) after each first occurrence in a paper, to make the meaning perfectly clear. Note that after calibration ranges will often be used, since deviations may not be symmetrical about the mean.
3. Calibrations should be made using the calibration curves of Stuiver and Pearson (1986) or Pearson and Stuiver (1986), depending on period. Both curves are published in *Radiocarbon*, 28, 2B. (Any suitable curve can be chosen for calibrating the period older than 5000BP.)
4. In order to maintain continuity with older literature, it may sometimes be necessary to present uncalibrated dates in terms of 'ad' or 'bc' (where 1950 BP = 0). We do not encourage this because dates presented in this way may not correspond closely with the calendrical AD/BC scale.
5. Dates obtained by other methods, e.g. TL, Uranium Series, or Fission Track, are best referred to in years 'before present' or 'years ago', rather than by radiocarbon conventions.
6. Old dates: Ma for 'millions of years' and ka for 'thousands of years' are advised as abbreviations recognized internationally.

European
journal of Archaeology

Journal of the European Association of Archaeologists

Editor **John Chapman** *University of Durham*

The **European Journal of Archaeology** seeks to promote open debate amongst archaeologists committed to a new idea of Europe in which there is more communication across national frontiers and more interest in interpretation.

When you subscribe you will automatically receive free membership of the **European Association of Archaeologists**.

Contents: Volume 1, Issue 1

■ Late upper Paleolithic subsistence strategies in southern Iberia: tardiglacial faunas from Cueva de Nerja (Málaga, Spain) **Arturo Morales, Eufrasia Roselló and Francisco Hernández**

■ Reconstructing prehistoric metallurgical knowledge: the northern Italian Copper and Bronze Ages **Mark Pearce**

■ Iron Age Iberian sculptures as territorial markers: the Córdoban example (Andalucia) **Teresa Chapa Brunet**

■ Embracing uncertainty and challenging dualism in the GIS-based study of a palaeo-flood plain **Mark Gillings**

**Three times a year: April, August, December
First issue April 1998 • (ISSN:1461-9571)**

Visit the SAGE website: http://www.sagepub.co.uk/

Order Form for New Subscribers - Free EAA membership included

SAGE Publications, 6 Bonhill Street, London EC2A 4PU, UK
Subscription Hotline +44 (0)171 330 1266 / Email: subscription@sagepub.co.uk

USA orders to be sent to:
PO Box 5096, Thousand Oaks, CA 91359

Name _____

Address _____

_____ 8J01

❏ Yes! I want to subscribe to the **European Jn'l of Archaeology** starting with Volume 1 (1998)

❏ **Individual Rate** £35/$56

❏ **Institutional Rate** £105/$168

❏ Please send me a brochure on the journal

Methods of Payment

❏ I enclose a cheque (made payable SAGE Publications Ltd) for: ____

Please invoice my credit card
❏ Mastercard ❏ Visa   Amount: ____

Card No: [ ][ ][ ][ ][ ][ ][ ][ ][ ][ ][ ][ ][ ][ ][ ][ ]

Expiry Date: [/   ]

Signature: _____ Date: / /

Journals from SAGE

Companion Encyclopedia of Archaeology

2 Volume Set

Edited by **Graeme Barker** and **Annie Grant,** both at Leicester University, UK
In twenty-six authoritative and clearly-written essays, this Companion explores the origins, aims, methods and problems of archaeology. Each essay is written by a scholar of international standing and illustrations complement the text.

January 1999: 1264pp: illus. 134 line drawings & 83 b+w photos
Hb: 0-415-06448-1: **£160.00**

Encyclopedia of the Archaeology of Ancient Egypt

Edited by **Kathryn Bard,** Boston University, USA

The Encyclopedia of the Archaeology of Ancient Egypt is the first reference work in English ever to present a systematic coverage of the archaeology of this region from the earliest finds of the Palaeolithic period through to the 4th century AD.

March 1999: 968pp: illus. 120 photos, plans and drawings
Hb: 0-415-18589-0: **£150.00**

Further information is available from Darell Carey, Marketing Executive, Routledge, 11 New Fetter Lane, London EC4P 4EE
Tel. 0171 842 2099. Email reference@routledge.co.uk.
Information about all Routledge titles is available on the Internet at www.routledge.com

www.ingramcontent.com/pod-product-compliance
Ingram Content Group UK Ltd.
Pitfield, Milton Keynes, MK11 3LW, UK
UKHW010021280225
455677UK00023B/735